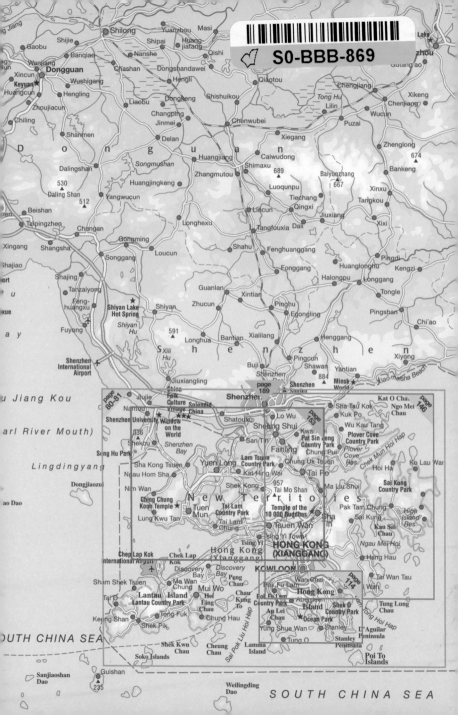

INSIGHT CITY GUIDE

HONG KONG
MACAU & GUANGZHOU

※ INSIGHT GUIDE
HONG KONG

Editor
Tom Le Bas
Art Director
Klaus Geisler
Picture Editor
Hilary Genin
Cartography Editor
Zoë Goodwin
Production
Kenneth Chan
Editorial Director
Brian Bell

Distribution

UK & Ireland
GeoCenter International Ltd
The Viables Centre, Harrow Way
Basingstoke, Hants RG22 4BJ
Fax: (44) 1256-817988

United States
Langenscheidt Publishers, Inc.
36–36 33rd Street 4th Floor
Long Island City, NY 11106
Fax: (1) 718 784-0640

Canada
Thomas Allen & Son Ltd
390 Steelcase Road East
Markham, Ontario L3R 1G2
Fax: (1) 905 475 6747

Australia
Universal Publishers
1 Waterloo Road
Macquarie Park, NSW 2113
Fax: (61) 2 9888 9074

New Zealand
Hema Maps New Zealand Ltd (HNZ)
Unit D, 24 Ra ORA Drive
East Tamaki, Auckland
Fax: (64) 9 273 6479

Worldwide
Apa Publications GmbH & Co.
Verlag KG (Singapore branch)
38 Joo Koon Road, Singapore 628990
Tel: (65) 6865-1600. Fax: (65) 6861-6438

Printing

Insight Print Services (Pte) Ltd
38 Joo Koon Road, Singapore 628990
Tel: (65) 6865-1600. Fax: (65) 6861-6438

©2005 Apa Publications GmbH & Co.
Verlag KG (Singapore branch)
All Rights Reserved

First Edition 1980
Tenth Edition 2005

ABOUT THIS BOOK

This guidebook combines the interests and enthusiasms of two of the world's best-known information providers: Insight Guides, whose titles have set the standard for visual travel guides since 1970, and Discovery Channel, the world's premier source of nonfiction television programming.

The editors of Insight Guides provide both practical advice and general understanding about a destination. Discovery Channel and its Web site, www.discovery.com, help millions of viewers explore their world from the comfort of their own home.

How to use this book

The book is carefully structured both to convey an understanding of Hong Kong and its culture and to guide readers through its sights and activities:

◆ The first section of the book describes Hong Kong's history and culture in lively, authoritative essays written by specialists.

◆ The main Places section provides a full run-down of all the attractions worth seeing. The principal places of interest are coordinated by number with full-colour maps.

◆ A list of recommended restaurants is included at the end of each chapter in the Places section, and those in the main urban areas of Hong Kong Island and Kowloon can be located on the pull-out restaurant map.

◆ Photographic features illustrate various facets of Hong Kong, from the iconic Star Ferry to the colourful festivals, idiosyncratic superstitions and high-rise architecture that make this such an exciting destination.

The contributors

This edition of *Insight Guide: Hong Kong* was co-ordinated by **Tom Le Bas** at Insight's London office, who restructured the book into its practical and reader-friendly City Guide format, and wrote the Best Of, Architecture, Traditional Beliefs and Nature photo essays.

Ed Peters, a journalist and long-term resident of Hong Kong who has contributed to several previous editions of the guide, fully updated the Features and the Places sections. The revamped Travel Tips were compiled by **Ruth Williams** (Accommodation, Children's Activities, A–Z and Language) and **Dinah Gardner** (Transport and Activities). The restaurant reviews were written by **Roger Cave**, former editor of the *Asia Hotel and Catering Times*. **Mischa Moselle** wrote the panel on the Cantonese penchant for Western nicknames. Thanks to **Stephanie Ng** and **Mary Anne Le Bas** for assistance with the Traditional Beliefs photo essay and other material in the book.

Past contributors whose work remains in this edition include **Saul Lockhart**, **Leonard Lueras**, **Philippa Conway**, **Paul Hicks**, **Suzanne Lidster**, **Angelica Cheung**, **Angie Ching Yuan and Bill Williams**. The photographers include **Richard Jones**, **Graham Uden**, **Rick Senley** and **Dave Wilkinson**.

This edition was proofread by **Neil Titman** and indexed by **Helen Peters**.

◆ The Travel Tips listings provide all the practical information you will need, divided into five easy-to-use sections: Transport, Accommodation, Activities (cultural, shopping, sports), an A to Z directory covering everything from budgeting to tour agents, and Language. The final section includes a short phrasebook and a list of recommended reading.

◆ A detailed street atlas is included at the back of the book, complete with a full index.

◆ Information can be located quickly by using the index printed on the back cover flap. The flaps are designed to serve as bookmarks.

◆ Photographs throughout the book are chosen not only to illustrate geography and buildings but also to convey the moods of Hong Kong and the life of its people.

CONTACTING THE EDITORS

We would appreciate it if readers would alert us to errors or outdated information by writing to:

Insight Guides, P.O. Box 7910, London SE1 1WE, England. Fax: (44) 20 7403-0290. insight@apaguide.co.uk

NO part of this book may be reproduced, stored in a retrieval system or transmitted in any form or means electronic, mechanical, photocopying, recording or otherwise, without prior written permission of *Apa Publications*. Brief text quotations with use of photographs are exempted for book review purposes only. Information has been obtained from sources believed to be reliable, but its accuracy and completeness, and the opinions based thereon, are not guaranteed.

www.insightguides.com

Contents

Travel Tips

THE BEST OF HONG KONG

Setting priorities, saving money, unique attractions...
here, at a glance, are our recommendations, plus tips
and tricks even the locals won't always know

FIRST THINGS FIRST...

For those visiting Hong Kong for the first time, a list of
must-do priorities to help you get your bearings.

- **A ride on the Star Ferry** Essential for any first-time visitor, this is an absolute bargain. It's best to go first class (upper deck). *Page 96.*
- **Central walkways** Get up onto the above-street-level walkways and head inland to the Landmark building, then go back down to the steamy streets into one of Hong Kong's premier nightlife areas. *Page 87–8.*
- **A tram trip** Make sure you get a seat at the front of the top deck, and enjoy a marvellous wind-cooled tour of Hong Kong Island's north shore. *Page 97.*

- **The Peak** Incredible vistas await (weather/smog permitting – best chances are after heavy rain). *Pages 91–3.*
- **The Kowloon waterfront** For the best views of that famous skyline, take a stroll along the waterfront from the Star Ferry pier and clock tower. *Page 127.*

TOP: the harbour as seen from the Peak. **BELOW** a trip on
the Star Ferry should be on every tourist itinerary.

HONG KONG FOR FREE (OR ALMOST FREE)

- **Junk trip** Free to all foreign passport holders, take a trip around the harbour on an old Chinese junk. *Page 226.*
- **Free museums on Wednesdays** All day Wednesday, every Wednesday. Applies to most major museums in Hong Kong.
- **HK magazine** Top notch listings magazine, available in most cafés and bars.

- **Internet access** Several cafés (Pacific Coffee Co, etc) have free internet access for customers. Major post offices also offer this service, as do public libraries. *Page 231.*
- **Local phone calls** are free in Hong Kong (mobile calls are very cheap). If you need to make a local call you can ask in a shop and they will probably let you use their phone. *(see also money-saving tips, page 9.)*
- **Horse racing at Happy Valley** Admission fee is a nominal HK$10, great value for what can be an exhilarating night out – although of course it can work out very expensive... *Page 109.*

HONG KONG'S BEST SHOPPING

- **Shiny shopping malls**
Hong Kong is well
supplied with
upmarket malls
perfect for seeking out
Armani, Dior and co.
In Tsim Sha Tsui, the
gigantic Harbour City
on Canton Road is
unrivalled. In Central,
choose between the
Landmark, Princes
Building, Pacific
Place and the new
IFC2 mall. Posh
hotels, of course, have
their own shopping
arcades.

- **Grimy markets** At
the other end of the
scale, Hong Kong's
street markets are
worth seeking out for
local colour and, of
course, that fake
Rolex you have
always promised
yourself. Temple
Street market in Yau
Ma Tei is a perennial
favourite. Bargaining
is expected. Specialist
markets include the

Jade Market in
Wanchai, and Cat
Street for bric-a-brac.
- **Antiques** Don't
expect bargains, but
the shops along
Hollywood Road are
full of interesting
chinoiserie.
- **Clothing bargains**
Causeway Bay is
particularly good for
clothes and footwear.
For factory outlet
clothing try around
Wanchai MTR
station. Cameron and
Carnarvon roads in
Tsim Sha Tsui are
also worth a look.
Get a made-to-
measure suit at one
of the many tailors in
Tsim Sha Tsui.
- **Electronics** People
tend to think of Nathan
Road's "Golden Mile",
but while there is no
denying the
abundance, prices can
be keener elsewhere.
Price electronics at a
branch of Fortress or
Broadway first, and try
Stanley Street, Central,
for cameras;
department stores can
also be cheap. Sham
Shui Po is the place
for computer software
and accessories.

ABOVE: one of four long-distance trails in Hong Kong.

BEST WALKS

- **Kowloon waterfront
to Kowloon Park**
Admire the famous
skyline, then head
north via subways to
the heart of Tsim Sha
Tsui – Nathan,
Peking, Hankow
roads and the breath-
ing space of Kowloon
Park. *Pages 126–131.*
- **Star Ferry Pier
(Central) to
Lan Kwai Fong**
(see page 6).
- **Central/Western
back streets** Explore
the area around
Staunton Street, hub
of the lively SoHo
nightlife area, then
return downhill to the
authentic Chinese
atmosphere on
Gage, Graham and
Peel streets. *Pages
99–103.*
- **The Peak Circle
Walk** Along Lugard
and Harlech roads is a
gentle but rewarding
stroll. Some more
strenuous hikes can
also be enjoyed from
here. *Page 93.*

- **MacLehose Trail**
Take your pick of
walks along this 100-
km (62-mile) trail
running across the
mountains of the New
Territories. Highlights
are Tai Long Wan, a
beautiful beach at the
eastern extremity, and
Tai Mo Shan, the
SAR's high-
est peak
(957 metres /
3,140 ft).
Page 152.
- **Tai Po Kau**
One of
the largest
remaining
forests in the
New Territo-
ries, little
known, but
beautiful.
Watch out for
monkeys. *Page 148.*
- **Po Lin Monastery**
The massive bronze
Buddha draws the
crowds to this moun-
taintop sanctuary. Sev-
eral trails lead into the
peaceful grassy hills
around. *Page 159.*

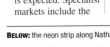

BELOW: the neon strip along Nathan Road in Tsim Sha Tsui.

- **Disneyland** opened in September 2005 and has naturally become an instant must-visit for kids. *Page 161–2.* Nearby is the **Ngong Ping 360 cable-car ride** from Tung Chung to Po Lin Monastery. *Page 159–60.*

- **Ocean Park** is always a hit with families. A variety of attractions include rides for all ages including a thrilling rollercoaster, a cable car, an aquarium and performing dolphins. *Page 119.*
- **Outlying Islands** The ferry ride, the seafood and the beaches make for an enjoyable day out. *Pages 158–165.*
- **Ice skating** at Taikoo Shing. A well-equipped ice-rink,

ABOVE: the cable-car at Ocean Park.
RIGHT: Disneyland is a major crowd-puller.

within an excellent shopping mall. Another skating rink is located in Festival Walk, Kowloon Tong. *Page 227.*
- **Science Museum** The usual hands-on interactive exhibits entertain and educate. Nearby is the **Space Museum** with its IMAX cinema. *Pages 126, 129.*
- **The Peak** is a top attraction for all ages. The Peak Tram is exciting, the views are amazing, and then there is always Madame Tussaud's and the shaded Peak Circuit walk to enjoy. *Pages 91–3.*
- A trip to a **dim sum restaurant** is an essential part of the Hong Kong experience, and one that always seems to go down well with children. *Pages 60–61.*

ABOVE: the view from the top of IFC2, Hong Kong's tallest tower.

AMAZING HONG KONG

- With 7,422 high-rise buildings (over 13 storeys), Hong Kong has more skyscrapers than any city in the world, easily beating second place New York's 5,445, and nearest Asian rival Singapore's 3,503. Shanghai trails way behind with 550. Four of Hong Kong's five tallest skyscrapers are in the top 15 of the world's tallest buildings.
- Ongoing reclamation work has halved the size of Hong Kong's harbour in the last hundred years or so. The scarcity of flat land and subsequent high values mean that land sales account for a large proportion of government revenue.
- Punters at the Hong Kong Jockey Club's Sha Tin Racecourse check the racing statistics and watch the thoroughbreds going through their paces on the world's longest television screen. Measuring 70.4 m (231 ft), the LED screen is as long as a Boeing 747. An average of 40,000 people bet on every race,

giving the Jockey Club a race-day turnover in excess of HK$1 billion.
- Any journey from the airport on Lantau to the Kowloon peninsula will take you on the world's longest road and rail suspension bridge, the Tsing Ma Bridge. Completed in 1997, the bridge has a main span of 1,377 m (4,518 ft).
- A 2005 global survey revealed that Hong Kong has more night owls than anywhere else in the world except Portugal. Sixty-six percent of the city's population is still awake after midnight and 31 percent stay up past 1am.
- In 2001, a Hong Kong jeweller built the world's most expensive toilet in 24-carat gold decorated with amber, emeralds, sapphires and rubies. The jeweller claimed that his HK$27 million convenience was inspired by Lenin, who said that toilets should be built to remind people of the waste of capital warfare.

BEST FESTIVALS AND EVENTS

- **Chinese New Year** is the time to see dragon dances, firecrackers, spectacular illuminations and fireworks over the harbour. *Page 166.*
- **The Bun Festival** on Cheung Chau features stilt-walkers and colourful costumes. *Page 163.*
- **The Dragon Boat Festival** takes place in early summer, with dragon boat races at various places around Hong Kong. *Page 166.*
- **The Mid-Autumn Festival**, with its beautiful lantern parades and moon cakes, is best experienced at Victoria Park. *Page 111.*
- **The Rugby Sevens** People wear wacky costumes and drink lots of beer at this annual tournament. *Page 226.*
- **The Arts Festival** at the beginning of the year features a wide range of concerts and theatre from around the globe. *Page 218.*

ABOVE: a dragon dance at Chinese New Year.
BELOW RIGHT: an Octopus Card saves time and money.

ABOVE: spilling onto the street in Lan Kwai Fong.

BEST NIGHTLIFE

- **Lan Kwai Fong** Long-established nightlife hub in the heart of Central with a wide range of restaurants and bars.
- **SoHo (SOuth of HOllywood Road)** This area adjoining Lan Kwai Fong has developed over the past few years, together with BoHo (BelOw HOllywood).
- Lots of trendy bars, clubs and restaurants.
- **Wan Chai** Faded for a time but now back on form. More down to earth than the Central nightspots.
- **Tsim Sha Tsui** A mix of touristy and local bars and restaurants. A new nightlife zone is developing around Minden Avenue east of Nathan Road.

MONEY-SAVERS

Octopus Card
Recommended to anyone who is staying more than a day or so, this stored-value card costs HK$150 (which includes a refundable $50 deposit). Unused credit is also refundable. The card can be used on almost all forms of transport, and – handily – to purchase museum tickets and even items in convenience stores. It is also possible to top up the credit (up to HK$1000) from a bank account or credit card. For enquiries, tel: 2266 2222 or visit www.octopuscards.com

Museum Pass
Available from HKTB visitor centres and participating museums; gains the holder open access to Hong Kong's main museums. Of most use for residents, but the 6-month pass costs only HK$50 and will pay for itself with just a few trips to museums. Also gives 10 percent off purchases at museum shops and cafés.

Mobile Phones and Phone Cards
If you are staying for a few days and need to make local calls on your mobile, invest in a SIM for your phone, sold in 7-11 convenience stores for around HK$100. Another worthwhile purchase if you are calling abroad from Hong Kong is a phone card – the kind that gives you an access number. These can give you as much as 5 hours calling time to the UK and US for only HK$50, and can be used on your mobile.

Miscellaneous
In restaurants, ask for filtered tap water rather than bottled mineral water. Taxis are quite cheap, but costs can add up quickly – try to avoid rush hours and cross-harbour tunnel routes as far as possible.

HONG KONG, CHINA

Few cities ignite the senses as does Hong Kong, and the appeal is as strong as ever following the return to Chinese sovereignty

Hong Kong pulsates with the visual energy of a fireworks display. It resonates to the din of a dim sum restaurant's peak hour. Polymesmeric, at times chaotic, intriguing, puzzling, endlessly exciting and in parts possessed of an astounding alternative beauty, Hong Kong is a place that precipitates the strongest emotions. More than one visitor has noted that this must be one of the earth's acupuncture points.

Hong Kong is fuelled and inspired by constant immigration, from mainland China, from elsewhere in Asia and the four corners of the world, with seven million souls simultaneously focused on top dollar and bottom line in an area rather smaller than the English county of Berkshire and less than half the size of the American state of Rhode Island. Cosmopolitan yet integrally Chinese, Hong Kong's inhabitants are defined by what's written on their business cards. Off duty, they may go shopping, play tennis and basketball on courts perched atop skyscrapers, or pinball their way between the bars and clubs crammed hugger mugger in the numerous nightlife zones; everyone here is all too aware that Time's winged chariot doesn't so much hurry near as overtake on the inside lane.

Hong Kong took an extended bath in the limelight at the end of the 20th century, with a dignified and heroic return to Chinese sovereignty in June 1997. When Prince Charles and Chris Patten, the widely admired last colonial governor, sailed off into the sunset aboard the royal yacht *Britannia*, it marked the end of a colony, an era and an empire.

It's all history now. Hong Kong is a Special Administrative Region (SAR) of China, with a key role to play in the spectacular growth of the Chinese economy. Yet despite the handover, it remains markedly different from the mainland. The SAR maintains its own identity, a blend of Chinese with a strong cosmopolitan flavour, an eye for the main chance and a stolid imperturbability when economic times get tough.

For the first time, Hong Kong is starting to face some real competition from its neighbours. The economic revolution in the Pearl River Delta has catapulted entire new cities like Shenzhen onto the world map. And Macau's lackadaisical ambience has been given a makeover with the arrival of a clutch of casinos which are being dubbed the "Las Vegas of the East". Does the former Crown colony have the stamina to keep up? The smart money is saying: you bet. ❑

PRECEDING PAGES: the glittering harbour; the bustle of Wan Chai.
LEFT: Hong Kong's crowded urban areas have the world's highest population densities.

A BARREN ISLAND

Initially regarded by the British as an ill-chosen gain of limited value, Hong Kong soon became an important part of the Empire – and one that was only reluctantly relinquished

To most people, Hong Kong's history starts with the Opium Wars in the 1840s. However, archaeological studies have uncovered evidence of human habitation along this stretch of the southern Chinese coast dating back some 6,000 years.

Most of the excavated stone tools, pottery and other artefacts have been found preserved in coastal areas, suggesting a strong dependence on the sea. Bronze appeared in the middle of the second millennium BC, and weapons and tools such as axes and fish hooks have been excavated from local sites. There is evidence, too, in the form of stone moulds from the islands of Chek Lap Kok, Lantau and Lamma, that the metal was worked locally. Rock carvings, most of which are geometric in style, have also been discovered around Hong Kong Island and on some of the smaller islands.

An increasing number of people from the mainland came to settle in the region during the Qin (221–206 BC) and Han (206 BC–AD 220) dynasties. Coins of the Han period have been found in Hong Kong, and a brick tomb was uncovered at Kowloon's Lei Cheng Uk *(see page 141)* with a collection of typical Han tomb furniture. Other findings included pottery and iron implements. Little has been discovered from the next 1,000 years, but engraved writings, coins and celadon pottery suggest strong links with the Chinese Song

dynasty during the 13th century AD. The many Ming-style blue-and-white porcelain works discovered on Lantau suggest increasing contact with the mainland during the Ming (1368–1644) and Qing (1644–1911) dynasties.

The coming of the Europeans

The West began to show an interest in China and Asia during the 15th and 16th centuries due to the increased trade in products such as silk and tea. The Portuguese were the first to arrive, trading with China at various points along the coast and establishing a settlement at Macau in 1557. The British, on the other hand, did not appear in force until the 17th century.

LEFT: houses on the Peak; this picture was taken in 1937, before the reforestation programme.
RIGHT: early colonial buildings on the harbour, 1856.

In 1685, Emperor Kangxi, who reigned when the Qing dynasty was at the peak of its power, opened Guangzhou for limited trade. Ships began arriving from the British East India Company stations on the Indian coast, and Hong Kong – with its sheltered deep-water harbour – began to establish itself as a trading hub. Fifteen years later the Company, by then the world's largest commercial organisation, received permission to build a storage warehouse outside Guangzhou.

At first, trade with Western countries was in China's favour. Traders paid huge amounts of silver for fine Chinese tea and silk products, for which there was great demand in Europe. Isolated from the outside world, the Chinese were proud of their ancient civilisation and regarded themselves as a highly civilised race, whereas foreigners were considered to be barbarians. Tough terms were imposed on foreign traders: they could only live in restricted areas in Guangzhou, and were only allowed to stay during the trading season. They could not bring in arms, warships or women, and they had to pay for everything in hard cash, normally silver. Learning the Chinese language was forbidden, and traders also had to put up with the Chinese system of royalties, bribes and fees. Local merchants were appointed by the emperor to keep an eye on foreigners. But despite these restrictions, the southern coastal region prospered.

The East India Company tried to balance its huge purchases from China by increasing its sale of opium to the Chinese, and by the end of the 18th century the volume reached 2,000 chests a year. Alarmed at the outflow of silver, the emperor banned the drug trade completely in 1799. But neither foreigners nor Guangdong merchants were willing to give up the profitable business, and they resorted to smuggling. By 1816, annual opium imports amounted to at least 5,000 chests. After the East India Company lost its monopoly on the opium trade in 1834, traders from other countries rushed to get rich quick from the lucrative, illegal trade.

To try to eliminate opium for good, in 1839 the emperor appointed Lin Zexu as a special commissioner to Guangzhou. Lin blockaded foreign factories, and refused to let anyone leave until all stocks of opium had been surrendered. Large quantities were burned in the port city of Humen, at the mouth of the Zhu Jiang (Pearl River), and dealers and ship owners were forced to sign a pledge promising to stop importing opium or else face execution.

After a six-week siege, the British government's representative, Captain Charles Elliot of the Royal Navy, finally agreed to surrender more than 20,000 chests of opium.

When word reached London, the British government was alarmed. The Foreign Secretary, Lord Palmerston, instructed Lord Napier (Chief Superintendent of Trade) to deliver a letter of protest to Lin Zexu. But under Chinese law Napier had no right to enter

Guangzhou, because only merchants were so privileged, and his rank only permitted him to pass a petition, not a letter, to Lin, who had by now been promoted to viceroy.

Deadlocked, Napier returned to Macau and Lin stopped all trade with the British. Napier sent two frigates up the Zhu Jiang to force a passage past Guangzhou's forts, but the ships were cut off and stranded. (Napier died three weeks later of natural causes.) The British community, mainly traders and their families, retreated from Guangzhou to Macau, but were warned by the Portuguese governor that he could not be responsible for their safety. During the summer of 1839, the British took refuge aboard ships in Hong Kong harbour.

Still reluctant to give up the lucrative opium business, British forces poured into Guangzhou to force Lin to reopen the province to opium trade. He refused, and in a diplomatic gesture to demonstrate his authority over British traders who had retreated to Macau, he made an official visit to the Portuguese enclave.

At this point, the British decided to resort to more resolute measures. Claiming that their citizens in Guangzhou were in danger because of the Chinese government's anti-opium movement, Palmerston proposed two solutions: either a commercial treaty in favour of

On 26 January 1841, the British flag was raised at Possession Point on Hong Kong Island, and the island was officially occupied by the British. Five months later, British officials began selling plots of land and the colonisation of Hong Kong began.

Neither China nor Britain was happy with the terms of the Chuen Pi agreement, however. The Chinese government and its people saw the loss of a part of its territory as an unbearable humiliation, and Qi Shan was ordered to Beijing in chains. The British government, particularly Palmerston, was unhappy with Hong Kong, which he contemptuously, and famously, described as "a barren island with

British traders, or British occupation of a small island where her citizens could live under their own flag, free from control of the Chinese government.

When negotiations broke down between Lin's representative and Captain Elliot in 1840, the British fleet attacked Guangzhou and occupied the city's forts, thus sparking the First Opium War. Intimidated by the British, the Qing commissioner, Qi Shan, who had replaced Lin, agreed in January 1841 to the Convention of Chuen Pi, which ceded Hong Kong Island to Britain.

ABOVE: a panorama of Victoria Harbour from 1860.

barely a house upon it", and refused to accept it as the station that Elliot had demanded as an alternative to a commercial treaty.

Blaming Elliot for failing to make full use of the troops sent to China, Palmerston replaced him with Sir Henry Pottinger, Hong Kong's first governor, in August 1841. Pottinger soon realised Hong Kong's potential future, even though Britain had treated it as just another pawn in ongoing negotiations with the Chinese. He encouraged long-term building projects and awarded land grants.

To capitalise on Britain's foothold in China, Pottinger ordered his troops north up to the Chang Jiang (Yangzi River) and threatened to attack Nanjing (Nanking). The Chinese capitulated in August 1842, and signed the Treaty of Nanjing, which officially gave Hong Kong island to the British "in perpetuity". (The Chuen Pi Convention, agreed earlier by the two sides, had not been signed and so was never accepted as an official agreement by the British.) Under the Treaty of Nanjing, which China naturally regarded as "unequal", five Chinese ports, including Guangzhou, were opened for foreign trade. The treaty included the supplementary Treaty of the Bogue (Humen) in October 1843, under which the Chinese were permitted to come and go in Hong Kong for trading purposes.

ernment, lost again. By the summer of 1858, allied British and French troops had advanced far to the north, forcing the Chinese government to sign the Treaties of Tianjin (Tientsin). The terms gave foreigners the right to send diplomatic representatives to China and travel freely throughout China.

Hostilities were renewed the following year when Chinese soldiers fired on the first British envoy to China as he made his way to the court in Beijing. Fighting continued until 1860. The British consul in Guangzhou secured the perpetual lease of the Kowloon peninsula all the way north to what is now Boundary Street, including Stonecutter's Island.

With the silting of Macau's harbour and the weakening of Portuguese power in Asia, Hong Kong began its growth into one of the greatest port cities the world had ever seen.

The early colonial period

In its early days, the new British colony grew slowly, but further Anglo-Chinese conflict was soon to change this. In 1856 a dispute over the interpretation of the two earlier treaties led to the outbreak of the Second Opium War, and during the two-year conflict, many companies in Guangzhou transferred their offices to Hong Kong, considerably strengthening the fledgling colony. China, weak with a corrupt gov-

By this time, other countries – Russia, France, Germany and Japan – were waking up to the importance of having easy access to China. Not to be outdone by the British, they began to make similar incursions to secure footholds all along the Chinese coastline. In 1862, a Sino-Portuguese treaty gave Macau a colonial status similar to that of Hong Kong. A second treaty in 1887 confirmed it as a Portuguese colony in perpetuity.

The British were concerned that their territory in Hong Kong was vulnerable to attack from the north, and wished to gain control of the mountainous area north of Kowloon as far as the Shenzhen River. In 1898 they got their way, securing the lease of what became known as the New Territories (as well as some 230 islands) for a period of 99 years. There was later regret at having signed this treaty, which only leased the land, while Hong Kong Island and the Kowloon peninsula were British in perpetuity. (It would later be impractical for Britain to keep Hong Kong Island and Kowloon when the New Territories lease ran out in 1997.)

At first, Chinese warships were allowed to use the wharf at Kowloon City, and Chinese officials were permitted to remain in office. However, a year later, the British took over the city completely. The New Territories was declared a part of Hong Kong, although it kept a separate administrative body from the urban area. Under a laissez-faire style of British rule, Hong Kong people were left alone to concentrate on their businesses.

During the late 19th and early 20th centuries, the colony developed rapidly, becoming a magnet for immigrants and a centre of trade with Chinese communities abroad. Several public-service companies were established, including the Hong Kong and China Gas Company in 1861, the Peak Tram in 1885 and the 137-km (85-mile) Kowloon-Canton Railway (KCR) in 1910. The paucity of land for building due to the steep terrain meant that land-reclamation projects got under way as early as 1851. In 1904, the first land reclamation was completed in what is now the area of Chater, Connaught and Des Voeux roads. In 1929, another reclamation project was completed in Wan Chai. Today around six per cent of Hong Kong's land has been reclaimed from the sea.

Turbulent times

From the beginning of the 20th century, China experienced a series of political upheavals. In 1900, a peasant uprising known as the Boxer Rebellion seriously challenged the authority of the creaky and corrupt Qing government, which collapsed for good a few years later. In 1911 Sun Yat-sen established the Republic of China. Although Sun travelled to Hong Kong many times to enlist support for his cause, his revolution did not have much impact on the

British colony, apart from the fact that many people came to Hong Kong to escape the unrest further north.

Between 1920 and the late 1940s life in China was dominated by wars. The long-running civil war between Mao Zedong's Communist Party (founded in 1921) and the Nationalists (Guomintang), led by Chiang Kaishek, divided the country. The Japanese invasion in 1937, and World War II, brought terrible suffering. In December 1941 Japanese troops attacked Hong Kong from the north; Allied forces withdrew from the New Territories and Kowloon to Hong Kong Island. After a week of resistance, Hong Kong

surrendered on Christmas Day. The Japanese occupation lasted for three years and eight months. Under an agreement between Japan and Portugal, Macau became the only "neutral pocket" in China, and many Europeans found refuge here during the war.

During the occupation, Hong Kong's trade virtually stopped, the currency lost its value and food supplies were disrupted. But most residents remained loyal to the Allied cause. Chinese guerrillas fought against the Japanese invaders in the New Territories, while peasants helped foreigners to escape.

In August 1945, after the Japanese surrender, the Royal Navy arrived in Hong Kong to

LEFT: the British negotiate to open China's ports.
RIGHT: Sun Yat-sen remains a Chinese national hero.

re-establish British rule, and a provisional government was created.

After the war, Hong Kong Chinese who had escaped to those mainland areas beyond Japanese control returned in large numbers. China's civil war, which resurfaced in 1946 soon after the Japanese surrender, drove more people – many of whom were affluent Shanghai entrepreneurs and property owners – into the British territory. By 1949, the population had reached two million.

In October 1949, Mao Zedong declared the establishment of the People's Republic of China, and the defeated Nationalists fled to Taiwan. The United Nations imposed an

desperately to keep them out because the numbers were becoming alarming.

During the Vietnam War in the late 1960s and early 1970s, US Navy vessels, en route to or from Vietnam, were a familiar sight in Victoria Harbour. Hong Kong became a favourite destination for American soldiers on leave, and troops spent their dollars liberally in the bars and nightclubs of the Wan Chai red-light district and in Tsim Sha Tsui.

In subsequent years, China was ravaged by the Cultural Revolution, and the turmoil drifted into Hong Kong, where tensions erupted into a series of disturbances in the mid-1960s, and also to Macau where Red Guards waged a

embargo on trade with China, with the intention of killing the new Beijing government in its cradle. Hong Kong's economy suffered from the embargo, and since revenue from the port was not enough to support the rapidly increasing population, the colony was forced into industrialisation. Entrepreneurs from Shanghai established themselves in the colony by setting up textile factories. By the 1960s, the textile and garment industries accounted for more than half of the colony's exports.

Famine swept China in the early 1960s due to misguided socialist policies, and brought another wave of immigrants to Hong Kong. This time, the colonial government tried

propaganda war with posters and slogans, calling on the Chinese residents to start a revolution. The chaos almost paralysed Hong Kong's economy, but by the end of 1967, the unrest had been more or less quelled.

Rapid development

During the late 1970s and 1980s, Hong Kong's economy developed at an amazing pace, as it expanded its role as an entrepôt with its neighbours and as China's trading partner. This was made possible by greater stability in China, and the rapid economic advance there due to Deng Xiaoping's pragmatic policies. As China's window to the world and the world's gateway to China, Hong Kong began to play a more important role. An increasing number of businesses moved their manufacturing operations north to the mainland, where labour and raw materials were cheaper.

To keep pace with economic development, infrastructure throughout the colony was improved, and the territory was transformed into a modern, efficient and cosmopolitan city. A higher standard of living made it possible for the government to increase investment in education, housing and other social welfare projects. An efficient civil service system introduced by the British government played a major role in the economic boom, aided by the Independent Commission Against Corruption (ICAC), set up in 1974.

Three years earlier, Sir Murray MacLehose had become the first Hong Kong governor to be appointed from the British diplomatic circle. London's choice of MacLehose, a diplomat who was familiar with China and spoke Mandarin and Cantonese, demonstrated Britain's concern over Hong Kong and its future. He and his successors Edward Youde and David Wilson were professional diplomats and China experts; the last governor, Chris Patten, was, however, a career politician.

With the city becoming increasingly crowded, Hong Kong ended an immigration policy in 1980 that allowed Chinese refugees to remain in the colony if they managed to reach an urban area. From this time on, all illegal immigrants were sent back.

By the 1980s, the Hong Kong government enjoyed near complete autonomy from London, and even had the power to conclude certain negotiations with foreign powers. The colony regularly negotiated its own economic agreements with other countries, and was admitted into several international financial institutions such as the Asian Development Bank.

However, amid all the prosperity was an inescapable anxiety over the future, with the 1997 expiry of the 99-year lease on the New Territories – which made up 90 percent of the total land area – looming large. Most Hong Kong people would have preferred to stay

under British rule rather than embrace the Communist regime. Although they were unhappy with the fact that British companies and expatriates had enjoyed privileges in business and in government positions, most locals appreciated the fundamental policies by the British government that enabled people to compete in a free market. Having escaped earlier from the authoritarian system in socialist China – or in some cases, having suffered political persecution on the mainland – they feared going back to the Communist system. But their destiny was not in their own hands.

China had always maintained its stance that it would take back Hong Kong when it was

"ripe". Although China had refused the Portuguese government's offer to hand back Macau in the 1970s, for fear of causing instability in Hong Kong, circumstances had changed by the early 1980s, and Chinese leaders began thinking about getting Hong Kong back, and expunging 150 years of humiliation.

It was under such circumstances that British Prime Minister Margaret Thatcher paid a visit to Beijing and Hong Kong in 1982. During the trip, she discussed with Chinese leaders the issue of Hong Kong's future. Thatcher believed she could get the Chinese to allow Britain to extend the 99-year lease on the New Territories. History was to prove otherwise. ❑

FAR LEFT: Bonham Strand, Western District, c. 1900.
LEFT: the Japanese arrive, December 1941.
RIGHT: illegal immigrants from mainland China, 1978.

THE RETURN TO CHINA

Generations of Hong Kong people grew up living under
British rule. Then, in a single day, they were living according
to the dictates of the Chinese Communist Party

In the early 1980s, life in Hong Kong was dominated by the issue of its return to China. Even now, although the former British colony is a part of the People's Republic of China, its relationship with the mainland still dominates all other issues.

In the years leading up to the 1997 handover, mainlanders flooded into the territory. In 1996, the governments of Hong Kong and Beijing had agreed to limit immigration to the colony to 150 people per day. But this new wave was different from previous flows of immigrants. Most notably, it included some of the mainland's top business executives and professionals, lured by Hong Kong's opportunities.

Several opinion polls taken shortly before the handover showed that most Hong Kong people would prefer to remain under British rule if they could control their own destiny, although it was deemed politically correct to say they loved the motherland. And although many were sceptical that Beijing would keep its promise to let Hong Kong's political system continue for another 50 years, most people had decided to accept the reality and adapt.

Negotiating the return

The issue of Hong Kong's return to China arrived on the political agenda with British Prime Minister Margaret Thatcher's visit to Beijing in 1982. This launched the discussion on what would happen to Hong Kong after the 99-year lease on the New Territories, nine-tenths of the colony, expired in 1997. The reaction to the news that the colony's future

was being negotiated was typical of Hong Kong – the local stock market nosedived.

In September 1984, after two years of often acrimonious negotiations, Britain and China came to an agreement, the Joint Declaration, which formally agreed the return of the colony to China in 1997. The Declaration stipulated that Hong Kong's way of life would remain unchanged for 50 years, that the territory would become a Special Administrative Region (SAR) and continue to enjoy a "high degree of autonomy" – except in foreign affairs and defence – and that China's socialist system and policies would not be imposed. As Deng Xiaoping put it, "Horses will keep racing, and nightclub dancing will continue."

Plans were drawn up for Hong Kong's administration in the years running up to 1997. Key points included elections to the Legislative Council (Legco), the District Boards and new Regional Councils. The Hong Kong government expressed its intention to train local policymakers during the years preceding 1997 to prepare the territory for its role as an SAR.

Beijing soon appointed a committee of 59 members, only 23 of whom were from Hong Kong, to draft the mini-constitution – known as the Basic Law – for the SAR. Britain announced it would phase out its garrison, while China said the People's Liberation Army (PLA) would be stationed in Hong Kong after the handover.

During Hong Kong's first Legco elections in 1985, initiated by the British, 24 of the 56 members took their places through indirect elections. Out of a total population of 5.5 million at the time, only 70,000 people were eligible to vote under Hong Kong's restricted system of indirect elections. Of that number, only 47,000 registered to vote and only 25,000 actually went to the polls. Nevertheless, this election was enough to touch off a debate about whether the Hong Kong government would allow open elections in 1988, as had been previously promised.

Strained relations

China began to worry about the territory's fledgling attempts at democracy, and the ensuing debate about the future of Hong Kong. Beijing's top man in the territory, Lu Ping, insisted that Britain was deviating from the Joint Declaration and arousing fear and anxiety amongst Hong Kong's people. Amid the political tension, however, Hong Kong's economy continued to thrive.

The British government wanted direct elections to be held before 1997. Increasingly irritated, Beijing eventually declared that political changes not consistent with the Basic Law would be nullified in 1997. Deng Xiaoping added that universal suffrage might not be beneficial for Hong Kong.

LEFT: lowering the Union Jack on handover day.
RIGHT: Margaret Thatcher takes tea in a resettlement estate during her 1982 visit.

In June 1989, the Chinese government crushed a pro-democracy demonstration centred in Beijing's Tiananmen Square. Horrified by Beijing's brutality, one million people took to the streets in Hong Kong. The massacre exacerbated the Hong Kong brain drain, with more than 50,000 leaving the territory annually after the incident. At the end of the year, Britain said it would grant British citizenship to just 225,000 Hong Kong Chinese before Hong Kong reverted to China.

London tried to keep earlier promises of democratic reform without provoking China's displeasure at free elections for Legco. Pushed by budding political awareness among its citi-

zens, the Hong Kong government agreed to speed up the process, saying it would put 18 seats up for direct elections in 1991.

After numerous consultations, the two governments agreed in early 1990 that members elected to Legco in 1995 would serve until their term ended in 1999, two years after the handover, and that they would be among the 400 people who would select Hong Kong's first post-1997 handover Chief Executive. China later reneged on the agreement after Governor Chris Patten carried out electoral reforms against Beijing's wishes; China replaced the elected Legco with a Beijing-appointed provisional legislature.

Funding the new airport

To boost the economy and restore confidence battered by the Tiananmen Square massacre, the Hong Kong government announced it would build a new airport on Lantau Island, scheduled for completion in early 1997 at an estimated cost of HK$78 billion. But China attacked the scheme, insisting that it should be consulted because its future SAR government might be saddled with debt.

The Hong Kong government announced it would fund the HK$7.8 billion Lantau fixed crossing (a series of bridges to the new airport) as there was no international financing. China took the announcement as a direct challenge.

The argument over the airport project began to move beyond the question of finance to the broader issue of Hong Kong's autonomy. If Hong Kong did not have the autonomy to build a new airport, then its say in other matters would be in doubt. Hong Kong and British government representatives paid many visits to Beijing to win approval for the airport project, all the time trying not to appear they were grovelling. Beijing was unrelenting.

Finally, Beijing and London announced that an understanding about the airport had been reached. But like the 1984 Sino-British Agreement, its conclusion was without Hong Kong's participation. The agreement gave

China's support for the airport project in exchange for fiscal guarantees and membership on the board of the airport authority. A few days after the announcement, Hong Kong's Hang Seng Index hit an all-time record high – a sigh of relief from the business community that the two governments had worked out their differences.

But the optimism did not last long. In June 1991, Hong Kong's new Bill of Rights backing the "rights and freedoms" guaranteed in the 1984 Sino-British Agreement became law, despite China's insistence that the move was against the principles stated in the Basic Law, Hong Kong's post-handover constitution.

The political instability encouraged more residents to emigrate. In 1990, about 60,000 of Hong Kong's most accomplished professionals moved overseas, mainly to Canada and Australia. Britain called on its allies to accept Hong Kong immigrants; the United States amended its immigration laws to increase Hong Kong's quota to 10,000 annually until 1994 and 20,000 thereafter. The Hongkong Bank, the territory's largest, moved its headquarters to Britain, generally seen as reflecting the company's lack of confidence in Hong Kong's future.

The first direct elections in Legco's 150-year history took place in September 1991. For the first time, the incumbent government faced opposition and the potential of legislative defeats from the opposition under barrister Martin Lee. China, in a not-too-subtle move, advised voters to take candidates' "attitudes toward the mainland" into account when casting their votes. The comment was widely interpreted as a call to vote for the pro-Beijing candidates and not those of the pro-democracy camp represented by Lee's United Democrats. Unimpressed, voters demonstrated their independence by giving 15 of the 18 seats up for direct election to pro-democracy candidates.

The last governor

In April 1992, Britain's Conservative Party chairman Chris Patten was named Hong Kong's last governor – the first time a politician instead of a diplomat had been given the post. Patten's arrival heralded the most tense period in relations between Britain and China.

Unlike his predecessors, who had arrived decked out in full ceremonial dress (plumed helmet and all), Patten wore a dark business suit – discreetly modernising the image of the office of governor in Hong Kong in the process. Despite, or perhaps because of some of his unorthodox ways, Patten soon proved to be a popular leader. Instead of sitting in his office, he went out into the streets to meet ordinary people, listened to their opinions, and held question-and-answer sessions in public during which he addressed politically sensitive issues with a candid, sometimes controversial attitude.

Patten announced proposals for increased spending on welfare, health, housing and the environment. The most controversial move, however, was his proposal to reform the politi-

1997, the last day of Britain's rule. Beijing also pointed its accusing finger at the private sector, including the British company Jardines, which it accused of supporting Patten's political agenda and damaging the international community's confidence in Hong Kong's future.

In 1994, Legco passed Patten's proposed electoral reforms by a narrow margin, inviting strong condemnation from China. The reforms were a halfway point between full direct elections for all members of the legislature and a more muted electoral plan. Legco remained far from being a directly elected legislature, but the change was still enough to draw more criticism from China.

cal system. China wanted no such shift towards greater democracy, and openly attacked Patten's political reforms. As a result, the Hang Seng Index dropped about five percent in October 1992, and brokers warned that unless Patten made a U-turn on his push for greater democracy, the stock market could suffer further.

Beijing declared that all contracts, leases and agreements signed or ratified by the British Hong Kong administration without the approval of China would not be honoured after 30 June

LEFT AND ABOVE: street demonstrations in Hong Kong following the Tiananmen Square massacre in 1989. **RIGHT:** Chris Patten, the last governor.

The electoral reform was Patten's last major act in office. As China began to play an increasingly important role in Hong Kong society and the business sectors competed with each other to get on Beijing's good side, Patten was sidelined. Beijing simply refused to talk to him, making it difficult for him to take any further action.

Sunset over the Empire

The SAR's first chief executive was selected by a Beijing-appointed committee at the beginning of 1997 from among three candidates. Tung Chee-hwa, a shipping tycoon who had received financial help from China in his earlier business days, was the obvious candidate from early on. Ironically, Tung had previously been a member of the colonial government appointed by Patten.

Despite the many humiliating insults the Chinese leaders threw his way during his five years in office, Patten's political reforms and personal charisma won him the respect of Hong Kong's residents. At the British farewell ceremony on the night of 30 June 1997, Patten's forceful farewell speech received long applause from the crowd, and people shouted "We will miss you" as he and Prince Charles boarded the royal yacht *Britannia* for England.

The handover meant the immediate dismantling of the elected Legco, with Beijing refusing to recognise its legitimacy, reneging on an earlier promise; the official reason given for this move was that Patten had changed the electoral process and therefore the pledge was invalidated. After taking office on 1 July 1997, Tung formulated a voting system for Hong Kong's first legislative election, set for May 1998, when the Beijing-appointed provisional legislature was replaced. It gave the biggest say to business groups, a move believed to have been designed to sideline the most popular party, the Democrats.

THE HANDOVER

The handover of Hong Kong back to China on 30 June 1997 saw more parties, spontaneous street celebrations and fireworks in one night than at any other time in the territory's history. Most Hong Kongers, Chinese and Western residents alike, forgot the political implications for the night and celebrated the historic occasion with a festive spirit and a sense of humour. At midnight, all major figures who either had, or were to have, a hand in Hong Kong's future gathered in the new extension to the Hong Kong Convention and Exhibition Centre. But the man who had won the territory back for the Chinese was conspicuously missing – Deng Xiaoping had died just months earlier.

Just before midnight, the Union Jack made its slow descent down the flagpole as the British military band played "God Save the Queen". Then, the red-and-yellow Chinese flag was raised as a Chinese military band played its national anthem. Chris Patten shook hands with the crowds of people near the pier in Central before sailing away on board the royal yacht *Britannia*. Inside the Convention Centre, Hong Kong civil servants swore allegiance to the People's Republic of China in Mandarin.

In the early morning of 1 July, People's Liberation Army troops crossed over the border into the New Territories, welcomed by hundreds of villagers lining the roads.

Future anxieties

Although China's recent economic development has helped to change Hong Kong people's opinions of their northern compatriots, the mutual prejudices will take years to overcome. Beijing has kept its promise not to interfere in Hong Kong's internal affairs during the early post-handover period, but some aspects of society have changed. More locals are learning Putonghua (Mandarin), the language of mainland China; more mainland artists are putting on shows and exhibitions in Hong Kong; and local businessmen are competing feverishly to get a share of the huge market to the north.

The school curriculum has also changed. The Basic Law and Putonghua have become new subjects, the aim being to strengthen the sense of belonging to China. Cantonese has replaced English as the language of instruction in most schools, and, unsurprisingly, many observers have commented that local English-speaking ability has suffered as a result.

Before the handover, a popular view was that Hong Kong under Communist China would undergo political changes, while remaining stable and prosperous economically. What happened in the months after the handover was just the opposite. There were few political confrontations, apart from some dissent concerning the make-up of the SAR's first legislative body, and the PLA kept a low profile in its barracks. However, in late 1997 and through 1998 Hong Kong experienced a major economic crisis, as did many Asian countries. The Hang Seng dropped 6,000 points – about 40 percent.

There was a slow recovery from 1999, but even by 2003 the economy was still in the doldrums, unemployment had soared and, in an ironic reversal of history, many locals began seeking work on the mainland. From March to May 2003 the SARS virus epidemic caused panic across the region – the Hong Kong public wore surgical masks and plastic gloves outdoors, and tourist numbers dried to a trickle. SARS may now be in the past, but you can still see plenty of people wearing masks. This is because the air pollution is now so bad, despite government initiatives, that on many days it is

a genuine health hazard. Clear days are now unusual – most likely immediately after summer rainstorms – and for much of the year Hong Kong is shrouded in thick haze and smog.

The dictum of "one country, two systems" has been called into question a number of times in recent years, notably when the government asked Beijing to overturn the Court of Final Appeal's ruling on the right of abode, and then on July 1st 2003, when more than 500,000 demonstrators marched peacefully to protest against plans to introduce controversial anti-subversion laws. Following another big demonstration a year later, the government backed down and Tung Chee-hwa stepped

down in early 2005. His replacement, Donald Tsang, is a devout Catholic and career civil servant. A relatively popular figure, with a background in finance, Beijing hopes he will prove to be a stablising influence.

Hong Kong's first post-handover chief secretary, Anson Chan, commented that in 100 years, Hong Kong and China would merge into one system, the Hong Kong system. She may be right. Few believe that China can significantly change Hong Kong. But to most local people, impatient and expecting immediate results, and used to the efficiency that created an economic wonder in just a few decades, 100 years is far too long to wait and see. ❑

LEFT: getting into the party spirit for the handover.
RIGHT: the Falun Gong movement has been a thorn in the government's side.

Decisive Dates

c.4000 BC The first stone-age settlements are established on the south China coast.

1557 Portuguese traders establish a colony at Macau.

1685 Emperor Kangxi allows limited trade in Guangzhou (Canton). Ships begin arriving from the British East India Company.

1773 British traders unload 1,000 chests of opium in Guangzhou.

1799 China's opium consumption reaches 2,000 chests a year, forcing Beijing to ban the drug, which then drives the trade underground.

1834 The British East India Company loses its monopoly on the opium trade to other European nations.

1839 China appoints the anti-opium viceroy, Lin Zexu, to clean up drugs in Guangzhou. He confiscates some 20,000 chests of opium from the British. Hostilities mount until November, when British ships blow up four Chinese junks, sparking the first Anglo-Chinese War, which became known as the First Opium War.

1840–1 Negotiations between China and Britain break down, and the British fleet attacks Guangzhou and occupies the city's forts. The two sides agree on a preliminary resolution (the Convention of Chuen Pi), which cedes the island of Hong Kong to the British. But neither government is happy with the terms and both refuse to ratify it.

1842 The Opium War ends and British possession of Hong Kong is confirmed by the Treaty of Nanjing, which cedes Hong Kong Island to Britain "in perpetuity". Sir Henry Pottinger becomes the first British governor of Hong Kong.

Colonial period

1856–60 The Chinese cede Kowloon (Tsim Sha Tsui) and Stonecutter's Island "in perpetuity" to Britain. But hostilities continue, culminating in the Second Opium War.

1862 A Sino-Portuguese treaty grants Macau colonial status similar to Hong Kong's.

1898 Britain forces China to lease the New Territories, which includes some 230 outlying islands, for 99 years, beginning 1 July 1898.

1911 Dr Sun Yat-sen overthrows the Qing dynasty and establishes the Republic of China.

1912 Emperor Puyi abdicates, signalling the end of Imperial China.

1931 The Japanese occupy Dongbei, or Manchuria.

1932 The Chinese Communists declare war on Japan.

1941 On Christmas Day the British surrender Hong Kong to the Japanese.

1945 World War II ends. China's ongoing civil war between the Communists and the Nationalists (Guomintang) resumes.

1949 The Nationalists are defeated and flee to Taiwan. The Communists found the People's Republic of China (PRC).

1966 Rioting flares up in Hong Kong over a price increase in the first-class Star Ferry fare. China begins its disastrous Cultural Revolution.

1971 The PRC replaces Taiwan in the United Nations General Assembly (Taiwan had become the sole representative of China in the United Nations after the PRC was founded in 1949). Sir Murray MacLehose becomes the first Hong Kong governor to be appointed from the British diplomatic corps.

1972 Opening of the first cross-harbour tunnel.

1973 The first New Town, Tuen Mun, is completed.

1974 The Independent Commission Against Corruption (ICAC) is set up to stamp out crime and corruption.

1978 China starts to reform its economy and open its doors to the world.

1979 Hong Kong's US$1 billion Mass Transit Railway (MTR) opens.

1982 British Prime Minister Margaret Thatcher visits Beijing and Hong Kong in September and begins discussions on Hong Kong's future. China decides to develop Shenzhen, a small town on Hong Kong's northern border, into a Special Economic Zone.

Handover countdown

1983 China reveals its plan for Hong Kong to become a Special Administrative Region (SAR) after the territory is returned in 1997. Hong Kong will keep its own capitalist system, judiciary and police, but the head of Hong Kong will be a Hong Kong Chinese. The Hong Kong dollar is pegged to the US dollar at a rate of 7.8.

1984 The British Ambassador to China and the Chinese Vice Foreign Minister initial "A Draft Agreement on the Future of Hong Kong", ending two years of acrimony. The Hong Kong government starts to plan for the territory's administration in the years running up to 1997.

1985 Britain and China ratify the Sino-British Joint Declaration. A Sino-British joint liaison group is created in regard to Hong Kong's future. The colony holds its first election for the Legislative Council (Legco), drawing criticism from China, which insists that any political changes not accepted by Beijing will not be respected after the handover.

1988 The proposed Basic Law, Hong Kong's post-handover constitution, is published.

1989 One million people take to the streets to protest against the Tiananmen Square massacre. The government announces plans for a new airport, criticised by Beijing. Forced repatriation of Vietnamese boat people begins.

1991 Beijing and London announce an agreement regarding the new airport. Later, British Prime Minister John Major visits Beijing, the first Western leader to do so since the Tiananmen massacre in 1989.

1992 Hong Kong's 28th and last British governor, Chris Patten, arrives in the territory and proposes political reform. The move draws attacks from Beijing.

1994 Legco passes Patten's proposed electoral reforms. Beijing and London continue to squabble.

1997 China resumes sovereignty on 1 July, Tung Chee-hwa is appointed chief executive, Legco is temporarily replaced by the Provisional Legislature and Hong Kong becomes an SAR. The stock market dives in response to the Asian economic crisis.

Post-handover

1998 Elections held for Legco. Chek Lap Kok airport opens.

1999 The rule of law is undermined as government asks Beijing to overturn the Court of

Final Appeal's ruling on the right of abode. Typhoon York, Hong Kong's first "direct hit" since 1983, kills two and injures over 500.

2003 The economy continues to flounder, particularly from March to May when the deadly SARS virus spreads to Hong Kong. Proposals for national security laws ("Article 23") spark mass protests on 1 July. The government backs down and shelves the plans indefinitely.

2004 Up to half a million protestors again march on 1 July, calling for more democracy and local control over local affairs.

2005 Tung Chee-hwa resigns. His successor is set to be Donald Tsang, a career civil servant with a background in finance. ❏

LEFT: a view of Hong Kong harbour from 1800.
RIGHT: the SARS outbreak caused panic in 2003.

HONG KONG'S PEOPLE

Outsiders may see Hong Kong's people as materialistic
and sometimes brusque. But there are reasons
for this, including an obsession with success

The people of Hong Kong are variously
described as being the most business-
minded, materialistic, competitive and
restless population on the planet. Few other
cities have such a complex, unsettled society.
It is a place that moves at lightning speed
because time is money, and every minute costs.
Love it or hate it, life in Hong Kong is addic-
tive, and even those who have escaped to more
peaceful places – vowing never to return – have
been drawn back like iron filings to a magnet.
Even the most jaded visitor usually finds something seductive about it.

Hong Kong's seven million people are
packed into just 1,103 sq. kilometres (426 sq.
miles), and certain areas have some of the
world's highest population densities. During
rush hour, overwhelming crowds of commuters
squeeze themselves into trains and buses.
Lunch hour is a feeding frenzy as thousands of
office workers dash for restaurants, jostling and
barging their way into tiny noodle shops and
delicatessens. Elbowing strangers, jumping
queues and honking horns in traffic jams (often
complemented by deafening construction sites
and roadworks) are unavoidable features of
daily life here.

As a major trading port situated on the fertile
Pearl River Delta, Hong Kong has long been a
magnet for immigrants in search of a better life.
New arrivals continue to flood in from China
and overseas, all sharing one dream: to make

money quickly and to enjoy spending it. This
continual injection of new blood is what gives
Hong Kong its excitement and intensity.

For those seeking a settled, peaceful existence, Hong Kong will be a hard slap in the
face. This place resounds with rags-to-riches
tales of entrepreneurs who built up their business empires from scratch, and this promise
of success is in the minds of almost every
immigrant who heads here.

Ethnic backgrounds and identity

Hong Kong is, and always has been, Chinese.
In spite of more than 150 years of colonial rule,
the Chinese, who now make up 98 percent of

PRECEDING PAGES: race day at Sha Tin racecourse.
LEFT: Hong Kongers love their dogs.
RIGHT: mah-jong is a popular, sociable game.

the population, never had a sense of allegiance to the British Crown. Those of the older generation, who originated from elsewhere, often identified with their home provinces or towns in China rather than Hong Kong. On the whole, however, local Chinese are more inclined to view themselves as Hong Kong citizens rather than Han Chinese. This sense of identity has increased in the post-handover years, along with what could be termed an embryonic civic pride – Hong Kongers no longer regard their city simply as somewhere to live and make money. Greater political and even environmental awareness – an example is the campaign to save the harbour – are

symptoms of a maturing city growing in confidence and sophistication. This is in part due to the fact that the local population is ever more likely to have been born and raised here rather than being refugees.

On the other hand, there is a great deal of frustration amongst ordinary people – despite the fact that Beijing has kept its distance, the feeling is that people have little or no say in local affairs. The angst is compounded by rising unemployment and a feeling of economic uncertainty that has persisted since the 1998 financial crisis.

The vast majority of Hong Kongers are Cantonese, and their dialect, cuisine and customs make up the fabric of society here. The Cantonese language often sounds harsh and argumentative to unaccustomed ears, but its humour, slang and interspersed English words make for lively conversation. Cantonese is also centuries older than Mandarin (*putonghua*), the official language of China, which evolved later in the courts of Mongol emperors during the Yuan dynasty (1271–1368). Therefore, the original rhythms and sounds of classical Tang- and Song-dynasty poetry are probably closer to modern-day Cantonese.

The Cantonese have traditionally been regarded as rebellious, ungovernable people given to spontaneous action if angered, and they have always been feared and mistrusted by successive emperors and regimes. The Nationalist revolution, which toppled the Qing dynasty in 1912, was instigated by a Cantonese – Dr Sun Yat-sen. In 1966, public discontent in Hong Kong erupted into serious rioting, ostensibly against an increase in Star Ferry fares. At the height of the Cultural Revolution in 1967, hundreds of Communist supporters besieged Government House. More recently, in 1989 one million protested against the Tiananmen Square massacre, and over 500,000 turned out to express their disgust with proposed government security measures in 2003.

Hong Kong's oldest landowners, the Hakka ("guest people"), immigrated from central and southern China centuries ago, fortifying villages against marauding pirates. Hakka women are forbidden from inheriting land, which is passed down through the male line, so that the family can retain ownership of its land. The Tanka and Hoklo "boat people" once spent their lives on junks off Aberdeen, Yau Ma Tei and other typhoon shelters, but most of them have now come ashore to earn a living. The Tanka are allegedly the descendants of General Lu Tsun, who revolted against the emperor; after his death, his people were persecuted and deemed unworthy to live on land.

The Hoklo originate from Fuzhou (Fujian province) and were mainly fishermen and manual labourers. They celebrate the sea goddess Tin Hau's birthday on the 23rd day of the third moon, sailing in elaborately decorated fishing boats to her temples to pray for protection at sea.

From the 1930s onwards, thousands of immigrants began arriving from other parts of China, especially Shanghai and Fuzhou. Shanghai and Chiu Chow (Shantou) people, renowned for their business acumen, clung together in powerful clan networks and established successful family firms. As a result, many of Hong Kong's top professionals hail from these regions. The Chinese government contained a formidable Shanghai clique under former president Jiang Zemin, once mayor of Shanghai, and it is likely that the appointments of Hong Kong's first chief executive, Tung Chee-hwa, and chief secretary, Anson Chan, were partly due to their roots in Shanghai.

mainland wives and children of Hong Kong men to register as local citizens. In 1997, 66,000 of these illegal immigrant children known as *siu yunseh* (little snakes) were deported, causing fierce debate over residency rights. Since then, priority has been given to these women and children in the quota of new arrivals allowed, but they still sometimes need to bribe mainland officials.

Nowadays, mainlanders can enter Hong Kong on an entry permit, and numbers have been increasing – from 25,000 a year in the late 1980s to 55,000 in 2002. This mainland influx is the main factor in Hong Kong's population rise in recent years.

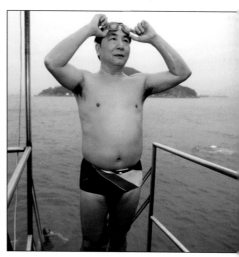

Between 1978 and 1980, some 500,000 illegal immigrants from mainland China braved the tidal waters, or climbed hills along the Sino-British border under the cover of darkness. Pitted against them were battalions of the People's Liberation Army (PLA) and Chinese coastal gunboats, which cooperated with Hong Kong's security forces. Once derided as *ah tsan* (country bumpkins), many of them are now assimilated into the local culture. Previously, it was also difficult for

LEFT: grandmother and granddaughter, Central Market.
ABOVE: Hakka woman in the New Territories.
RIGHT: swimming in Clearwater Bay.

Foreign devils and ghost people

Hong Kong's cultural diversity is largely a result of the many different foreign nationals who have made their home here, either temporarily or permanently. Indeed, the two percent of the population that is not Chinese have made valuable contributions to cuisine, arts, culture and religion in Hong Kong, while assimilating local customs and traditions.

American, Australian, Canadian, British and other European expatriates – *gweilo* ("ghost person" or "foreign devil") as they are known in Cantonese – make up the majority of the foreign business community. During British rule, expatriates were often given preferential treatment in the workplace, commanding much higher salaries than the Chinese. Today, these inequalities are less apparent.

One of the more established foreign communities in Hong Kong comprises the descendants of early merchant traders and soldiers who followed the Union Jack from the Indian subcontinent to Hong Kong: Indians, Sri Lankans, Pakistanis, Bangladeshis, Sikhs and Parsees. Their descendants, many of whom speak fluent Cantonese and hold Hong Kong passports, are not recognised as Chinese nationals, even though they were born in the territory. However, most of them have now been granted British citizenship. The survival of this community is largely due to a family-oriented approach to running cost-effective, profitable companies. A few thousand ex-Gurkha troops, who once served in the British army, are now working as security guards in Hong Kong, while their locally born offspring staff many Lan Kwai Fong and SoHo nightspots.

Hong Kong is home to a large number of Filipina *amahs* (domestic helpers). There are also many Filipinos working as singers and musicians. On Sundays and holidays, thousands of *amahs* gather in Chater Garden, Statue Square and surrounding streets in Central on their day off work.

WHAT'S IN A NAME

One of Hong Kong's odder cultural quirks is the range of eccentric English nicknames chosen by the Hong Kong Chinese: Photosynthesis, Frandie, Wealthy, Biscuit, Xerox, Tweetie… This is in part the result of a desire to embrace the English-speaking world, and in part a way of identifying with a particular respected figure, a hobby or interest.

Emulation of the successful accounts for the plethora of Jackie Chans in the territory, and may also explain some of the Wilsons, after the colony's penultimate British governor. Seemingly gaudy names such as Lucky or Wealthy or the no-nonsense Money represent the aspirations of a people who have only enjoyed prosperity for a couple of generations.

Humour is apparent with names that echo the individual's Chinese name, leaving the glorious Winky Winky Wong Wing-kee. Sometimes the name puns on the family name, as in Gypsy Lee or Ivan Ho. Hobbies or interests can play a role, scientific processes clearly being of fascination to Photosynthesis Wong. Fandie, Ankie and Banda represent a desire to be the only person in the entire world to have a certain name. And then there are the downright odd but memorable, such as Onions, Squash or Catherine (a man).

Several thousand Vietnamese boat people, who started arriving in 1975 after the Communist North Vietnamese took power, have stayed on. In the 1970s and 1980s, asylum was granted to over 100,000 refugees, many of whom had no hope of resettlement abroad. But after international discussions to resolve the issue, it was concluded that all Vietnamese were to be removed from local refugee camps by the end of 1995. Those deemed "economic migrants" were repatriated to Vietnam, by force when necessary, while political refugees, who comprised about 10 percent, were resettled elsewhere overseas.

can be achieved through sheer will and hard work. Their attitude is, "If you don't have any money, then go out and earn some!" rather than relying on government support or charity to provide financial assistance.

With this work ethic in mind, many parents work at least nine or 10 hours a day, six days a week to provide for their children who will, one day, look after them in old age. Most of the family budget goes towards children's clothing, healthcare and education, so that they may enjoy what their parents never had in their youth. Children are expected to support their elderly parents and to honour the memory of deceased parents by regularly

Traditional values

Traditional Chinese values such as humility, perseverance, reverence for ancestors and respect for elders have been adapted to Hong Kong's modern, capitalist society. In fact, its community is based upon a paternalistic, family-oriented system that was perpetuated by China's most venerable sage, Confucius. He believed that a person should always examine motives carefully before acting, since all individuals are directly responsible for their fate. Therefore, the Chinese believe that anything

LEFT: happy on handover day, 1997.
ABOVE: Hong Kong has a lively nightlife scene.

visiting their graves and making offerings.

The Chinese tend to be rather reserved about displays of affection; love is expressed through acts of kindness rather than through words or embraces common in other cultures. Family values are very strong, and parents dote on their children by spending time and money on them. On Sundays and holidays, parents take the whole family, with grandparents in tow, for Western-style buffets, *yum cha* ("drinking tea"), or dim sum. After lunch, families wander around the streets and shopping malls and buy new toys and clothes for the children.

Successive famines, wars and political upheaval in China have taught the Hong Kong

Chinese not to be complacent about financial security. They are eagle-eyed at spotting opportunities for making money; here "filthy lucre" really does seem to buy happiness, since material security is vital to one's sense of well-being. There is no other place in the world where people, rich or poor, are as business-minded and clued-up about property, stocks and horse-racing. It's no coincidence that *kung hei fat choi* – literally "congratulations on your wealth" – is a common greeting at Lunar New Year. As in most places in the world, of course, the quest for wealth is also motivated by self-respect or "face". Driving expensive cars, wearing designer labels and

campaign, aimed at promoting tourism after the disastrous slump in numbers following the SARS epidemic, has achieved good results.

Security overseas

After the 1984 Sino-British agreement to return Hong Kong to China in 1997, emigration became a constant feature of life in the territory. During the 1980s and 1990s, tens of thousands left each year to secure foreign passports, mainly from Canada, Australia and the United States. The price of such security meant sacrificing businesses, family and friends, and starting from scratch in an alien country. Many emigrants returned to Hong

living in a beautiful apartment are all ways of raising self-esteem.

At the end of a meal, diners will fight to pay the bill, since generosity also gains face. Face and *guanxi* – lifelong obligations of mutual assistance – are crucial to relationships. That's why the Chinese prefer to give business to family and friends rather than deal with strangers, who might prove to be unreliable. In friends there is certainty.

Many foreigners visiting Hong Kong have complained that the people are sometimes brusque to the point of rudeness. This was often a result of cultural misunderstandings, but sometimes not. A government awareness

Kong after establishing permanent residence overseas, shuttling back and forth annually to retain their status in both places. In theory, Beijing insists that all ethnic Chinese Hong Kong residents are Chinese nationals; therefore, they are not entitled to foreign consular protection. However, Hong Kong residents are free to travel on foreign passports, since attempts to change their status could lead to economic disaster.

Property and cost of living

For financial reasons, Hong Kongers often marry later than mainland Chinese – for women, 25 is a typical age, for men, 28.

Because of high property prices, most people, even married couples, have no choice but to live with their parents until they have saved enough money. Cramped living conditions, however, make life difficult for would-be lovers. Moments alone are rare, and the prying eyes of relatives are not conducive to romance. Among the few romantic retreats are public parks, and at night the benches are often taken by courting couples. Another option is the love motel rented by the hour in Kowloon Tong, or on one of the outlying islands, a popular escape for couples looking for a few hours of undisturbed passion.

Hong Kong is a capitalist society where Darwin's theory of the "survival of the fittest" predominates. Local tax laws give residents incentive to be among those that not only survive, but thrive. Residents keep most of what they earn – the highest income-tax rate is 15 percent, and only around two percent of the working population pays this, with over half paying no income tax at all.

However, Hong Kong has a high cost of living due to rising inflation, limited land, the expense of importing raw materials and food, and high duties imposed on petrol and cars. In spite of this, luxury cars score high points in the "face" game, and people will gladly blow all their cash on a Mercedes-Benz or BMW even if they can't then afford much else. The cost of a parking space in certain residential blocks is the price of an apartment in other countries, and like property or stocks, speculators buy and sell spaces at enormous profit.

The government has generated substantial revenue from auctioning land to private developers who are willing to pay astronomical prices, and from taxes imposed on the sale and purchase of property. Before the 1998 Asian economic crisis, the property market remained the fastest and most consistently reliable way of earning a buck. By 2004, after a period of uncertainty following the crisis, property prices were on the up again, and attracting investors once more. Meanwhile, land prices have always been high, a result of the shortage of suitable land for construction. The

government makes huge profits on land sales – a situation which fuels the desire for more and more land to be reclaimed from the sea.

Old factory areas such as Cheung Sha Wan and Tsuen Wan, and rural land in Sheung Shui and Fan Ling, have been developed into residential areas at minimal cost. However, the main problem of developing high-density residential areas in the New Territories is that of infrastructure – efficient transportation and employment opportunities are essential to encourage people to move in. The earliest New Towns, as these developed areas are called, lacked these facilities, although the situation is now much improved.

HOU Q: THE CUTE OBSESSION

In tandem with much of the rest of Asia, Hong Kong is in thrall to Japanese pop culture, and its obsession with all things cute – what is termed in Japan as *kawaii*, in Hong Kong as *hou Q*. The epitome of this is "Hello Kitty", the ubiquitous cat created by the Japanese company Sanrio which adorns over 20,000 products from clothing to stationery. Sociologists say the fascination with Japanese style is fuelled by Asians' need to find a modern image of themselves, to form their own popular culture rather than borrow from the West. Or, as an 18-year-old Hong Konger expressed it: "Japanese society is very fast-paced and always changing. Everything is very cute and stylish."

LEFT: tai chi in the park.
RIGHT: Hello Kitty is a common sight in Hong Kong.

A more cost-effective solution to the shortage of space for building new public housing has been land reclamation, as there is no need to compensate tenants or buy property. Over half of Hong Kong's population lives in public housing. The largest single housing project is Yau Oi Estate, in Tuen Mun. It has 9,153 units housing over 35,000 residents. Families living in public housing benefit from low rents, as well as shared income from family members, so they are relatively well-off compared to low-income families in other parts of the world. However, lower-middle-class families are often caught: they do not qualify for public housing, and most property prices are

through public funds and private donations. There are no government-aided schemes for comprehensive healthcare, except in extreme cases when people cannot afford private healthcare and insurance, and their employers do not provide medical insurance. This has led to substantial growth in private medical and life insurance funded by both companies and individuals.

Crime

Hong Kong's over-the-top action movies often give the impression of a crime-ridden city and a perpetual hunting ground for chopper-wielding tattooed thugs and armed robbers. In

way out of their budget. Since the 1990s, the Hong Kong government has allocated "sandwich-class" housing for these families in the form of affordable rental or private property.

Social welfare and health

Primary medical care is largely dominated by market forces in Hong Kong, while the government subsidises secondary healthcare in hospitals. The problem of overcrowded public wards and long waiting lists has drawn a great deal of criticism. But despite these problems, affordable government medical care is assured for the entire population

reality, one of the pleasures of Hong Kong is its lack of crime – the streets are safe at any time, and the chances of being mugged or pickpocketed are significantly lower than almost anywhere in Europe or America.

Organised crime does exist, though. The triad crime syndicates (their emblem symbolises harmony between Heaven, Earth and Man) rely on a hierarchical structure, with ranks denoted by numbers that begin with four, representing the four elements, compass points and seas. The most high profile gangs are "14K" and "San Yee On", whose illegal activities include loan-sharking, gambling, narcotics, prostitution, smuggling and extortion.

Hong Kong has an estimated 40,000 drug users, 96 percent of them heroin addicts, so the government takes a particularly tough stance on narcotics. Possession of marijuana carries the same penalties as hard drugs: a criminal record and possible imprisonment. Still, Hong Kong's "work hard, play hard" culture, coupled with its affluence, has meant that recreational drugs are readily available.

Education

Hong Kong's educational system is every bit as competitive as its business community. Children suffer tremendous pressure to get into prestigious schools. The most sought-after are English or bilingual schools, because English is widely used in business, medicine and law. A number of students commit suicide each year because they fail an important exam. Parental pressure often proves too much for children, who spend much of their time doing homework, cramming for exams and studying foreign languages for overseas study. Tutors are hired to prepare toddlers for kindergarten entrance exams, an ordeal that sometimes requires two hours of testing to determine a child's Chinese, English and arithmetic skills.

The government regularly carries out studies to ascertain the standard of English spoken by teachers, to ensure that students get every opportunity to become confidently bilingual. The core competency remains Chinese, English and maths. It's hardly surprising that the most popular, over-subscribed university courses are in science, business and engineering – more easily rote-learned, they tend to lead to more financially rewarding careers than the arts and humanities.

The future

During the 1989 pro-democracy movement in China, over 500,000 demonstrators took to the streets in Hong Kong in a show of solidarity. Hong Kong residents donated millions of dollars to the cause, and sent tents to Beijing for student protesters camped out in Tiananmen Square. After the 4 June massacre, more than one million people in Hong Kong took to the streets in protest. Preconceptions of a socially compliant population evaporated overnight. Post-1997, and particularly in the last few years, political awareness has developed further, and street protests have become a regular feature as local people have become increasingly frustrated at the lack of control over their affairs and the perceived sense of injustice.

The economic success of Hong Kong can be credited above all to one thing: its industrious people. Any heavy-handed attempts to restrict freedoms could still result in an unprecedented exodus of a talented, highly educated workforce, with disastrous conse-

quences for China, negating the benefits brought about by the reforms, modernisation and acceptance into world markets that have been so encouraging for the region as a whole.

Stories of the economic success possible in Hong Kong and its remarkable hinterland of Shenzhen and the Pearl River Delta (not to mention Shanghai), have reached even the remotest parts of China, and the tide of migrants heading south and east is gaining momentum. Most China-watchers believe that for Hong Kong to continue to thrive, it is here that China's economic reforms must coincide with the advance of democracy rather than its suppression. ❏

LEFT: Filipinas form the largest foreign community.
RIGHT: a Lantau windsurfer downs a beer.

BELIEFS AND SUPERSTITIONS

Ancient beliefs such as fortune-telling and feng shui, as well as more traditional religions, continue to colour daily life in Hong Kong

ABOVE: mirrors deflect bad feng shui.

Few modern-day city residents take their traditional beliefs more seriously than the Hong Kong Chinese. A constant undercurrent, counterpoint to the brash, modern metropolis, these values have been formed over the centuries through an interaction of the three primary Chinese religions or philosophies – Buddhism, Daoism and Confucianism – overlayed with elements of animism, superstition and folk tradition. Adding further to this esoteric mix is the Chinese tradition of ancestor worship. Some aspects of the core beliefs overlap with each other (for example, many temples are both Buddhist and Daoist).

These religions are complemented by the more overtly superstitious beliefs so important in Hong Kong. Feng Shui *(see page 46)* is based around the central Chinese concept of *qi* (the energy, life force or spirit that is believed to exist in nature and all living creatures) – an underlying principle in Chinese medicine *(see pages 49–53)*. Numerology *(see page 47)* is a more straightforward superstition. Throughout all of these overlapping beliefs, however, two themes are universal – the desire for prosperity and longevity.

Yet it is often said that Hong Kongers worship one thing and one thing only: money. And it is true that the almost evangelical pursuit of personal wealth seems to be hard-wired into much of the population. Deity worship is often used in the pursuit of worldly gains – including advice on stock-market and horse-racing tips (witness the large number of offerings to the god of good fortune, Wong Tai Sin, at his temple).

ABOVE: busy Wong Tai Sin temple, dedicated to the Daoist god of healing and good fortune, is famous for its fortune-tellers *(see page 139)*.

BELOW: a typical Chinese temple entrance features a spirit wall inside the main doorway to block the path of evil spirits. The red lanterns also offer protection, as well as symbolising well-being and happiness.

ABOVE: ancestor worship is an ancient Chinese tradition. When someone dies, his or her soul is thought to enter the underworld and come under the threat of evil spirits. Offerings are made and "spirit money" burned to protect the ancestor, who will in return offer protection to his or her descendants. It is considered important to keep the grave clean – as observed on the Ching Ming and Chun Yuen festivals. Eventually the remains are dug up and cremated.

ABOVE: Daoism is China's only true native religion, founded in the sixth century by Laozi (pictured), a semi-mythical philosopher. Chinese "popular" religions are often a blend of elements taken from Daoism, Buddhism and Confucianism.

ABOVE: temples in Hong Kong are dedicated to a particular deity, generally from the Daoist pantheon. Kwan Tai (pictured) is the god of loyalty and integrity, and widely venerated by the Hong Kong police. One of the most popular deities is Tin Hau, goddess of the sea and worshipped throughout China, where she is variously known as Tianhou (in Mandarin Chinese), A-Ma (in Macau) or Matsu (in Taiwan).

BELOW: most people agree that IM Pei's iconic Bank of China Tower is an impressive and attractive structure, but there is one negative aspect: its strikingly sharp angles channel bad feng shui onto its neighbours. Feng shui ("wind and water") is an ancient Chinese form of geomancy, and an important consideration when a new tower block is being planned – a feng shui master will advise on which direction it should face and where desks, beds or even a vase should be placed to attract the best luck and prevent bad fortune. A sheltered position, facing the water and away from a hillside, is considered auspicious, but although the Bank of China was built with these principles in mind, the fact that its aggressive angles arrowed hostile energy towards, amongst others, Government House and the HSBC Building, was not considered. The construction of the Cheung Kong Centre, at an angle askew to the Bank and between it and the HSBC, and a strategically placed willow tree at Government House, have improved neighbourly relations.

ABOVE: red papers with blessings inscribed on them are burned at ancestral graves or other shrines to release the blessing. Red is considered a lucky colour by the Chinese.

ABOVE: paper money is burned so that ancestors can benefit in the other world, in which they need money and consumer goods (cars, flats, TVs etc. are all made in paper form for this purpose). Offerings of incense and food are also important.

LUCKY NUMBERS

Hong Kong may be the only place in the world where someone would pay US$1.7 million for a vehicle licence plate. In 1994, local tycoon Albert Yeung did just that – investing in a licence plate bearing the single digit nine, considered lucky because the Cantonese word for "nine" sounds like the word for "eternity", "longevity" or "perpetuity".

Other lucky numbers include two, which stands for "easy", three for "living or giving birth", six for "longevity", and eight for "prosperity". But it is the combinations that are in most demand. For example, 163 means "live forever" or "give birth non-stop"; 168, "prosperity all the way"; and 162, "easy all the way". Lucky licence-plate numbers became so much in demand that, in 1973, the government's transport department began auctioning them off to the highest bidders. The number eight has consistently drawn the highest bid. Today, all licence plate numbers considered lucky in Cantonese are reserved and available only through auctions.

The superstition over numbers also applies to street, apartment and telephone numbers. For example, the price for an apartment on the 14th floor can be 20 percent cheaper than that for the same flat on the 18th floor, because 14 in Cantonese means "definitely dies", while 18 means "definitely prospers". Some buildings get around this problem by simply omitting a 14th floor, going straight from the 13th to the 15th.

ABOVE: fortune-telling can be a lucrative business in Hong Kong. Clairvoyants, usually in residence at a temple, read palms or the feet or face to predict the future. Other methods include using *chim* sticks (at temples such as Wong Tai Sin), or game-like activities such as throwing coins or other objects at a target – an example being the Wishing Tree near Tai Po, where people throw oranges attached to streamers in the hope that they will lodge in the branches and thus confer good fortune.

Following a fortune-teller's advice to the letter can impinge on daily life. In order to appease the fortune god, it may be deemed necessary to shave off all one's hair skinhead-style, or to wear a bright red belt at all times.

ABOVE: tai chi balls (also known as healthy balls) are moved around the hand to massage the acupressure points and circulate *qi* energy through the entire body.

TRADITIONAL MEDICINE

Chinese remedies have been practised for 4,000 years and, aided by the international popularity of acapuncture, have been gaining increasing respect around the world

Whenever traditional Chinese medicine is mentioned nowadays, many people immediately think of acupuncture. In some countries, orthodox Western medicine is still somewhat reluctant to accept acupuncture as part of an alternative approach. However, it is increasingly accepted by many physicians, and many "pain centres" around the world offer acupuncture as a therapy. In 1997, medical authorities in the United States approved it as a legitimate – and insurable – treatment for pain.

Yet medicine in China is not just traditional medicine. In fact, Western-style medicine is the primary form of medical treatment in Hong Kong and the rest of China. The large metropolitan hospitals in all cities use the Western approach *(xiyi)* to treatment almost exclusively. The hospitals for Chinese medicine *(zhonggi)* are smaller and less well-equipped. Nowadays, the Chinese will usually visit a doctor trained in Western medicine if they feel that they are seriously ill and wish to be diagnosed. If no organic failure is found, the patient will see a traditional doctor, who is far more likely to be able to restore the lost harmony in the body.

Traditional Chinese medicine entails more than just acupuncture. The knowledge of remedies *(zhongyao)* is an important factor. Patients are treated with different kinds of massage and chiropractics *(tuina)*, as well as breathing and movement therapies, such as *taijiquan* (shadow boxing) and *qigong* (breathing therapy).

LEFT: a typical Chinese medicine shop in Western.
RIGHT: ingredients come from all kinds of animals.

Traditional cures are not only administered at hospitals or pharmacies. Wandering around a Chinese town, one will see farmers in the street selling herbs and produce. Often it is not obvious that these are remedies. For example, *giou qize*, a small and oval-shaped fruit, carmine red and rather bitter, is used to relieve congestion of the liver and to get rid of anger. It is also believed to lower blood pressure.

The pharmacy

Pharmacies tend to have a unique odour, a mixture of 1,001 scents. There are all sorts of exotic animals, insects and vegetables: birds' eggs, snakes wound up in spirals, dried monkeys, toads, tortoises, centipedes, grasshoppers, dried fish, octopi, antlers, rhinoceros horns and the genitalia of various unfortunate – and often endangered – animals. And then there are the myriad herbs, blossoms, roots, berries, mushrooms and fruits – dried and preserved. In fact, there is hardly a plant, mineral or animal substance in the world that is not used as a remedy or preventative. All traditional Chinese pharmacies are well-stocked with ginseng roots, often shaped like a human figure. In fact, the character for ginseng contains the sign *ren*, which means person.

The *Encyclopaedia of the Traditional Chinese Pharmacopoeia*, published in 1977,

dred schools". It was a time when ideas were born that were to have a profound influence on life in China. The two most important schools of thought at the time were those of Confucianism and Daoism. Both shared the wish for harmony, but their views on how this was to be achieved differed.

Harmony was interpreted as the interaction of opposite forces, such as the adjustment of human behaviour to ecological and social conditions. If this harmony was unbalanced, then this would lead to social or physical illness. Belief in the opposite forces of *yin* and *yang*, the "five phases of change" and the idea of *qi* – the life force – were the most influential in

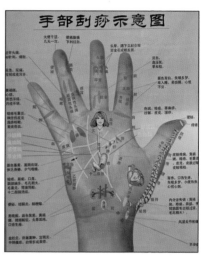

runs to 2,700 pages listing 5,767 substances with medicinal or preventative properties.

Historical roots

The foundations of traditional Chinese medicine were laid over 2,000 years ago, in the era of the Warring Empires, when China was split up into many quarrelling fiefdoms and kingdoms. This stage in Chinese history, marked by fighting and misery, lasted several centuries, and it is hardly surprising that people began to search for a solution to their woes. Innumerable thinkers, philosophers and social reformers with many diverse ideas emerged – a collection of thought referred to as the "hun-

the theoretical background of traditional medicine, and formed the framework of medical thinking.

At a time when very little knowledge of human anatomy and physiology existed, these theories provided points of reference. They explained the relationship of the human microcosm to the macrocosm of the environment, but also the effect that physical and emotional changes have on each other.

Thus, the feeling of fury was related to sudden gusts of wind and with elemental force; fury was also connected with a sour taste, and with muscles and sinews that can become cramped due to aggression.

The *Inner Classic of the Yellow Emperor*, which is around 2,000 years old, mentions that people with gall-bladder problems must have fallen ill due to unsatisfied ambition and pent-up anger. So a special form of medicine and treatment evolved that concentrated particularly on the functional body. And as Chinese influence grew, these treatments and techniques spread around the East Asia region.

Acupuncture

One effect of acupuncture that is undisputed and valued by a billion Chinese is the relief of pain. While others rely on drugs to moderate physical pain, the Chinese go to the

also said to relieve such allergies as hay fever.

When entering an acupuncture clinic, you will notice one of the dominant aromas of the Chinese pharmacy – that of the *moxa* herb, which is the same thing as Artemisia, or mugwort. It is considered especially helpful in treating illnesses that, in Chinese medical terminology, are classified as "cold" – for example, stomach and digestive complaints without fever, certain rheumatic illnesses, chronic pains in the back and cramped neck and shoulders. The mugwort is placed onto the acupuncture point or on the end of the acupuncture needle, or moulded into the shape of a cigar and rolled back and forth over the skin.

acupuncturist. Cases of acute back pain, for example, can be cured by sticking just one needle in the *renzhong* point between the top lip and nose.

A new form of painless acupuncture, which does not use needles, is administered by ear. Small, round seed kernels are stuck onto certain points of the ear and massaged by the patient from time to time. This method is not only very successful in treating pain, but is

FAR LEFT: varieties of Chinese tea.
LEFT: diagram of pressure points.
ABOVE: acupuncture needles.
RIGHT: Muay Thai boxers on Tsim Sha Tsui promenade.

Exercise

At some stage while travelling in China, visit a public park at dawn to witness the Chinese exercise arts of *taijiquan* and *qigong*. *Taijiquan* is the most common type of exercise, so-called shadow boxing. *Qigong* is often translated in the West as breathing therapy.

Both exercises are based on the belief that the human body is endowed with the life energy, *qi*. If this can be harnessed and controlled, a person can influence the course of certain ailments that afflict the body. Body and breathing exercises are thus preventative forms of "medicine".

During the Cultural Revolution in China, *qigong* was banned because it was said to be too close to superstition. But in 1980, new *qigong* groups sprang up, and soon gained a large following. Some forms involve hardly any movement: breathing and "sinking into oneself" are of prime importance. Other forms, like the "wild goose" variety, entail a great deal of movement and are aesthetically appealing.

In both *taijiquan* and *qigong*, changes in mental and emotional states follow a certain pattern of movement. The most extreme of these is the "crane *qigong*", which involves violent, sometimes cathartic emotional outbursts. Practitioners may scream, cry, laugh, dance or jump around as they experience *fagong*, abandoning oneself to spontaneous movements.

dizziness and high blood pressure. Bird's nest, usually taken as a soup, allegedly cleanses the blood and the complexion.

Verifying such claims is difficult. The scientific method, which involves controlled experiments using known values and quantities, doesn't lend itself well to the analysis of claims that a food item can help cure physical illnesses. Moreover, to be valid, a result must be independently verifiable. Consideration must also be given to the placebo effect, where a valid result occurs because one believes in something's efficacy. Many say the success of Chinese cures is simply a question of mind over matter. However,

It's in the diet

For much of China's history, herbalists have attributed medicinal value to various foods. At times, the distinction between food and treatment can blur. The Chinese have little doubt of the efficacy of different foods for treating ailments and healing certain parts of the body. Consider three traditional delicacies: shark's fin, abalone and bird's nest. These are exquisite parts of an extensive cuisine, eaten for their sensory delights. Yet each is claimed to have medicinal value. Shark's fin and abalone are said to benefit internal organs, including the heart and kidneys. Abalone also regulates the liver and reduces

recent research on the health effects of soy beans and green tea, for example, suggests that components in these two items have substantive medicinal value, possibly against some forms of cancer.

Herbal remedies have gradually gained respect around the world. Western nutritionists have always stressed that certain foods provide necessary vitamins and minerals that are good for the body – carrots for good eyesight, calcium for strong bones. Traditional Chinese medicinal foods simply take these scientific remedies one level further. ❏

ABOVE: communal morning exercises.

The Animal Parts Trade

The Chinese have been using animal parts for medicinal purposes for well over 1,000 years. Yet for all its growing appeal across the world as people look for alternatives to Western drugs, there is a darker side. Wildlife, under pressure from intensive industrial and economic development in recent decades, is now being pushed to the brink of extinction by the increased demand for body parts.

The demand for tigers, for example, is forcing three of the world's five remaining subspecies ever closer to extinction, threatening the long-term survival of the species as a whole. Various tiger parts are used in Chinese medicine: eyeballs to treat epilepsy, the tail for various skin diseases, bile for convulsions in children, whiskers for toothaches, the penis for male impotence and the brain to combat laziness and pimples. Yet of all tiger parts, it is the bones that are most valued. Tiger bone is often used to treat rheumatism, but can also be used for treating weakness, stiffness or paralysis.

Recent studies estimate that there are only 30 to 80 South China tigers, 150 to 200 Siberian tigers and 600 to 650 Sumatran tigers left in the wild. In addition, tigers have vanished from much of their former range worldwide, and may now number as few as 5,000. Without radical intervention, tigers may disappear altogether in the near future.

Rhinoceros, bear and even shark populations are also rapidly shrinking. Rhinoceros horn is reputed to be an aphrodisiac. Only about 12,500 rhinos remain in the wild, with another 1,000 in captivity. About half of these are white rhinos and the remaining half consists of four other species. Without assistance, these could soon be extinct. Also greatly threatened by Chinese demand, bears from as far away as North America are valued for their bile, used to treat a variety of ailments, and paws, which are used in soup. Like bear's

paw, shark's fin, though not used exclusively for medicine, is a delicacy. Served most commonly as shark's fin soup, this broth is believed to benefit the internal organs. Sharks are caught and their top fin sliced off. They are then tossed back into the ocean, alive, to drown. In some areas, the shark population – essential to the ecosystem, as the shark is the top predator – is declining.

In recent years, human populations and expendable incomes have increased dramatically in Asia, along with a resurgence of interest in traditional cures. Use of traditional medicines is seen as a status

symbol and also as a way to hold on to traditional customs amidst rapid social and economic changes.

While the effectiveness of these endangered animal products in medicine is still disputed, researchers confirm the benefits of the active ingredients present in a considerable number of Chinese prescriptions.

As endangered animal populations plummet, the use of their parts to feed an ever-growing demand is no longer sustainable. One way or another, the trade in endangered animal parts for medicine must stop. This means finding an alternative to alternative medicine. ❏

RIGHT: tigers are threatened by the Chinese medicine industry.

WHERE FOOD IS AN ART

Cantonese cuisine has been exported around the world for decades. Much of what is unique about it, however, is rarely found outside southern China

It has been said that when the Chinese are confronted with something they have never seen before or do not understand, their first impulse is to try eating it. This folk philosophy has helped inspire one of the greatest cuisines the world has known.

Each region of China naturally evolved a distinctive cooking style that reflected its topography, climate, flora and fauna, the temperament of its people and their contact with outsiders. Foods of northern and western China developed separately from those of the southern and eastern coastal "rice bowl". Southern Chinese (mainly the Cantonese, but also sub-groups such as the Hunanese, Chiu Chow and Hakka people) like to complain that Beijing-based food lacks smoothness and subtlety. Beijing folks, meanwhile, argue that southerners grind, chop and dilute the flavour out of their food.

Whatever their regional biases, Chinese everywhere talk about their food the way foreigners might talk about art. This is probably because Chinese cuisine is regarded as an art form. And even if they aren't conscious of their food as a major cultural accomplishment, no Chinese can ever avoid talking about it. The most common Cantonese greeting, for example, is *sik tzo fan mei* – meaning "Have you eaten?" Every dialect is rich in food symbolism. "You are breaking my rice bowl", wails the Chinese whose livelihood is threatened.

LEFT: the elegant simplicity of dim sum.
RIGHT: lunchtime noodles at a neighbourhood *dai pai dong.*

Even to learn simply how to say rice in Chinese requires an annotated dictionary. Consider the linguistic variables of Cantonese: plain rice is *mai*; cooked rice is *faan*; rice porridge (commonly called congee) is *juk*; and harvested but unhusked rice is *guk*.

The traditional Chinese concept of a meal is very much a communal affair and one that provides strong sensory impact. Dishes are chosen with both taste and texture in mind – a stomach-pleasing succession of sweet-sour, sharp-bland, hot-cool and crunchy-smooth.

In a land that has experienced recurrent famine and natural disasters, wastage is not acceptable. Children are warned by their parents that if they leave any rice in their bowls, they will marry a pock-marked spouse – and the more grains left in the bowl, the more pock-marked the partner will be.

In spite of traditional poverty and privation, the Chinese nearly always insist on fresh food. Many Chinese still shop twice or three times a day for fresh meat and vegetables. Cooks do not start with a particular dish in mind, but rather go to the market to buy what's fresh and in season, then create the meal.

To many outsiders, some Chinese foods seem bizarre, if not downright repulsive. The search for rare delicacies is common to all Chinese, but the Cantonese have pushed it to

the authentic cuisine often has little to do with what they have been served in Chinese restaurants abroad. Take, for example, two supposed Cantonese dishes: sweet-and-sour pork is said to have been invented by the ever-resourceful inhabitants of Guangzhou solely for sweet-toothed foreigners. And chop suey was reportedly invented in San Francisco when a customer entered a restaurant at closing time, and the cooks threw their leftovers into a pot, served it up and in quiet jest called this oriental goulash "chop suey". Also, despite the Chinese preoccupation with luck and superstitions, American-style fortune cookies do not exist here.

the extreme. Among them are monkey's brain, bear's paw, snake, dog, pigeon, frog, sparrow, sharks' fin, birds' nest and lizard. Unfortunately for the average Hong Kong Chinese who savours such fare, many of these delicacies are either illegal or virtually impossible to obtain. Hence, many are rare and expensive.

Cantonese cuisine

The Cantonese live to eat and, at its most refined level, their gastronomy achieves a finicky discrimination that borders on cultism.

Overseas visitors who are familiar with Chinese food in Western countries soon learn

In the Cantonese method of preparation, food is cooked quickly and lightly, usually stir-fried in shallow water or an oil base in a wok. The flavour of the foods is thus preserved, not cooked away, in preparation. Many dishes, particularly vegetables or fish, are steamed. This discourages overcooking and preserves a food's delicate and natural flavours. Sauces are used to enhance flavours rather than overwhelm them. The sauce usually contains contrasting ingredients such as vinegar and sugar, or ginger and onion.

The Cantonese are very fond of seafood. Fish is typically steamed whole with fresh ginger and spring onions and sprinkled with a little soy sauce and sesame oil. Cantonese consider fish eyes and lips to be delicacies. However, it is considered unlucky to turn over a fish to reach the meat underneath as it symbolises a capsized boat.

Prawns and crabs – steamed or in a black-bean sauce – are also popular Cantonese dishes. The term "jumping prawns" signifies that they are alive, but it doesn't mean you are expected to eat them that way. Shark's fin soup – golden threads of gelatinous-like shark's fin in a broth – is the centrepiece of Cantonese banquets, despite ecological concerns *(see page 53)*.

Chicken is commonplace and, in keeping with the Chinese sense of economy and vari-

batter and served in a lemon sauce flavoured with onions, ginger and sugar.

For starters, choose something from the display of barbecued meats in the restaurant's display window. Cantonese barbecuing methods are unrivalled. Try goose, duck or, best of all, tender slices of pork with a golden and honeyed skin served on a bed of anise-flavoured preserved beans.

Also experience the taste sensation of double-boiled soups with duck, mushroom and tangerine peel, and a winter speciality called Monk Jumping over the Wall. This is a blend of abalone, chicken, ham, mushrooms and herbs so irresistible that monks are said

ety, a single bird is often used to prepare several dishes. Chicken blood, for example, is cooked and solidified for soup, and the liver is used in a marvellous speciality called Gold Coin Chicken. The livers are skewered between pieces of pork fat and red-roasted until the fat becomes crisp and the liver soft and succulent. The delicacy is theni eaten with wafers of orange-flavoured bread. Cantonese chicken dishes can be awkwardly bony for chopstick beginners, but lemon chicken is prepared boneless with the skin coated in a crisp

LEFT: seafood spread. **ABOVE:** photo call at the Cathay Pacific Worldwide Chinese Chef workshop.

HONG KONG'S BAKERIES

Bakeries occupy a special place in Hong Kong hearts, dispensing breakfast and snacks from the ubiquitous egg-custard tarts *(daan taht)*, doughnuts and doughy sausage buns to a wide range of colourful celebratory cakes and pastries. Young parents take their offspring to the same bakery they patronized when they were children, and after a spell overseas, Hong Kongers drop by their friendly neighbourhood cake shop, a reflex reaction which confirms their homecoming. And when a rental hike forced the closure of the famed Tai Cheung Bakery on Lyndhurst Terrace (Central) after 51 years of business, protesters took to the streets.

to break their vows of vegetarianism once they smell it.

Snake is a traditional winter dish, often served as an energy-enhancing soup. Dog meat is also a winter dish but is illegal in Hong Kong, so there are special tours across the border specifically to eat dog meat. Yet another Cantonese winter dish to sample is a casserole of chicken and Chinese smoked pork sausage. These sausages are sold in pairs and usually are served steamed on a bed of rice. In autumn, restaurants serve rice birds – culled from paddy fields at harvest time. These are quite often eaten together with succulent Shanghai hairy crabs. Frogs are also found in

the rice paddies, and these "field chickens" are often served at banquets in southern China. In Hong Kong markets they are sold live in plastic bags, and restaurants prepare them in many delicious ways, including deep-fried frog's legs cooked in a crunchy batter mixed with crushed almonds and served with sweet-and-sour sauce.

Other Chinese cooking styles

Cantonese restaurants dominate in Hong Kong, but there is no shortage of other forms of Chinese cooking, from Peking Duck and Mongolian hotpot to the spicy cuisines of Sichuan and Hunan.

TOOLS AND TECHNIQUES

Many foreigners struggle with chopsticks. Small and loose rice grains are a particular menace. Thankfully, it's perfectly acceptable to raise the rice bowl to your lips and shovel the elusive morsels into your mouth. Scraping and slurping are not considered a faux pas.

Chopsticks are thought to have been adopted for eating because of a Confucian distaste for knives – potentially dangerous weapons – on the dining table. If they prove impossible, it is perfectly acceptable to use the porcelain spoon provided for soups as a scoop for other courses. And no one minds if you make a mess – it is even permissible to wipe your hands on the edge of the tablecloth.

A typical meal starts with a cold dish, which is followed by several main courses. Soup – usually clear, light broth – may be eaten after the heavier entrées to aid digestion. However, a thick and full-bodied soup may be served as a main dish, and a sweet soup often serves as a dessert at the meal's end. There are no rules when it comes to ordering your meal. The main thing is to enjoy the food.

One mistake some foreigners make is swamping their rice with soy sauce, a crude act that robs it of its character and function. A meal should include enough spicy and savoury dishes to make the relative blandness of steamed rice an essential balancing agent.

Over the centuries, culinary elements from all over eastern Asia have been liberally adapted and absorbed into Chinese cuisine, and it's difficult to trace the origins of some dishes. Peking Duck, prepared by roasting the duck over an open charcoal fire and slowly basting it with syrup until the skin is a deep, crispy brown, was originally Mongolian. Mongolian hotpot, called "steamboat" in Singapore and Malaysia, is in fact of central Chinese Moslem origins. It is probably the second best-known of the northern dishes, and as a winter food, is served between November and March in northern-style restaurants.

A surprise for many at their first northern Chinese meal is that rice is not served unless specially requested. Wheat is the common grain staple in the north, so northerners traditionally eat steamed bread *(pao)* or tasty onion cakes instead of rice. One of the spectacular treats at a northern Chinese meal is handmade noodles called *lie mien*, often deftly made at the table by the chef, who turns dough into strands of noodles within seconds.

Chiu Chow cuisine is also known as Swatow food because this type of cooking originated around the city of Swatow in eastern Guangdong province. Seafood addicts enjoy such dishes as oysters fried in egg batter and clams served in a spicy sauce of black beans and chillies. Grey mullet is a favourite cold dish, and pomfret fish smoked over tea leaves and freshwater eel stewed in brown sauce are other highly recommended seafood wonders.

A Chiu Chow restaurant is also an appropriate place to try banquet-style food such as shark's fin soup and bird's nest soup, for which the dried saliva lining the edible swiftlet's nest provides the base. The owner of one restaurant in Hong Kong reputedly rents a mountain in Thailand that is said to harbour the finest collection of swiftlet nests in Southeast Asia. The nest itself is virtually tasteless, but its nourishing saliva linings are believed to rejuvenate the old. This delicacy is also eaten as a dessert flavoured with coconut milk or almonds.

Baked rice birds are a seasonal fowl dish stuffed with chicken liver and served by the dozen. Minced pigeon, meanwhile, is cooked with water chestnuts and eaten wrapped in crisp lettuce leaves spiked with a healthy dollop of plum sauce.

After Cantonese, the cuisine of the central province of Sichuan is perhaps the best-known to foreigners. The food is the most emphatically flavoured in all of China. Much of this emphasis comes from chillies, which appear in many guises: dried and fried in chunks, together with other ingredients; ground into a paste with a touch of added oil; as chilli oil; and crushed to a powder. Other ingredients important to Sichuanese cuisine are Sichuan "pepper" (the dried berry of the prickly ash or fagara), garlic, ginger and fermented soybean. Popular dishes

include *mala doufu* (spicy tofu) and *gongbao* chicken (with chilli and peanuts).

A typical Sichuan eating experience is hotpot, or *huo guo*. Diners sit around a table with a pot of seasoned broth heated by a gas fire (charcoal was used in the past). Each diner adds bits and pieces of prepared vegetable, meat, fish and beancurd. The food cooks very quickly and can be fished out of the broth using chopsticks or a special strainer, then dipped in sesame oil, peanut sauce or a beaten egg.

The cuisine of the lower reaches of the Yangzi River, especially around Huaian and Yangzhou, gave rise to the term *huaiyang* to describe the food of China's eastern seaboard.

LEFT: cleaning up at the local *dai pai dong*.
RIGHT: a favourite winter warmer, snake soup *(se gung)*.

This fertile area, known as the land of fish and rice, produces a wide range of crops as well as abundant fish, prawns, crab and eel. Huaiyang cooks often steam or gently simmer their food, rather than using the faster deep-frying style. Signature dishes include pork steamed in lotus leaves, Duck with Eight Ingredients, and Lion's Head Meatballs. For the most part, the cooking of Shanghai, Jiangsu and Zhejiang is usually regarded as being part of Huaiyang cuisine.

Eating in Hong Kong today

Nowadays, while Cantonese cuisine predominates in Hong Kong and just across the border, there is a vast array of other fare on offer. Stand

beneath the escalator in Cochrane Street in Central, and within a 100-metre radius there's an Irish pub, a fiery Sichuanese whose chef sings opera at the end of the meal, one of the city's most revered Shanghainese restaurants, a Russian eatery and modern-British gastro, an ice-cream parlour ecstatically named XTC and a scarlet-hued sushi joint with platters humming round the bar on a conveyor belt.

Food hawkers still ply their trade on street corners – although officialdom frowns on such *dai pai dong* and is seeking to eradicate them – and a browse round a convenience store like 7-Eleven or Circle K leads past microwaveable dim sum and curries, pot noodles, pun-

gent packets of dried fish and fruit; and boxed drinks that might be mistaken for medicine.

The budget-minded can feast for a few score dollars on seafood noodles at a seaside restaurant on one of the outer islands, or you can splurge in a five-star hotel, diving in and out of cosmopolitan buffets or settling down to a lengthy repast with maître d' and sommelier shimmering discreetly in the shadows.

Hong Kong's long-established Indian community has resulted in a good supply of curry houses all over the main urban areas, notably in Tsim Sha Tsui's Chungking Mansions. Also very easy to find and usually excellent are the numerous Thai restaurants, as well as plenty of other Southeast Asian cuisine – not just Malaysian and Singaporean but Vietnamese and Burmese too. Japanese food is also very well represented. As in any large cosmopolitan city, there is no shortage of European (mainly French and Italian) and American restaurants (McDonalds are everywhere, and very cheap), as well as other cuisines from Persian to Argentinian.

Dim sum

Dim sum is a Cantonese invention, extremely popular with Hong Kong's Chinese population, expats and tourists alike. The term means "little heart" or "touching the heart", and refers to food that comes in small portions on equally small plates. Traditionally served mid-morning, these days it is possible to find dim sum up until about 2 or 3pm, although the earlier the better, as later on some items won't be available. In a dim sum restaurant, an infinite variety of offerings arrive at the table relentlessly. Servings are kept warm inside bamboo canisters stacked high on trolleys, which are wheeled from table to table by waiting staff. In the more traditional dim sum house, the waitresses will sing traditional verses of praise about the food.

Don't ask the waiters to clear the table as the dishes and canisters pile up. While in an ordinary Chinese meal the dishes are cleared after each course, in a dim sum lunch the dishes are usually left on the table until it's time to tally the bill. The waiter counts the number of dishes served; each variably sized dish is of a certain price. The meal is usually filled out with noodles and other dishes. ❑

LEFT: dumplings at a street stall in Guangzhou.

Dim Sum

Below are some of the most popular varieties of dim sum, whic[...]
able in any dim sum restaurant as long as it is not too clos[...]
The dishes are usually accompanied by a pot of Chinese t[...]
(leave the lid open to request more), and a variety of
condiments including soy sauce, chilli sauce *(laht jiu
jong)* and hot sauce *(lat jiu yow)*.

HA GAO: this succulent shrimp dumpling is many people's favourite dim sum.

CHA SIU BAO: barbecued pork dumplings, filling and delicious.

JAR WON TON: deep-fried wonton filled with pork or shrimp, or both.

SIU MAI: come in several varieties, usually filled with pork and shrimp.

CHA SIU SO : barbecued pork pastry, caution advised as it can be hot.

DIM SUM PLATTER: includes spring rolls *(chun goon)* and sesame prawn toast.

THE PERFORMING ARTS

Spend any time in Hong Kong and one will encounter a diverse catalogue of performing arts, including traditional opera, lion dances and Cantopop

A lthough Chinese opera is no longer the most popular performance art in Hong Kong and China, it remains an integral part of Chinese entertainment and culture. Originating from China's earliest folk music and dances, modern-day Chinese opera – a story put to music and dance – emerged during the Song dynasty (960–1279). Although Chinese opera came to be associated with festivals and state occasions at the 18th-century imperial court in Beijing, it was also popular among the common people.

In Hong Kong, a performance of Chinese opera is customary during important festivals on the Chinese calendar. Performances are usually held in bamboo-and-mat theatres temporarily erected in public areas. Chinese opera has many cultural and regional variations. Cantonese operas, which are naturally the most popular in Hong Kong, are quite different from Chiu Chow operas. Beijing operas are performed in the court's official dialect, Mandarin.

The repertoire is drawn from folklore, legends and historical events. The backbone of the performance is the actor-singer. In the same way as their Western counterparts, Chinese operatic singers undergo many years of intensive training to achieve a properly pitched falsetto. Singing artists are often accompanied by a traditional Chinese orchestra. Percussionists occupy one side of the stage, while the wind-and-string section sits opposite, leaving the main area of the stage

clear for the primary performers. To foreign ears, the sounds of a Chinese opera seem bizarre and discordant, with the high-pitched dialogue, deafening gongs and drums echoing from the music pit.

There were no actresses during Chinese opera's early development, because women were not allowed to make public appearances, so male actors took the female roles. As in Western opera, however, that tradition has died.

Make-up, movements, props and specific costume colours identify an actor's age, sex and personality the moment he or she appears on stage. Actors in Beijing operas wear extremely heavy make-up, a cosmetic style

LEFT: the painted mask is critical in Chinese opera.
RIGHT: colours of the face identify the character.

derived from the use of painted masks in older operatic forms. A white patch on the nose indicates a comic character of low rank; a completely white face suggests evil and treachery; a red face identifies a courageous but dim-witted man; and a black-faced actor is an ordinary person. There are eighteen types of opera beards, each symbolising a different personality.

Headdresses are also a vital part of Chinese opera costume; the more important the character, the more elaborate the headdress. Costumes are exaggerated in style to achieve as great a theatrical effect as possible. Each colour identifies the rank, status and personality of the

Most of the traditional opera performances in Hong Kong are called *sumkung* (god's eulogy), as they are performed to celebrate special festivals or the birthdays of different gods. Many of these performances are related to Daoism and Buddhism. For example, during the Ghost Festival, operas are staged together with other activities to expiate the sins of the dead. On each occasion, performances can last up to five days.

To revive the popularity of Chinese operas, some artists have taken measures to rejuvenate both form and content. The most active reformer in Hong Kong is veteran Leung Hon-wai, who has formed his own operatic group

different operatic roles: purple for barbarians, yellow for emperors. Props are usually minimal, the idea being to leave as much as possible to the audience's imagination.

Chinese operas also incorporate mime, dance, sword-play and acrobatics. For the principal artists, gesture, movement and attitude are all as important as their spoken lines.

It is perfectly acceptable for audiences to arrive late for a performance, leave early, walk around and chat, or even eat during a show, which may run from three hours to a whole day. When an actor sings especially well, the audience is expected to respond by shouting out praise and applauding.

and employed writers to produce new scripts, while a symphony orchestra was introduced to bring a more modern tempo.

Ironically, the first major reform of Chinese opera was started on the mainland by the late Chinese leader Mao Zedong's wife, who persecuted intellectuals during the Cultural Revolution. Under her instructions, traditional opera troupes put on "revolutionary model plays". They sang the praises of the Communist Party and condemned the evils of capitalism. Delicate young girls yearning for love were replaced by iron ladies sweating away in the fields. Symphonic music was introduced to add a stronger mood, while Western opera-singing techniques were applied to make revolutionary leaders stand out.

Rigid political propaganda aside, these revolutionary plays introduced modern elements to traditional Chinese operas and convinced veteran artists that new stories could work.

Lion and dragon dances

A lion dance, in which two performers wear and manipulate a lion costume, is also an integral part of festive occasions. This *qongfu*-related entertainment form is usually performed at festivals, or on special occasions such as the opening of a new business or a corporate anniversary.

who move the large cloth or paper puppet from within. Also, in the lion dance, performers can move the head in various ways, as well as the eyes, mouth and ears.

There are generally two types of Chinese lions – northern and southern. The differences are in their appearance and the way they move. While the northern lion has a furry yellow coat and a semi-rigid mouth, the southern version has a movable mouth and a more colourful body, but no long hair for fur.

Music and film

Despite efforts to adapt to modern times, interest in traditional arts has been replaced by pop

Since the lion is considered a holy animal and seen as a spirit that has its own importance in Chinese mythology, lion dances are believed to bring good luck. Sometimes performances are accompanied by firecrackers to scare away evil spirits. There may also be a dragon dance to accompany the lion. The difference between the two dances is simple: the dragon is held aloft by a group of performers, who move the giant puppet from outside. They walk in set patterns to make the dragon look like it is flying. But the lion dance has a crew of only two,

LEFT: resplendent costumes embellish the operatic performance. **ABOVE:** New Year dragon dance.

music and movies. Mainland Chinese immigrants in the 1950s and 1960s brought to Hong Kong not only money and entrepreneurial skills, but also arts, culture and the Mandarin language. During the 1950s and 1960s, most of the well-known artists in Hong Kong were from Shanghai. In the 1970s, when contact between Hong Kong and Taiwan increased, Hong Kong's music scene was dominated by Taiwanese songs, mostly written by college students on the island ruled by the Guomintang (Nationalist) party.

In the mid-1970s, some Hong Kong-born singers with a clear local identity started a movement to promote Cantonese pop songs, and by the early 1980s the first generation of Cantonese pop stars – dubbed "Cantopop" stars by the local press – appeared. Since the late 1980s, this local scene has been dominated by teen idols – young male and female singers in their late teens or early twenties – whose popularity depends more on their looks than their voices. In the 1990s, the biggest local pop stars were described as "emperors" and "empresses", with the most famous performers called the "four heavenly emperors" – singers Leon Lai, Jackie Cheung, Andy Lau and Aaron Kwok. Each has their own coterie of fans who track their idol's every public appearance. When heart-

the city gets more affluent, the government and its citizens are beginning to appreciate the high-quality arts.

There are eight professional performance companies in Hong Kong and hundreds of amateur groups. The most prominent players include the Hong Kong Philharmonic Orchestra, Hong Kong Repertory Theatre, Hong Kong Chinese Orchestra and the Hong Kong Dance Company. Founded in 1985, the Academy for Performing Arts in Wan Chai is one of the top performing-arts schools in Asia. Major cultural events include the annual Hong Kong Arts Festival and the Fringe Festival.

throb singer/actor Leslie Cheung died – a suicide jump from the top floor of the Mandarin Oriental hotel in 2003 – the city was practically paralysed by grief. Tribute websites continue to clutter the Internet, and his fans still parade wreaths in public. In the past decade, Hong Kong has become established on the international concert circuit. Various big-name rock bands have played at the Hong Kong Stadium and other venues in recent years.

Life for the more traditional professional artists has got tougher, since the local society is so commercially oriented that people do not have much time for serious art. However, as

The profile of Chinese cinema has risen considerably in recent years. Hong Kong films are gaining international attention, and local film talent has become more influential following the achievements in Hollywood of director John Woo, actor Chow Yun-fat and action-star Jackie Chan, as well as the highly acclaimed, idiosyncratic work of director Wong Kar-wai. Hong Kong remains one of only a handful of places in the world where locally made films (mainly action and romance) consistently outsell Hollywood productions. ❑

ABOVE: a scene from local director Wong Kar-wai's acclaimed *Chungking Express* (1994).

Chinese Arts and Crafts

Chinese arts and crafts have a long history. Traditional forms include porcelain, embroidery, brocade, carpets, jade products, carvings (wood, bamboo and ivory) and paper decorations called "scissors-cuts" – all with different styles and regional influences – as well as brush painting and calligraphy. In Hong Kong, the most reliable places to buy these items are the China Arts and Crafts shop in Wan Chai and the several department stores specialising in Chinese products on Hong Kong Island and Kowloon. For antiques, look no further than Hollywood Road and neighbouring Upper Lascar Row (more commonly known as Cat Street; *see page 101*)

Chinese **embroidery and brocade** have had a reputation for excellent quality since the days of trade on the Silk Road. The best silk products come from eastern and southeastern regions where the climate is suitable for raising silkworms, while the dry northwestern regions of the country produce fine-quality cashmere.

Silk embroidery from Suzhou, near Shanghai in eastern China, is especially well known for its fine workmanship and venerable history stretching back over 2,000 years. **Drawn work** from Shantou in eastern Guangdong also enjoys a good reputation overseas.

Scissors-cut is traditionally a product of rural China, where various kinds of colourful designs are created to decorate windows before Chinese New Year. Patterns include animals, fruit, flowers and characters from ancient Chinese folk tales or operas, often with themes of good harvests, prosperity and happiness.

Carvings of jade, ivory, wood, bone, rock and bamboo are a familiar sight in China. The best-known are jade carvings from Beijing, an art form that dates back to the Ming dynasty (1368–1644); ivory balls featuring legendary Chinese figures from Guangzhou; stone carvings from Shoushan in Fujian province; bamboo carvings from

Huangyan in Zhejiang province; and high-quality ink-slabs made in Duanxi and Zhaoqing in Guangdong.

The Chinese invented **porcelain** in the 7th century AD, a thousand years before the Europeans. The best variety comes from Jingdezhen County in Jiangxi province. The ceramics are fine and smooth, reminiscent of those made during the Yuan dynasty, and the colourful styles have inherited the rich artistry of the Qing dynasty during its most powerful and prosperous period.

Chinese landscape painting and **calligraphy** are generally mounted on a hanging

scroll. In days gone by, the scroll was rolled up, stored away, and brought out on special occasions to be slowly unfurled, revealing only parts of a scene, subtly drawing the observer into the picture. **Miniature paintings** on shells, feathers, tree bark, deer horns and even thin strands of wheat straw, are also popular souvenirs and gifts.

Artificial **decorative flowers** made in brocade, silk, paper, feather, plastic and synthetics are relatively new crafts coming out of China. Beijing is best known for its silk flowers, Liaoning in the northeast for its feather flowers, while Yangzhou in the east produces flowers made of grass. ❑

RIGHT: a large and complicated jade carving.

MODERN ARCHITECTURE

Few of the world's cities confront the visitor with their architecture as dramatically as does Hong Kong, with its constantly shifting skyline

Hong Kong is a city that likes to flaunt its wealth, and nowhere is this more apparent than in its architecture. The acute scarcity of land, particularly on the dense urban strip of Hong Kong Island, and subsequent high prices have pushed buildings ever higher into the polluted skies. In fact there are more tall structures (over 13 storeys) here than anywhere else on the planet. Showpiece buildings vie for the prime spot and the most eye-catching design, augmented by gaudy nighttime light displays.

This being Hong Kong, nothing stays still for long. At one time St John's Cathedral was the tallest building. In the early 1960s, the Mandarin Oriental Hotel took over the mantle, to be usurped by Jardine House (1973), the Hopewell Centre (1980), the Bank of China (1990), Central Plaza (1992), and IFC2 (2003).

But height isn't everything. With money to play with, architects have been able to produce some truly exciting designs. Prime examples are Norman Foster's widely admired Hongkong and Shanghai Bank building (said to have cost around US$1 billion), the Convention and Exhibition Centre, and I.M. Pei's unique Bank of China Tower.

LEFT: the IFC2 tower is currently the world's fifth-tallest structure.

BELOW: the Convention and Exhibition Centre was extended, at great expense, for the handover ceremony in 1997. The result is unusual and spectacular.

BELOW: the Cultural Centre on the Tsim Sha Tsui waterfront. Oddly, there are no windows through which to admire the view across the harbour.

ABOVE: Central's skyline never fails to captivate. The IFC2 tower, completed in 2003, looms over Jardine House, once Hong Kong's tallest.

BELOW: old and new side by side, Flagstaff House is dwarfed by the Lippo Centre towers.

HIGH DEMAND, HIGH PRICES

The construction industry is big business in Hong Kong, and the government draws much of its revenue from the sale of land (income taxes are low). With supply exhausted and demand as high as ever, land has to be reclaimed from the sea, with construction companies willing to fork out staggering sums for the right to build on the new plots.

In contrast to the high-tech buildings themselves, the giant webs of scaffolding used in their construction are made entirely of bamboo. Extremely strong and durable, bamboo goes up four times faster than steel – no nails or screws are used – and withstands typhoons better. There are around 250 experienced bamboo scaffolders in Hong Kong, who clamber about barefoot hundreds of feet above the streets. Few use proper safety equipment, however, and there are several deaths each year.

Hong Kong Island has long held a monopoly on these super-tall glass and steel towers, but Kowloon is catching up. With the end of height restrictions following the closure of Kai Tak Airport, development is rapid – and the Union Square tower (on the West Kowloon reclamation) is set to take over from IFC2 as the tallest building in town by 2007. The New Territories are also getting in on the act, with the completion of the 319m (1,046ft) Nina Tower at Tsuen Wan.

BELOW: much of urban Hong Kong is characterised by run-of-the-mill 1950s, '60s and '70s apartment blocks such as here in Mongkok. The typical living space is cramped, around 45–65 square metres (500–700 sq.ft).

MONEY IS EVERYTHING. OF COURSE

Making money is Hong Kong's *raison d'être*:
the fast buck is revered and the tycoon's status
stops just short of beatification

Even with its limited resources and space, prosperity and affluence are among the first impressions a visitor gets after arriving in Hong Kong. Local people are renowned for their materialism, and it is easy for casual visitors to sneer, but it does not take long to understand the reasons behind it. Consider what it takes to survive in this city. A new university graduate makes about HK$7,000 a month, but the rent for an apartment can cost the same amount, if not more. That (small) apartment – 400 sq.ft, two bedrooms – can't be bought for less than US$200,000 – even though rental prices have fallen in recent years. The belief among Hong Kong's people is that if you do not go into business for yourself, you will spend 30 years of your life earning only enough to pay for a matchbox-sized flat.

Hong Kongers have a sharp eye for business. As soon as they have saved enough money by working for other people, many of them venture into their own businesses. If they prosper, they move from somewhere like Kennedy Town, a cheap(er) area in Western District, to the more privileged Mid-Levels. If they fail, they get a regular job and make a comeback once they have saved enough money. Hong Kong is rich with the stories of tycoons who have ascended to the summit, fallen into the financial abyss, then climbed to the top once more, attaining legendary status in the process.

Overview

The government's basic policy of minimum interference and maximum support for business has long been a key factor underlying Hong Kong's continued economic success. There are few places in the world where it is easier to set up and register a business. Contributing to Hong Kong's economic prowess are a low tax environment, free and fair market competition, a sound legal and financial framework, a fully convertible and secure currency, a highly efficient network of transport and communication, a skilled workforce, the enterprising spirit of locals, a high degree of internationalisation and cultural openness.

Business decisions are left to the private sector, and the government has rarely sought to influence commerce through regulations, tax policies or subsidies. The tax system is simple, with the corporate tax rate at 17.5 percent, lower than international standards. The bureaucracy is small and efficient.

As a compact city inhabited by seven million people, Hong Kong is one of the planet's most densely populated places. Compensating for the lack of natural resources are Hong Kong's excellent deep-water harbour and a strategic location on China's doorstep.

Hong Kong currently operates some of the busiest ports in the world. The international airport at Chek Lap Kok was used by 26.75 million passengers in 2003 and 2.64 million tonnes of freight, while the vast container port at Tsing

To provide a stable currency, the government introduced a linked exchange-rate system in 1983 that pegged Hong Kong's currency to the US dollar. The system was designed to align interest rates with those in the United States' reliable and stable economy. The currency exchange rate was fixed at approximately HK$7.8 to US$1. However, during the 1997 financial crisis that cascaded through Asia, many people questioned the wisdom of linking Hong Kong's currency to the US dollar so rigidly, and there is still periodic doubt as to whether the "peg" should remain, as it overvalues the Hong Kong dollar.

Yi, next to the Airport Express rail line, handles over 20 million containers every year.

Hong Kong has established itself as a major international trade and financial centre with a sound economic base. In January 2004, its foreign currency assets stood at US$ 124 billion, making it the world's fourth-largest holder of foreign currency reserves, only beaten by the rest of China, Japan and Taiwan. It is the world's twelfth largest banking centre in terms of external assets, and the seventh largest foreign-exchange trading centre.

LEFT: gold has an appeal in Hong Kong.
ABOVE: the trading floor at a large financial institution.

Manufacturing

For the first century of British rule, Hong Kong developed as a trading port through which China did business with the rest of the world, but this role rapidly diminished following the end of World War II, as communist China became increasingly isolationist. In a short time, the economy switched its focus to manufacturing. A large number of Shanghainese entrepreneurs fled here after the Communist Party came to power in 1949. Bringing capital and business skills, they re-established themselves by setting up factories making textiles and toys. A sizeable workforce was on hand to provide the labour.

Manufacturing gradually diversified into electronics, printing, publishing, machinery, fabricated-metal products, plastic products (the famous "made in Hong Kong" cheap toys), watches and jewellery. Yet this proved to be a relatively short-lived stage in Hong Kong's economic history. Since the late 1980s, most companies have moved their processing operations to China, where labour is considerably cheaper. By 1999, the manufacturing sector accounted for just 5.7 percent of GDP, down from 24 percent in 1984. What little remains is mostly in the garment industry, and these days Hong Kong functions primarily as a finance and service-industry centre.

knowledge of the Chinese way of doing business – naturally edged out their British rivals.

Apart from the free-market spirit and the rule of law established by British administrators, Hong Kong owes its economic success, to a large extent, to the opening of the mainland economy in the late 1970s. Suddenly, the territory's strategic position as the international community's gateway to China, and China's trade window to the outside world, became far more important. Both China and Hong Kong – whose total merchandise trade is in excess of HK$3,548 billion – have benefited from their fast-developing economic ties. China accounts for nearly half of Hong Kong's total trade in

Economic ties with China

Until the late 1970s, the Hong Kong business sector was dominated by British companies, known as *hongs* by the Cantonese. The four leading British *hongs* were Jardine Matheson, Wheelock Marden, Hutchison Whampoa and the Swire Group. But more recently, energetic and ambitious Hong Kong Chinese groups, with investments in shipping, property and the textile industry, have built new empires and taken over some of the British-founded concerns. Considering mainland China to be the biggest market in the world, Hong Kong entrepreneurs – with their blood and emotional ties to the mainland and their

goods, making the mainland one of its largest trading partners. China's share in Hong Kong's re-export trade (export of goods made abroad) is even higher at around 90 percent, making China both the largest market for and the largest source of Hong Kong's goods for re-exports. In 2003, Hong Kong was China's third largest trading partner (after Japan and the United States).

Financial links between the SAR and mainland China have also been increasing. The Bank of China, which has been in Hong Kong for decades, is now the second largest banking group after the Hongkong and Shanghai Bank (HSBC). The favourable geographical position and the absence of restrictions on capital flows have helped it develop into an international financial centre. Hong Kong's financial markets have a high degree of liquidity and transparent regulations – the founding of the Independent Commission Against Corruption (ICAC) in 1974 effectively stamped out a serious corruption problem that was stifling growth, and has been of enormous benefit to Hong Kong. About 80 percent of the world's top banks are represented here.

Hong Kong is also a major service centre for China, especially its southern provinces, providing financial and business support to mainland companies. For the international

US$100 billion, with 40 percent of that total in Guangdong province. Guangdong has an especially close economic relationship with Hong Kong because of its geographical location, cheap labour and because, unlike most of mainland China, the same dialect, Cantonese, is spoken.

Right on the border, the original Special Economic Zone, Shenzhen, is experiencing phenomenal growth: in 2004, its total output value climbed 17.5 percent from the previous year to reach US$33.25 billion. Growth in the IT sector was highest – up 28.1 percent to RMB 69.6 billion, accounting for almost half of the total industrial output.

business and tourist interests that are not familiar with China and mainland Chinese business culture, Hong Kong also serves as a bridge. In 2004, 195.56 million people passed through the Immigration Department's control points, up almost 18 percent from 2003.

The vast mainland market – with the world's largest population, in excess of one billion – has attracted an increasing amount of investment from Hong Kong, with a cumulative direct investment in China reaching

LEFT: manufacturers have relocated to mainland China. **ABOVE:** casino gambling is only allowed offshore in Hong Kong, but is hugely important in Macau.

Gambling

Gambling in Hong Kong is exclusively controlled by the Hong Kong Jockey Club, which takes bets on horses and football and runs the local lottery – the Mark 6. In Hong Kong it is illegal to place bets online, or overseas. Betting turnover in 2002–3 was HK$71 billion (approximately US$9 billion). After paying punters dividends of HK$58 billion, the HKJC contributes 11.7 percent of Hong Kong's tax revenue, making it the single largest taxpayer. Across the delta in Macau, the casino business is going from strength to strength as foreign investors cash in on the boom (see page 171). ❑

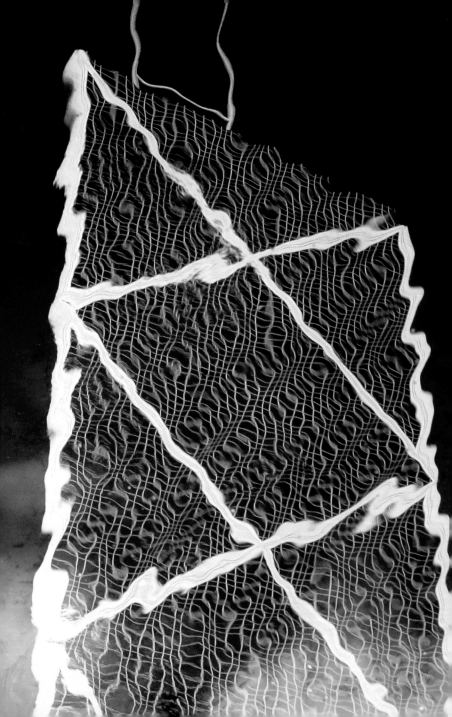

PLACES

A detailed guide to Hong Kong, Macau, Shenzhen and Guangzhou, with principal sites clearly cross-referenced by number to the maps

Today's Hong Kong can be divided into four parts: Hong Kong Island, the Kowloon peninsula, the New Territories and the numerous outlying islands. Hong Kong Island is 75 square kilometres (29 sq. miles) of topsy-turvy real estate. The earliest British settlements were established here; it is now dominated by great banks and counting houses, enormous futuristic buildings, opulent hotels, splendid residences on the Peak, surprisingly restful beach resorts, and the territory's oldest Chinese communities. Across the Harbour – by the Mass Transit Railway, Star Ferry or via one of three tunnels – is Kowloon, with its millions of people packed into just a few square kilometres. Tsim Sha Tsui district, the site of many hotels, bars and shops, is changing as fast as anywhere in Hong Kong, with massive developments above and below ground.

Beyond the mountains which ring Kowloon lie the anachronistically named New Territories, leased by the British for 99 years and handed back to China, together with the rest of Hong Kong, in 1997. A heady mix of empty hillsides, bucolic landscapes and bustling developments, it's a very different side of the Special Administrative Region. A further step into the outfield is granted by the 230-plus outlying islands, some changing for ever – Walt Disney's second Asian theme park opened on Lantau in 2005 – and others uninhabited and unaltered since the day the Union Jack was first planted. To the west across the silt-laden waters of the Pearl River mouth is the former Portuguese enclave of Macau, busily reinventing itself as East Asia's leisure capital. Across the border, the Pearl River Delta, anchored by the ever-expanding cities of Shenzhen and Guangzhou, is well on its way to becoming one of the great financial powerhouses of Asia. ❏

PRECEDING PAGES: crowded street in Mongkok; high-rise tower blocks at Tung Chung.
LEFT: the Bank of China Tower reflected in the waters of Victoria Harbour.

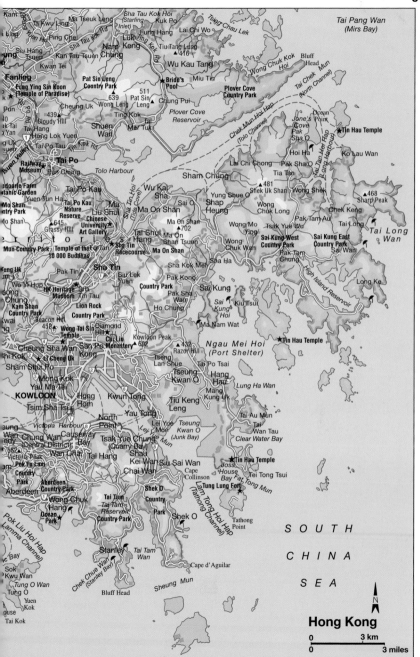

Tai Pang Wan
(Mirs Bay)

Kam Tin
Ta Kwu Ling
Ma Tseuk Leng
Sha Tau Kok Hoi
(Starling Inlet)
Sha Tau Kok Hoi
Lai Chi Wo
Tsing Chau Lek
ng
Yuen Long Ping Che
Siu Hang Tsuen
Kan Tau Tsuen Chung
Luk Keng
Fung Hang
Kuk Po
Sha Tau Kok Rd
Luk Ming Ko Rd
Tiu Tang Lung
Kwan Tei
Fanling
Nam Chung
Wu Kau Tang
Wong Chuk Kok Hoi
Bluff Head
Fung Ying Sin Koon
(Temple of Paradise)
Pat Sin Leng
Country Park
▲416
Miu Tin
Bride's Pool
Plover Cove
Country Park
Tai Chek Mun
(North Channel)
k
Pun
640
ok Tai
Wan
Uk
sueh
Cheung Uk
639
Wong Leng
511
Pat Sin Leng
Chung Pui
Plover Cove
Reservoir
Ocean Point
Jone's Cove
▲439
Cloudy Hill
Hong Lok Yuen
Tai Po Tau
Ting Kok
Mei Tuk
Tai Hang
Chek Mun Hoi Hap
Tolo Channel
Pak Sha O
Tin Hau Temple
Ko Lau Wan
Shuen Wan
Tai Po Kau Rd
Hoi Ha
Railway Museum
Ban Chung
Tolo Harbour
Lai Chi Chong
Pak Sha O
Long Harbour
Tai Po
Tai Wan Hoi Hap
adoorie Farm
tanic Garden
Yuen Tun Ha
Tai Po Kau
Nature
Reserve
Liu Shui
Wu Kai Sha
Sham Chung
Yung Shue O
▲481
Shek Uk Shan
Tia Tan
Wong Shek
▲468
Sharp Peak
lo Shan
▲645
Grassy Hill
Chinese
University
Art Gallery
Ma On Shan
Shap Heung
Wong Chuk Long
Chek Keng
Tai Long
un Country Park
Temple of the
10 000 Buddhas
Tai Tan
Tai Shui Hang
Ma On Shan
Ma On Shan Tsuen
Wong Mo Ying
Tsak Yue Wu
Pak Tam Au
Tai Long Wan
ung Uk
um
Wo Yi Hop
song
Chung
Pak Tin
Sha Tin Racecourse
Sha Tin
Wong Chuk Wan
Sai Kung West
Country Park
Sai Kung East
Country Park
Sai Wan
HK Heritage
Museum
Siu Lek Yuen
Sha Tin
Tin Tau
Sha Kok Mei
Pak Tam Chung
Kam Shan
Country Park
Lion Rock
Country Park
Pak Kong
Sha Ha
High Island Reservoir
Long Ke
Beacon Hill
458▲
Wong Tai Sin
Temple
Diamond Hill
Chi Lin
Nunnery
Pak Sha Wan
Sai Kung
wai
Cheung Sha Wan
San Po Kong
Kowloon Peak ▲602
▲432
Ho Chung
Sai Kung Hoi
Kiu Tsui
Tin Hau Temple
hi Kok
Li Cheng Uk
Razor Hill
Ngau Mei Hoi
(Port Shelter)
Sham Shui Po
Mong Kok
Tseng Lan Shue
Ma Nam Wat
Yau Ma Tei
KOWLOON
Hung Hom
Kwun Tong
Tseung Kwan O
Tai Po Tsai
Hang Hau
Tsim Sha Tsui
Tiu Keng Leng
Mang Kung Uk
Lung Ha Wan
aung
eung
edy
Wan
Chung Wan
(Central District)
Victoria Harbour
North Point
Causeway
Bay
Yau Tong
Lei Yue Mun
Tseung Kwan O
(Junk Bay)
Tai Au Mun
Tai Wan Tau
Clear Water Bay
552▲
Victoria Peak
am
Pok Fu Lam
Country
Park
Wan Chai
Tai Hang
Tsak Yue Mun
(Quarry Bay)
Shau Kei Wan
Siu Sai Wan
Chai Wan
Cape Collinson
Joss House Bay
Fat Tong Mun
Tin Hau Temple
Tei Tong Tsui
Aberdeen
Country Park
Wong Chuk Hang
Shek O
Country
Park
Shek O
Tung Lung Fort
Tai Tong Hoi Hap
(Tathong Channel)
Pok Liu Hoi Hap
Lamma Channel
Ocean
Park
Tai Tam
Tai Tam Reservoir
Country Park
Tathong Point
ic Bay
Sok
Kwu Wan
Stanley
Tai Tam Wan
Cape d'Aguilar
Chek Chue Wan
(Stanley Bay)
Tung O Wan
Tung O
Yuen
Kok
ouse
Bluff Head
Sheung Mun

S O U T H

C H I N A

S E A

N

Hong Kong

0   3 km

0   3 miles

CENTRAL AND THE

With its mass of skyscrapers wedged against the precipitous slopes of the Peak, Central District is Hong Kong's defining image

CHINA

Hong Kong

Central – still occasionally marked on maps as "Victoria", and Chung Wan in Cantonese – is Hong Kong's business and financial hub, at the heart of the incredible cliff-face of high-rise buildings that extends along the north shore of Hong Kong Island. Wedged between the harbour and the precipitous slopes of Victoria Peak, this is where the money is, the financial powerhouses, the glamorous high-end shopping malls, overlooked by the multi-millionaires' mansions up on the Peak. It all adds up to one of the most fascinating areas of modern Hong Kong.

This is not somewhere that rests on its laurels. The construction of gigantic new buildings is never-ending. Reclamation work is claiming great chunks of the harbour; one area reclaimed during the 1990s now accommodates the mammoth International Finance Centre *(see page 87)*, which has given the prestigious commercial district's orientation a decided tweak.

Central, like the rest of Hong Kong, doesn't have a great deal to offer in the way of conventional tourist sights. There are few old buildings or museums of interest, and despite the efforts of the tourist board to highlight the past with such innovations as the Sun Yat-sen Trail,

most of the "landmarks" en route are simply plaques recording some building or other that has long since disappeared. Instead, the fascination is in the contemporary, the everyday life of the place, its architecture, its amazing contrasts of scale, and the sheer energy that emanates from the crowded streets.

Yet while most of the pedestrians on Central's streets are attired for business, and giant video screens flash the latest news and financial figures from around the world

Map
on page
87

LEFT: the bright lights of Central.
BELOW: clothing stalls on the steps of Pottinger Street.

The rickshaws at the Star Ferry pier are for a quick ride around the block and no further.

BELOW: looking south from Statue Square.

to passers-by, there are still strong elements of former days, with wayside hawkers dangling novelties and knock-offs, incense sticks smouldering by tiny shrines, and delivery boys serenely pedalling through red lights with a cargo of fresh meat balanced in their bike's cast-iron basket.

The financial centre

The **Star Ferry Pier** ❶ is as good a place as any to begin exploring Central. The terminal is due to move northwards as reclamation (including a splendid public plaza, if official predictions are to be believed) proceeds, but – having been in business since the 19th century – the company is likely to take the upheaval in its stride. The green-and-white double-deckers are one of Hong Kong's icons, and the mini-voyage is one of the city's bargains, costing a mere HK$2.2 on the upper deck for an adult *(see page 96 for more details).*

In front of the busy Star Ferry Concourse are bright-red **rickshaws** pulled by the handful of wily ancients who still earn a living in this old-fashioned way. These two-wheeled chariots first appeared on the streets of Hong Kong in the late 1870s, but they actually originated in Japan. The first ones were designed and made by an American missionary, and the name comes from the Japanese *jinrikisha*, which means "man-powered wheeled vehicle". Today, they're only useful to provide photo opportunities for tourists or for a quick ride around the block – no further. Prepare to bargain hard.

Heading straight inland, an underpass will take you to **Statue Square** ❷ on either side of Chater Road. On Sundays, throngs of Filipina maids gather here on their day off in a festive, somewhat chaotic outdoor party. The 143,000 Philippine nationals, most of whom work here as maids, now form by far the single largest foreign community living in Hong Kong – over double the number of British, Canadian, Australian and American passport-holders, who together total around 70,000.

The square was once graced with a statue of Queen Victoria, long transplanted to Causeway Bay, and

replaced by a statue of Sir Thomas Jackson, an Irishman who managed the Hongkong and Shanghai Banking Corporation for 30 years around the end of the 19th century. Chinese and expatriate victims of World Wars I and II are commemorated at the **Cenotaph**, and Hong Kong's war veterans gather here on Remembrance Day every November.

The **Mandarin Oriental Hotel** ❸ is one of the oldest and grandest hotels in Hong Kong, and a favourite meeting place for the captains of industry. It's unusual to mention the Mandarin without the accompanying adjective "venerable", and at four decades old it's something of a treasure. Hong Kong's tallest building when it was completed, it is undergoing (2005– 6) a massive renovation to bring it up to scratch in the face of competition from new hotels which are springing up in the area.

This part of Central District is the financial hub of Hong Kong, home to the headquarters of several major banks. Facing Statue Square is Norman Foster's modernistic US$1 billion **Hongkong & Shanghai Bank Building** (HSBC Building) ❹, the most expensive building in the world when it was completed in 1985. A short distance along Des Voeux Road, past the gleaming **Cheung Kong Center**, is the dramatic 368-metre (1,209-ft) **Bank of China Tower** ❺, designed by the American-Chinese architect I. M. Pei and one of Hong Kong's most famous buildings. Opened in 1990, it is surmounted by two antennae resembling a pair of chopsticks, and its sharp angles point directly at other financial institutions, channelling bad feng shui onto them (*see page 46*). The 43rd floor observation area is open to the public (Mon–Fri 9am–6pm, Sat 9am–1pm; free). Behind it is **Citibank Plaza,** another cutting-edge-design office tower development, leading to the high-rise luxury apartments of the Mid-Levels (Pun Shan Kui).

East of Statue Square is the Hong Kong Club, a prestigious institution for the SAR's upper crust. The Club's blue-and-white building was demolished in 1981 and has been

Map on page 87

ORIENTATION:
This chapter covers the area from the former Prince of Wales Building and Hong Kong Park in the east to Central Market and the Mid-Levels Escalator in the west, and extends inland to the Peak.

BELOW: Central's streets are thronged with people.

A rare historic presence in Central District, the Legislative Council Building dates from 1912.

BELOW: buses, trams and people at rush hour on Des Voeux Road.

replaced by a modern skyscraper. Fortunately, the colonial-style former **Supreme Court Building**, which is now the **Legislative Council (Legco) Building** ❻, escaped a similar fate. Built in 1912, it is topped by a statue of the blindfolded Greek goddess Themis, and its Edwardian dome shows up brilliantly against IM Pei's postmodernist Bank of China Tower. The building was used as a torture chamber by Japanese police during World War II, and wartime shrapnel damage can still be seen on the eastern wall. It is not open to the general public.

Across Jackson Road, **Chater Garden** is a rare (but not especially pleasant) open space that may host demonstrators, dancing off-duty maids or munching office workers on their lunch break. Until the 1970s, the site was occupied by the Hong Kong Cricket Club. When the 1967 pro-communist riots shook Hong Kong, a photographer captured the ultimate clash of cultures – English colonels playing cricket against a backdrop of Mao posters draped all over the old Bank of China Building.

From Chater Garden, a walkway leads past the Bank of America Tower and the Ritz-Carlton hotel. Under another walkway and to the east of the Star Ferry Pier is **City Hall** ❼. The building not only houses administrative offices, but a concert hall, theatre and booking office. Just beyond is the ugly **former Prince of Wales Building**, which served as the headquarters of the British military until the handover. It is now the HQ for the People's Liberation Army. Reclamation work is ongoing between here and the Convention Centre in Wan Chai. While environmentalists worry about the adverse affects of filling in so much of the harbour, the government is trumpeting a brave new waterfront world, with a proper promenade and other public spaces which may be complete by 2010.

It is possible to get a preview of all this development at the catchily titled **Hong Kong Planning and Infrastructure Exhibition Gallery** (open daily 10am–6pm; free), just in front of City Hall. Inside is an

18.5-metre (60-ft) model of the city, while numerous computer animations and other exhibits showcase the planners' vision of the new Hong Kong.

West of the Star Ferry

On the other (west) side of the Star Ferry is **Jardine House 8**, whose distinctive 1,700-plus round windows have inspired the nickname "House of a Thousand Orifices". Opened in 1973 (when it was known as the Connaught Centre), it was for many years the tallest building in Hong Kong. Just behind this holey wonder is the General Post Office (GPO). Walkways lead across to **Exchange Square 9**, home of the Hong Kong Stock Exchange and featuring a collection of sculptures by Henry Moore and Ju Ming in the adjacent plaza, and the **International Finance Centre (IFC1) 10**, a combination of smart shopping malls and offices which sits atop the Airport Express

terminus. Just in front towards the harbour, and still part of the IFC complex, is Hong Kong's tallest building, the prosaically named **International Finance Centre Two (IFC2) 11**, finished in 2003. It stands at a staggering 420 metres (1,378 ft), which makes it currently the fifth tallest building in the world (39 metres/128 ft higher than the Empire State Building), and is capped by a mass of curving spires. Unfortunately people are not normally allowed up to the 88th floor to admire the views. There is an outside terrace (fifth floor only) with bars and cafés above the Lane Crawford department store. The adjacent tower block houses the brand new super-luxury ("six-star") Four Seasons Hotel, open from late 2005. To the north are the Outlying Islands ferry piers.

Central's streets tend to be busy and sweaty for much of the year; they are more easily navigated via the walkways which run from the

A street parade takes place at Chinese New Year through the streets of Central.

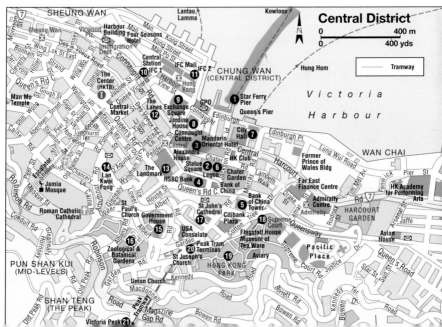

People assume that the dark-green forested backdrop to the famous view across Victoria Harbour is "natural". In fact, the hillsides were stripped of their original forest cover over the centuries, and it wasn't until the 1940s and 1950s that replanting took place. Early photographs (see page 16) clearly show the absence of trees, altering the scene almost as dramatically as the lack of buildings.

BELOW: silk jackets, scarves and accessories for sale on Li Yuen Street East.

GPO (first floor) past Exchange Square to the Macau Ferry Terminal, and via Swire House and adjacent buildings as far as the bottom of Lan Kwai Fong. Numerous (slightly world-weary) security guards en route are very obliging with directions. In the hot months, at least for those from cooler climes, it is quite an experience to walk through Central on these walkways – one minute you are perspiring in the unbelievable heat and humidity of a Hong Kong summer, the next you are instantly cool as the walkway passes into an air-conditioned mall; then, suddenly, you are out in the open again and the wall of damp heat washes over you like a wave. The contrast is heightened by the decibel level – soft piped muzak in the malls, traffic and piledriver din on the streets.

Heading inland from the GPO on these pedestrian thoroughfares takes you over Connaught Road Central to **Des Voeux Road**, named after Sir George William Des Voeux, governor from 1887 to 1891. The tram stop here, at the junction with Ped-

der Street, is one of Central's most photographed spots, a blur of traffic and people. **Queen's Road Central** was the area's original "Main Street", but a little footpath in front of the Queen's Road godowns (warehouses) and counting houses was turned into Des Voeux Road, which eventually upstaged it. These days both are (of course) very busy, although Queen's Road has more in the way of shops. Toward the western end of Queen's Road was the main branch of Lane Crawford, one of the most expensive luxury department stores in Asia. It closed in 2005, to be replaced by the new flagship store in the IFC complex.

To the west along Queen's Road, there are dozens of ship chandleries on the site where, decades ago, ships docked and refitted. Beyond this point Queen's Road quickly becomes less grandiose, whittling down from upmarket department stores to small traditional crafts shops as you head towards Western District beyond Central Market *(see page 98).*

Some of the side streets connecting Queen's and Des Voeux roads

are well worth exploring. **Li Yuen Street East** and **Li Yuen Street West,** also known as **The Lanes** ⑫, are narrow alleyways lined with stalls and shops that sell clothing, fabrics and counterfeit designer fashion accessories. The atmosphere is a complete contrast to the glamorous high-rises on the larger avenues near by. Bargaining is still expected here in these smaller streets, even though the neighbourhood is a bit more upscale than the outdoor markets, where haggling is de rigueur.

On **Pedder Street**, Shanghai Tang is one of Hong Kong's most successful home-grown fashion stores. British-Chinese entrepreneur David Tang, who first brought the territory the exclusive China Club, then Cuban cigars, turned his attention to making Chinese fashion chic. Across the street is **The Landmark** ⑬, a prestigious shopping complex opened in 1980 on the site of the old Gloucester Hotel. The Gloucester was demolished for the New Gloucester Building, which in turn was destroyed to

make way for The Landmark. Five floors surround a vast 6,000-square-metre (20,000-sq.-ft) atrium with 100 shops. The fountain in the middle is converted into a stage for performances on holidays and other special occasions. From The Landmark, walkways lead through to the **Prince's Building**, with a further abundance of marble and relentlessly upmarket shops.

Behind Queen's Road Central, which was the waterfront road before land reclamation began in the 1850s, the terrain rises steeply. D'Aguilar Street leads up to the nightlife centre of **Lan Kwai Fong** ⑭, which together with nearby SoHo *(see page 99)* is the prime nightlife area for Hong Kong's young and trendy. Modern cuisine, funky bars, clubs, English pubs and tiny snack shops generate dollars and testosterone in equal measure, and late-night revellers can get everything from pizza to sushi in the wee hours. At weekends many bars stay open until 5am or later.

Wyndham Street is lined with small antique and crafts shops, and

Map on page 87

Lan Kwai Fong is the narrow street at the heart of the eponymous nightlife area.

BELOW: the view from Hong Kong Park to the Lippo Centre and the harbour.

Black kites are a common sight all over Hong Kong.

BELOW: the interior of St John's Cathedral.

leads on to **Hollywood Road**, packed with shops selling top-dollar antiques, furniture, rattan and used books, and the nightlife areas of **SoHo** (SOuth of HOllywood) and **BoHo** (BelOw HOllywood). These areas have developed around the extremely useful, fatigue-preventing **Central Mid-levels Escalator**, which starts by Central Market (*for details see Western District, page 99*).

Colonial relics

The higher up one gets on this "rock", the more desirable the property and the higher the rents – a pattern established in the early colonial years, when the upper slopes were considered less prone to malarial mosquitoes than those closer to sea level.

Glenealy is mainly residential, and it snakes uphill and eastward onto Upper Albert Road and **Government House** ⓯, the grand home of the former colonial leaders of Hong Kong. The long-term fate of Government House is still unclear, but it is currently being used (with a marked lack of imagination) as a

state guest house and official banqueting hall, although it is rumoured that David Tang may take up residence. The mansion dates from the 1850s but was remodelled by the Japanese during World War II, who added a tower with a vague Shinto look. There is a clear view of the building through the wrought-iron gates, which are opened to the public only a couple of times a year, usually in spring and autumn (no set dates).

The area surrounding Government House is one of the few remaining parts of Hong Kong Island that retains a genuinely colonial feel. If you go any further up, the pocket of exotic greenery is quickly invaded by the high-rises of the Mid-Levels; lower down, the area is engulfed by banks and office towers. Opposite Government House is the **Zoological and Botanical Gardens** ⓰ (open daily 6am–7pm; free), a lush tropical area worthy of any urban retreat. The small zoo houses a variety of exotic wildlife, including an impressive collection of red-cheeked gibbons. It opened in 1864 and still retains

elements of its original Victorian gentility, with the added Eastern spirituality of elderly Chinese performing their tai chi exercises each morning. From here it is just a short stroll to Hong Kong's other colonial crumbs. The Victorian-Gothic **St John's Cathedral** , consecrated in 1849, is the city's oldest Anglican church, tucked away opposite the Citibank Plaza on Battery Path Road. The red-brick **French Mission Building**, behind the Cheung Kong Center, is more than 150 years old and now serves as the Court of Final Appeal.

Another example of bespoke architecture is **Flagstaff House**, home to the **Museum of Tea Ware** ⓘ (open Wed–Mon 10am–5pm; tel: 2869 0690; free) and completed in 1846. The building – of more interest than the museum – is reputedly Hong Kong's oldest surviving colonial structure, and was once the residence of the Commander-in-Chief of the British forces, when the area was Victoria Barracks. Today, the large expanse is the lush, green **Hong Kong Park** ⓘ, the site of,

amongst other things, an aviary (open daily 9am–5pm; free) and botanical gardens. It is overlooked by an observation tower, a great place from which to photograph the area. Enter the park from Cotton Tree Drive or through Pacific Place shopping centre on Queensway. The park is busy all day long, with tai chi practitioners first thing in the morning, joggers and office workers taking advantage of one of Central's few open spaces, and bridal parties posing against a backdrop of waterfalls and shrubs. Secluded benches lure courting couples, a rare opportunity for privacy in this crowded city.

The Peak

Make your way to the **Peak Tram terminus** ⓴ on Garden Road to ascend Hong Kong's most notable natural landmark, properly though rarely called **Victoria Peak** ㉑ (Shan Teng in Cantonese). "The Peak" is the residential aspiration of most of the population, not to mention the goal of more than three million visitors a year, equal to almost half the population of Hong Kong. Yet it

The Edward Youde Aviary in Hong Kong Park has an aerial walkway, and shelters a variety of endangered species from Southeast Asia.

BELOW: admiring the view from the Peak Tram.

The controversial Peak Tower has several floors of shops, cafés and restaurants as well as a viewing platform.

BELOW: the view over the harbour from the Peak is unforgettable, although clear days are increasingly rare.

wasn't always regarded with such awe. A travel writer once described it as "beautiful in the distance, but sterile and unpromising upon more close examination" (note that this was before reforestation took place – *see margin note on page 88*), and during the first six years of Hong Kong's history, hardly anybody travelled to those inhospitable heights. It wasn't until 1888, when the **Peak Tramway** (actually a funicular railway) was opened, that the area atop the hill became one of the most sought-after places to live in Hong Kong. Before the tram, sedan chairs transported lucky colonials to the top. Such coolie-powered transportation died long ago, but palanquins are still used during charity races once a year.

The vertiginous Tram is more than just a tourist attraction, rising to 396 metres (1,299 ft) above sea level in just seven minutes up gradients as steep as 27 degrees (1 in 2). The tram runs from 7am to midnight, and hasn't had a single accident since it began operation. It still has only two cars, each carrying 72 passengers and one driver, and is pulled up and lowered by 1,500-metre (5,000-ft) steel cables wound on drums. Eight minutes from the Garden Road terminus, the upper terminus at the **Peak Tower** is reached. Shaped like a wok or a pair of cupped hands, and for many people one of the ugliest buildings in Hong Kong, the Tower is full of tourist-oriented gift shops and attractions, including **Madame Tussaud's** (open daily 10am–10pm; entrance fee).

Of course, the main reason for coming up to the Peak is to marvel at some of the world's finest vistas. From the Tower's **viewing platform** the panorama sprawls, on the increasingly rare clear days, all the way to mainland China. Many people find the nighttime views even more incredible, a vast glittering swathe of electric light, most spectacular immediately below in Central and Wan Chai as the buildings attempt to outdo each other in their eye-catching displays. The Tower is being renovated to incorporate more shopping and dining outlets, and the rooftop is being converted into a huge viewing platform, to be completed by 2006.

Map
on page
87

There are a variety of superb walks from the Peak. The **Peak Circle Walk** follows Lugard and Harlech roads, affording magnificent views across the harbour and Kowloon to the north, Cheung Chau and Lantau to the west, and the great masses of junks and sampans at Aberdeen to the south, with Lamma Island beyond. This gentle 3-km (2-mile) walk, well signposted and shaded from the sun, takes about 45 minutes round-trip from the Peak Tower.

The area around the Peak Tower is in fact **Victoria Gap**, whereas the summit of Victoria Peak itself (552 metres/1,811 ft) lies to the west. Follow the Peak Circle Walk until you reach the **Governor's Walk**, which winds up to the attractive **Victoria Peak Garden**. The summit itself is out of bounds.

It is possible to walk back down to Central and indulge in some of the finer views and footpaths through The Peak's wooded slopes. The **Central Green Trail** – marked by 14 bilingual signboards highlighting points of interest – meanders from Barker Road down across May Road and then via paths named Clovelly, Brewin and Tramway back to the Garden Road terminus. A popular longer walk descends westwards through Pokfulam Country Park. For the more ambitious, the **Hong Kong Trail** heads east for some 50 kilometres (30 miles) all the way to Tai Tam and on to Shek-O. Nature-lovers can wander through forests of bamboo and fern, stunted Chinese pines, hibiscus and vines of wonderful, writhing beauty. Ornithologists log sightings of blue magpies, crested goshawks and kites.

The Peak is one of the world's most expensive places to live. Its best flats and houses are rented by banks and corporate giants for their top executives at astronomical sums. Swimming pools have been installed in lieu of verandas, but the area's wilderness, beautifully juxtaposed with stately residences, graciously survives. Cicadas buzz in the dense woods, shimmering tropical birds flit from tree to tree, and it is not uncommon for residents to have poisonous snakes removed from their gardens. ❑

The Peak has long been considered Hong Kong's most desirable area to live, and some properties date back to the 19th century.

RESTAURANTS

Cantonese

City Hall Chinese Restaurant
5–7 Edinburgh Place. Tel: 2921 2840. Open: L and D daily. **$$**
A raucous Cantonese institution, serving good dim sum from old-fashioned trolleys wheeled around by uniformed staff. A vast, well-lit space with views out across the harbour.

PRICE CATEGORIES

Prices are for a three-course dinner per person with one beer or glass of house wine:
$ = under HK$150
$$ = HK$150–300
$$$ = HK$300–500
$$$$ = over HK$500

Dumpling House
26 Cochrane St. Tel: 2815 5520. Open: L and D daily. **$**
Unpretentious, down-home eatery run by a collective of no-nonsense Cantonese women. Tasty dumplings and noodles dishes make up the menu. Packed with office workers at lunch. Very reasonably priced.

Luk Yu Teahouse
24–26 Stanley St. Tel: 2523 1970. Open: L and D daily. **$$**
This traditional Cantonese teahouse in the heart of Central is legendary for its bad-mannered management. Despite that, chauffeurs tend the lined-up Mercs outside while tycoons and criminal kingpins in dark glasses take their yum cha. Tourists take

second place, but the food can be excellent. Established in 1933.

Mak's Noodles
77 Wellington St. Tel: 2854 3810. Open: L and D (closes 8pm) daily. **$**
If wonton noodle soup is Hong Kong's national dish, this is the place to sample it. Pale pink, prawn-filled pillows of pastry float on a nest of noodles in a beef tendon broth tinged with fermented shrimp paste. Better by far than its imitative neighbours.

Ser Wong Fung
26 Cochrane St. Tel: 2815 5520. Open: L and D daily. **$**
A good example of a traditional family-run restaurant with an emphasis on seasonal Cantonese cuisine. A great and very economic place to try snake soup in winter. Rarely attracts tourists.

Yung Kee
32–40 Wellington St. Tel: 2522 1624. Open: L and D daily. **$$**
Visiting the Yung Kee is like taking a 1970s time warp. A true Hong Kong institution, with a rags-to-riches history spanning almost 70 years. Justly famous for its roast goose and the obligatory 1,000-year-old eggs. Also great for dim sum. Obliga-

tory for tourists, but popular with locals too.

Other Chinese

Bistro Manchu
33 Elgin St. Tel: 2536 9218. Open: L and D daily. **$$**
Authentic northern Chinese cooking with an emphasis on dumplings and a variety of intriguing vegetarian and "healthy" options. Clean, comfortable and colourful inside.

Yellow Door
6/F, 37 Cochrane St. Tel: 2858 6555. Open: L and D Mon–Fri, D only Sat. **$$**
Hard to find, but well worth the effort. Yellow Door is owned by one of Hong Kong's best-known artists – obvious from the simple but inventive interior. High-quality, authentic Sichuanese and Shanghainese menus are served at lunch and dinner respectively.

Japanese

Tokio Joe
16 Lan Kwai Fong. Tel: 2525 1889. Open: L and D daily. **$$**
Japanese style is increasingly influential in Hong Kong, and this lively sushi restaurant offers a youthful take on formal traditions in the heart of Lan Kwai Fong. Well known for its comprehensive selection of sake.

LEFT: Sichuanese dishes at Yellow Door.
RIGHT: most food is served as fresh as possible.

International

Harlan's

Shop 2075 IFC 2. Tel: 2805 0566. Open: L and D daily. **$$$$**
Brash and moneyed, Harlan's aims to attract Hong Kong's hoi polloi and succeeds. High-class "modern Western" cooking featuring fine ingredients prepared with panache. Scarily expensive.

Life

10 Shelley St. Tel: 2810 9777. Open: L and D daily. **$**
Popular vegetarian restaurant right next to the Mid-Levels Escalator. Attracts dreadlocks and gym-toned executives who munch on flapjacks and alfalfa between sips of passion fruit and carrot juice. Organic to its eyeballs.

Peak Lookout

121 Peak Rd. Tel: 2849 1000. Open: L and D daily. **$$**
This historic stand-alone building in its own grounds on Victoria Peak is like an alpine hunting lodge transported to the tropics. Offers great views over the south side of Hong Kong Island. Vivid, lively and colourful with a very international menu.

French

Le Tire-Bouchon

45a Graham St. Tel: 2526 5965. Open: L and D Mon–Sat. **$$$**
This long-standing French restaurant has the feel of a subterranean wine cellar. A traditional menu offers rich, tasty and satisfying food and vintages from a comprehensive cellar.

Italian

Di Vino

73 Wyndham St. Tel: 2167 8883. Open: L and D Mon–Fri, D only Sat, closed Sun. **$$**
Smooth and savvy wine bar and restaurant operated by a trio of charming Italians. Always has an interesting menu, and serves tapas-style appetisers gratis to guests.

Pizza Express

21 Lyndhurst Terr. Tel: 2850 7898. Open: L and D daily. **$$**
This Far East franchise of the famous chain serves well-prepared pizza and pasta from a straightforward menu. Simple, tasty and much loved by parents of small children.

Toscana

1/F Ritz-Carlton Hotel, 3 Connaught Rd. Tel: 2877 6666. Open: L and D Mon–Sat, D only Sun. **$$$$**
Sublime Italian dining in one of the most elegant hotel restaurants in town. Gifted chef Umberto Bombana established the kitchen over 10 years ago, and has delighted diners ever since with his breathtaking cooking. Very far from cheap, but a great investment. When in season, the white and black truffles are not to be missed.

Australian

M at the Fringe

1/F, 2 Lower Albert Rd. Tel: 2877 4000. Open: L and D Mon–Fri, D only Sat–Sun. **$$$**
A perennial favourite with a unique ambience and a dedicated clientele. The satisfying modern Oz menu overflows with French and Middle-Eastern influences. The rooftop bar above is a great place for a drink.

Mezz

M20–M28, Prince's Building, 10 Chater Rd. Tel: 2523 8989. Open: L and D Mon–Sat. **$$**
A popular, good-value fixture in a part of Central lacking in evening atmosphere. Modern Australian-inspired food. Try the lemon risotto with shaved parmesan or the lobster linguine.

Indian

Tandoor

1/F Lyndhurst Tower, 1 Lyndhurst Terr. Tel: 2845 2262. Open: L and D daily. **$$**
Probably Hong Kong's top Indian eatery features life-sized Sikh guards cast in solid silver at the door, with big screen Bollywood and live Indian music in the first floor dining room. A top-notch buffet is served for lunch.

Middle Eastern

Olive

32 Elgin St. Tel: 2521 1608. Open: L and D daily. **$$$**
Very popular Maghreb and Middle-East inspired restaurant. The menu features contemporised classics like bastilla, a rich pigeon pie seasoned with cinnamon, and Fatima's fingers, stuffed cigar-like tubes of crisp filled pastry. The long slim dining room has the air of a Casablanca souk.

● For a list of recommended bars in Central, see page 219.

STAR FERRY

Costing just a couple of Hong Kong dollars, the crossing of Victoria Harbour aboard one of the Star Ferries is a visual feast that is over in just eight minutes

From ancient to modern, from Rolls-Royce to rickshaw, Hong Kong offers every mode of conveyance for rich and poor. But the territory's quintessential transport is the Star Ferry. Shunting back and forth across Victoria Harbour, these green-and-white ferries link the community together in a way that is both symbolic and endlessly practical.

The fleet would win few prizes for glamorous design. Even the grandly named *Celestial Star* (other names include *Morning Star, Meridian Star, Shining Star* and *Twinkling Star*) is just one of a dozen juddering, smoke-belching people-movers. Yet the clanking gangways, weather-beaten coxswains and solid wooden decks have a timeless character.

The first of the current "Star" fleet made their maiden voyages in 1898, although earlier ferries began operating a quarter century before that. Until Hong Kong Island was connected to Kowloon by road tunnel in 1972 and the Mass Transit Railway (MTR) in 1979, the Star Ferry was the prime way to cross the harbour – these days it is generally quicker to use the MTR unless you are travelling between points close to the piers.

BELOW: the top deck is more expensive and gives slightly better views. Seat backs can be moved back and forth, depending upon which way the ferry and the view are headed. The main route is between Central and Tsim Sha Tsui, but there are also Wan Chai to Tsim Sha Tsui and Hung Hom to Central and Wan Chai services.

LEFT: tourists, local or otherwise, are easy to spot on the Star Ferry – they are looking at the scenery. Commuters, on the other hand, will be looking at the horse-racing news or reading a novel, looking up only when the ferry eases to the gate.

HONG KONG'S TRAMS

A kind of double-act with the Star Ferry, Hong Kong's fleet of electric trams was introduced in 1904, and has remained virtually unchanged since 1925 when the familiar double-decker cars came into service. However there are plans to modernise the fleet – a handful of vehicles have new seats and air-conditioning, although it is unclear if the old-style trams are to be phased out entirely.

As with the Star Ferry, riding the tram is not only one of the city's best bargains (a flat fare of HK$2 however far you go) but also a great way to sightsee – as long as you can get a seat on the top deck, preferably at the front where the views are accompanied by a refreshing breeze. It's a great vantage point from which to observe the city go about its business. A seat at the rear of the top deck is also good, and gives wonderful photo opportunities.

Redecorated annually according to advertising-agency whim, the trams – known locally as the "ding-ding" for the bells that announce their arrival – run along the northern coast of Hong Kong Island daily from 6am until midnight. The line heads east from Des Voeux Road Central along Queensway, through the heart of Wan Chai and past Victoria Park to North Point or Shau Kei Wan. A branch leads off to Happy Valley and the terminus south of the famous racecourse. Westbound trams are signed "Western Market" and "Kennedy Town". Trams can also be hired out for private parties.

ABOVE: as part of the reclamation work on the ever-shrinking harbour, the Star Ferry pier in Central is due to move northwards at some point before 2010. The new location will be next to the Outlying Islands ferry piers, in front of the IFC2 tower.

ABOVE: Star Ferries only ply between Hong Kong Island and Kowloon, but ferries to Lantau and elsewhere offer deck-top views and longer cruises.

WESTERN DISTRICT

The skyscrapers of the world of business and commerce dominate Central, but the traditional Chinese way of life still manages to thrive in Western District, making it a rewarding area to explore

Look down from the Mid-Levels Escalator near its base and your eye falls on the Graham Street market, with produce being weighed out by the catty (600 grams) and elderly ladies shouldering their purchases on either end of a stout pole. Cross an imaginary border here, and you enter Hong Kong Island's "China Town" – more Jackie Cheung than Roman Polanski, but still with a romantic celluloid tinge to it.

Western District is located just to the west of Central but is worlds away from the ultra-modern financial district. This was the first district to be settled by the British when they arrived in Hong Kong in 1841, although malaria soon scared them away, leaving this part of Hong Kong Island to the Chinese immigrants who arrived in the early 1850s. Despite its name, it is one of the least Westernised areas of Hong Kong and provides a rare hint of the old Chinese city.

The area begins officially at Possession Street and sprawls west to Kennedy Town, but for the purposes of this guidebook we have extended this to take in those parts of Central District to the west of Central Market and the Mid-Levels Escalator. The buffer zone where modern, upmarket Central abuts old, exotic China, typified by the aforementioned Graham Street, is one of Hong Kong's most fascinating – full of gobsmacking contrasts in scale and wealth.

One of Western's charms is that it is the last refuge of the artisan. Here one can marvel at craftsmen who create mah-jong tiles out of low-priced plastic or high-priced hand-carved husks. Find the Chinese herbalist, with his aromatic concoctions of snake musk, herbs, ginseng and powdered lizards, all part of pharmacopoeial potions dating back 4,000 years.

BELOW: a typical small shop in Western District.

SoHo and Hollywood Road

One can begin a walking tour of Western with a ride on the **Central-Mid-Levels Escalator ❶** that ascends to Conduit Road. The ride provides a broad view of the narrow streets and tenement blocks that lead into Western. This reversible escalator was completed in 1993, at a cost of HK$32 million, and at 800 metres (2,625 feet) is said to be the world's longest (although in reality it is comprised of over 20 separate sections). It was built to allow commuters to ride to and from work and thus ease some of the congestion of the streets that zigzag down the hillside. The escalator moves in one direction at a time: it goes down until 10.15am, after which it is switched to the "up" mode for the rest of the day. About 40,000 people use it each day.

The lowest section of escalator passes bustling Chinese markets on small, steep thoroughfares such as **Peel, Gage** and **Graham streets**. Further up, **Staunton Street**, together with Shelley and Elgin streets, has become the centre of

Hong Kong's alternative café culture, the hub of an area which has become known as **SoHo** (SOuth of HOllywood Road) ❷. Before the escalator was built, these narrow streets were rather run down and seldom visited by outsiders. Now they comprise a gallimaufry of cafés, restaurants and bars, offering an eclectic mix of ethnic cuisine – Vietnamese, Nepali, Portuguese, Cajun and French. The traditional Chinese grocery stores in the vicinity suddenly found themselves doing a roaring business in wine for consumption in the neighbourhood restaurants. The area is also home to some of Hong Kong's most avant-garde art galleries.

Further along Staunton Street is a red sign which marks the former headquarters of the Xingzhonghui, or Revive China Society, the revolutionary organisation established by Dr Sun Yat-sen in 1895 and dedicated to the overthrow of the Qing dynasty in China. It is one of 13 sites of interest in the Central and Western districts that form the **Sun Yat-sen Historical Trail**. Much of Dr

Map
on page
101

The Central–Mid-Levels Escalator, made up of several sections, gives easy access to the bars and restaurants of SoHo.

BELOW: delivery from Central Market.

The Center is a 73-storey building that comes alive at night in a hypnotic display. Bars of neon, girdling the whole structure, pulse through a wave of gradually changing colours.

BELOW: atmospheric Man Mo Temple.

Sun's revolution was in fact orchestrated from Hong Kong. Jose Rizal, the Philippine national hero, also lived in this area at around the same time. A few doors down is the rather more contemporary House of Siren, which hires out and makes to order costumes for Hong Kong society's most outrageous fancy-dress parties.

Immediately below Staunton Street lies **Hollywood Road ❸**, and around the escalator and the police station (dating from 1911) a score of bars and restaurants have sprung up. Known as **BoHo** (Below Hollywood) this has become the late-night trendy hangout, neatly joining up SoHo and Lan Kwai Fong. Plans are in hand to convert the police station to an arts centre, though they have yet to be given firm approval. Hollywood Road itself is well known for its abundance of shops selling all manner of Chinese (and other Asian) antiques – notably furniture, art and ornaments. Prices can be quite high, and – as always – it's best to shop around.

Follow this meandering road west to the corner of Ladder Street and the wonderfully dark and atmospheric **Man Mo Temple ❹** (open daily 9am–6pm; free), built around 1842 on what must have been a little dirt track at that time. Tourists regularly throng through Man Mo, but this doesn't inhibit the temple's regular worshippers from visiting to fill the temple with thick clouds of smoke from their joss sticks. The immense incense spirals hanging from the ceiling can burn for weeks. Man is the god of civil servants and of literature, and in Mandarin society, civil servants were the best-educated and most sophisticated group. Mo is the god of martial arts and war, and is more popularly known by his worshippers as Kuan Ti or Kuan Kung. Statues of the legendary Eight Immortals stand guard outside the temple; inside, two solid-brass deer (representing longevity) adorn the main chamber. Near the altar, there are two sedan chairs encased in glass. Years ago, when the icons of Man and Mo were paraded through Western on festival days, they were transported on these chairs.

While in Western, don't miss a cruise down one of the most quirky of all local shopping areas: **Ladder Street 5**. This road zigzags down steep inclines from Caine Road to Hollywood Road and down again to Queen's Road Central. Nobody knows when its broad stone steps were constructed, but records say that this 65-metre (118-ft) "street" was built so sedan-chair bearers could more easily carry their human cargo from Hollywood Road to residential Caine Road. Ladder Street contains some of Hong Kong's oldest houses, including shuttered buildings with wooden balconies and elaborate carvings.

Just downhill from where Ladder Street meets Hollywood Road is the street officially called Upper Lascar Row but much more commonly known as **Cat Street 6**, because the odds and ends you can buy here are known in popular Chinese as "mouse goods", and those who trade

in them are known as "cats". The lanes are filled with bric-a-brac, real and fake antiques, set out on myriad stalls. Bargaining is the rule here – whether for a safety pin, shoelace, or if you should be so lucky, a Tang-dynasty porcelain horse. The area was once famous for seamen's lodging houses and brothels, and it was a hang-out for criminals and low-life characters of all kinds. In nearby Lok Ku Street are the **Cat Street Galleries**, which are devoted to artwork and antique reproductions from all over Asia.

After exploring the markets around Cat Street, keep going west to **Possession Street 7**, so called because it was here that Captain Sir Edward Belcher landed in January 1841 to plant the Union Jack and take possession of Hong Kong for Britain. No monument marks the exact spot where the British flag was planted. The only memento to the HMS *Sulphur*, whose crew was

SoHo and BoHo are among Hong Kong's liveliest nightlife areas.

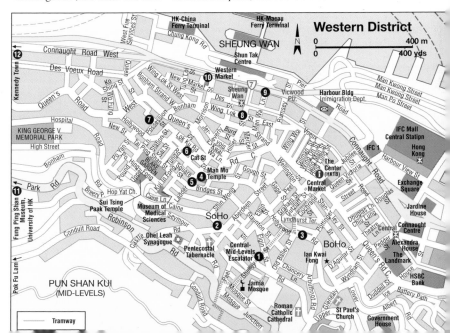

the first to step ashore, is Belcher Street, west of Possession Street.

Sheung Wan

Head back towards Central through the **Sheung Wan** area, along either Queen's Road West or Des Voeux Road. These two long streets are distinguished by their aromatic pharmacies, rice traders, traditional wedding-dress stores, and merchants selling paper lanterns and incense. Take a look at the fascinating range of dried seafoods, including abalone, sea cucumber and shark's fin, which can sell for several thousand dollars a kilo.

Between Bonham Strand and Des Voeux Road is colourful **Wing Lok Street ⑧**, with shops selling herbs, ancient medicines, preserved seafood and tea. One block inland from Bonham Strand is **Jervois Street**, once devoted to snake restaurants and wine shops. There are also a multitude of jade-carvers, calligraphers, opera costumers, fan-makers and pottery-shapers in the area.

Man Wa Lane ⑨, which runs north–south across these streets, is lined with the chop-makers who carve elaborate name stamps from blocks of stone. These chops are not only practical instruments (formal documents in Hong Kong require a "chop", used as a signature), but works of ancient Chinese craftsmanship. Perhaps only the Arabs have as much respect for calligraphy as the Chinese. Watching a Man Wa chop-carver sculpt a customer's name out of a small block of stone, ivory, jade or wood is an interesting experience. There are male and female chop styles: when background material is carved out, the chop is male; when the characters are carved out, it's female. The chop is also important in other Asian countries, particularly Japan.

This part of Western is for walking, for poking into little alleys and for getting lost in the web of side streets. Look for the key-cutters, tinkers, carpenters, cobblers and barbers in any alley. Their miniature factories operate in about six square metres (20 sq. ft) of space. Shops may be simple upended crates, with the materials of their trade stacked

ORIENTATION:
This chapter covers
the area from Central
Market and the Mid-
Levels Escalator in
the east to Kennedy
Town in the west.

BELOW: all kinds of odds and ends can be found along Hollywood Road and Cat Street.

outside. The craftsmen use drills and other tools of ancient design and timeless utility. Wander around and discover a veritable carnival of handicraft factories, teashops and restaurants.

On Morrison Street, close to the harbour, stands a red-brick Edwardian-style building called **Western Market ⑩**. It was opened in 1906 and served for more than 80 years as a food market. Recognised as a historical landmark, its elegant architectural features were preserved and restored, and in 1991 it was converted into a shopping complex. It offers a diversity of handicrafts, fabric and souvenir stalls, as well as a Chinese restaurant on the top floor, enlivened by weekend "tea dances".

From Western Market you can take a walkway across Connaught Road West to the Shun Tak Centre, which houses the Macau Ferry Terminal.

Further west

From Western it is possible to walk up toward the residential district of Pok Fu Lam. The hilly upper part of Western (which is actually part of the Mid-Levels) is quite different. Here the architecture is more Portuguese colonial than traditional Chinese – with tiled pitch roofs, stucco walls and projecting balconies. The **University of Hong Kong** has its campus here. On site is the **Fung Ping Shan Museum ⑪** (open Mon–Sat 9.30am–6pm, Sun 1.30–5.30pm; free), housed in an attractive Edwardian-era building and the oldest museum in Hong Kong. It houses a diverse collection of pottery and porcelain dating back to the seventh century, although the most prized possession is the world's largest collection of bronzeware from the Yuan dynasty.

Beyond the University is the residential district of Pok Fu Lam and, down by the harbour, **Kennedy Town ⑫** is one of Hong Kong's oldest Chinese settlements, and one of the cheapest places to live on Hong Kong Island. Also here is the result of another huge land reclamation project – the new **Western Harbour Crossing**, Hong Kong's third cross-harbour tunnel to Kowloon, completed in 1997. ❏

Map on page 101

Chop-carvers await business on Man Wa Lane, in the heart of Western District.

RESTAURANTS

Cantonese

Treasure Inn Seafood Restaurant
4/F Western Market, 323 Des Voeux Rd, Sheung Wan.
Tel: 2850 7780
Open: L and D daily. $$
Typical Cantonese restaurant, atypically located on the top floor of an extensively renovated four-storey listed colonial building constructed in 1906. The menu emphasises seafood, but the best time to visit is for dim sum, served until 5pm.

Korean

Korea House
G/F, 119–121 Connaught Rd, Sheung Wan.
Tel: 2544 0007
Open: L and D daily. $$
Established in 1965 as a focus for Hong Kong's Korean community. This off-the-beaten-track eatery serves authentic bulgogi and kimchee, just like Korean mamas used to make.

European

Café Ola
22 Ying Wo St, Sheung Wan.
Tel: 2851 0012
Open: L and D daily. $
Hidden gem serving excellent Western food at reasonable prices. The chef trained at the high-class Peninsula Hotel before setting up this family business. Browse the quirky collection of vinyl and spin a 33 while awaiting your order.

Le Vélo
9 Jervois St, Sheung Wan.
Tel: 3118 2895
Open: L and D Mon-Fri. $
This laid-back modern European café and

bakery produces great bread, a rarity in Hong Kong. The tiny dining room is packed for lunch, but relaxed and welcoming at other times.

● *For recommended bars in SoHo and BoHo, see page 219.*

● ● ● ● ● ● ● ● ● ● ● ● ●
Prices are for a three-course meal with one beer or a glass of house wine.
$ = under HK$150
$$ = HK$150–300
$$$ = HK$300–500
$$$$ = over HK$500

WAN CHAI AND CAUSEWAY BAY

Wan Chai and Causeway Bay offer an authentic taste of modern Hong Kong, with some of the SAR's best shopping and nightlife.

Last of Central lie two vibrant districts which embrace the hedonistic Hong Kong pleasures of eating, drinking and, of course, shopping. Wan Chai and Causeway Bay are, in general, architecturally undistinguished, but they are among the territory's most crowded and active areas, revealing the authentic flavour of modern Hong Kong. The tram line (which was on the waterfront when it was built at the beginning of the 20th century) runs right the way through these districts, and provides cheap and convenient transportation as well as numerous photo opportunities from the rearmost seats on the top deck.

Admiralty ❶, between Central and Wan Chai, used to be the site of a British naval station; now it is an agglomeration of gleaming office towers and shopping malls while massive reclamation work proceeds apace offshore. When the British first came to Hong Kong, they couldn't find a suitable site for a naval garrison, so HMS *Tamar* was moored offshore just east of Central. Many years later, after the Japanese occupation in World War II, the Tamar naval compound was moved ashore. After Hong Kong's return to China in 1997, the compound was turned over to the Chinese People's Liberation Army.

The epicentre of Admiralty is **Pacific Place**, one of Hong Kong's ritziest shopping malls, showcasing the top names in fashion and housing three of Hong Kong's best hotels: the Conrad, Marriott and Island Shangri-La. A new block, Pacific Place III, is being added on the other side of Justice Drive and the adjacent Star Street hosts some of the area's smarter entertainment spots.

From Admiralty, it is just a few minutes' walk to Wan Chai itself, originally a red-light district, though

Map on pages 106-7

LEFT:
typical Wan Chai scene, Johnston Road.
BELOW:
the air-conditioned glitz of Pacific Place. shopping mall

The Hong Kong Convention and Exhibition Centre is one of the city's most extravagant architectural statements.

more recently girlie bars have been eclipsed by trendy ones – more chic joints than clip joints, and one-night stands that involve no prior commercial discussions. By day, the area has a completely different personality. Thanks to exorbitant rents in neighbouring Central, many companies have spilled into Wan Chai, providing a steady clientele for its many restaurants and shops.

Close to the waterfront (north of multi-lane Gloucester Road), in an area sometimes known as Wan Chai North, are the **Academy for Performing Arts** ❷ and the **Hong Kong Arts Centre** ❸, two of the most popular venues for theatrical and cultural performances. The Arts Centre also has galleries, rehearsal rooms and a restaurant with views of the harbour.

Right on the harbour is the futuristic **Hong Kong Convention and Exhibition Centre** ❹, which underwent a HK$4.8 billion extension in order to serve as the venue for the formal handover ceremony in 1997 – the building work was completed days (some say hours) before the ceremony. The extra space sprawls over 6.5 hectares (16 acres) of reclaimed land (about the size of nine football fields), adding an extra 38,000 square metres (45,500 sq. yds) of function space to the existing convention centre. The complex is adjacent to the supremely elegant Grand Hyatt and the New World Harbour View Hotel, and fringed on the harbourside by a waterfront **promenade**. At its northernmost point are two rather odd-looking statues. The tall black obelisk is the **Reunification Monument** ❺, which was erected to commemorate the handover and signed in gold by former Chinese President Jiang Zemin. The plaque describes how the "ingenious concept" of One Country Two Systems was devised by the "Great Statesman Deng

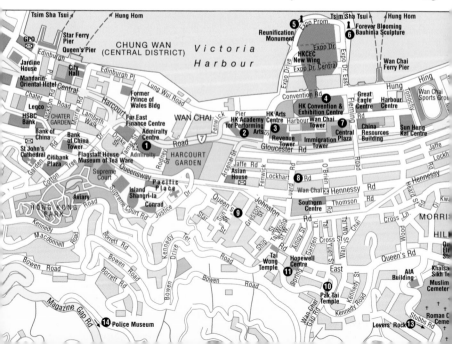

Xiaoping". Close by is the gaudy, golden **Forever Blooming Bauhinia Sculpture ❻**. The bauhinia flower is indigenous to Hong Kong and, as the territory's regional emblem since 1997, its five petals are printed on the Hong Kong flag. Further on past the tourist cruise operators is Wan Chai's own Star Ferry pier, with ferries to Tsim Sha Tsui.

The heart of Wan Chai

Elevated walkways lead south from the Convention Centre to the 78-storey **Central Plaza ❼** office tower, currently Hong Kong's second highest building at 374 metres (1,227 ft), and on into the heart of Wan Chai around the MTR station and **Lockhart Road ❽**.

From here westwards is a lively neighbourhood with numerous bars and restaurants housed beneath ageing office buildings. During the 1960s, Wan Chai was a favourite rest-and-recreation destination for

tens of thousands of troops fighting in the Vietnam War. It was during this period that the area earned its reputation as a tawdry but thriving red-light district. After a lean period in the late 1980s and early 1990s, during which Wan Chai's nightlife seemed to be in terminal decline, the area successfully reinvented itself. Some of Hong Kong's trendiest bars and restaurants are here, packed out almost every night with a mixture of expats, locals and out-of-towners, who start off in areas like Lan Kwai Fong and SoHo, then gravitate to Wan Chai to let rip.

There aren't many sailors roaming the streets of Wan Chai these days, so the diehard girlie bars on Lockhart Road have to fight hard for customers. If the reputation doesn't scare people away, the gruesome touts planted at the black-curtained doors probably will. Few people other than groups of men venture into these bars. The women who work in

The Bauhinia Sculpture is a favourite photo-stop for tourists from mainland China. There is a flag-raising ceremony here at 7.50 each morning.

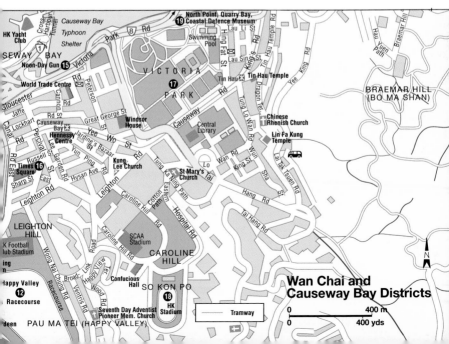

Wan Chai and Causeway Bay Districts

Shanghai hairy crabs are a seasonal delicacy during the autumn months.

BELOW: the annual Rugby Sevens tournament at Hong Kong Stadium takes place in March. The alcohol-fuelled festival atmosphere is legendary, with a range of wacky costumes on display.

these places are mostly Filipinas and Thais who have come to Hong Kong on temporary tourist visas. Chinese girls stay away from Wan Chai because they earn far more as "hostesses" in the karaoke bars in Kowloon that cater to affluent Asian business executives. There are still a few British-style pubs in the area, though they see a complete mix of nationalities, young and old. However, international-style bars – with plasma screens, slick service and a young clientele – are the more typical after-hours offering.

Three blocks to the south of Lockhart Road, **Queen's Road East** ❾ is remarkable for its rattan and rosewood furniture shops. This area also has two traditional Chinese temples that provide a glimpse of the old way of life in stark contrast to their modern surroundings. On Queen's Road East next to a narrow lane of steps leading up towards the Mid-Levels is the tiny, dark **Hung Shing Temple**. Legend has it that this temple, built on top of huge boulders, was named after a Tang-dynasty official who was renowned

for his extreme virtue and his ability to make predictions that proved to be of great value to traders. Perhaps by coincidence, several small banks in the neighbourhood are filled with groups of elderly "traders" who stare at computer screens to follow the share-price movements of the stock market.

Much more impressive is the **Pak Tai Temple** ❿ at the top of Stone Nullah Lane, a triple-halled temple noted for its 400-year-old, 3-metre (10-ft) statue of the deity Pak Tai, who assures harmony on earth. The temple itself was not built until 1863. There are usually old men and women pottering around in the dark recesses of the temple, lighting incense sticks or laying out offerings.

Just before Stone Nullah Lane along Queen's Road East, you will encounter the circular, 66-storey **Hopewell Centre** ⓫, once Hong Kong's tallest building. A rooftop restaurant offers an inspiring view of the city below but serves food that is far from inspirational. The Hopewell Centre also provides a shortcut to the Mid-Levels, because you can take the elevator to the 17th floor and step out of the building onto Kennedy Road.

At the eastern end of Queen's Road East is one of the oldest settlements on Hong Kong Island, developed after the early colonial settlers abandoned Western District because of malaria. This second settlement was named **Happy Valley**, reportedly because a cartographer's girlfriend accepted his proposal of marriage there. It was relatively distant from the sea, somewhat deserted and, most importantly, didn't have unhealthy, malaria-ridden rice farms in its vicinity.

Shortly after settling Happy Valley, the colony's residents created the greensward and edifice that has made the area world-famous amongst horse-racing fans: the Hong Kong

Jockey Club's **Happy Valley Race-course** ⓬. During the September–June racing season, it attracts up to 75,000 punters a race during week-nights and weekends. Races under the lights are particularly exciting, the atmosphere is frenetic, and the rewards for picking the right horse can be huge. Entrance is only HK\$10, and the thrill of standing at the rails while the horses gallop by, cheered and cursed in equal measure from myriad throats – with Brob-dingnagian high-rises surveying the scene from the horizon – is like nothing else on earth. This is the quintessential Hong Kong night out.

The racetrack itself is a state-of-the-art tribute to sport and gambling. Gigantic 20 x 5.8-metre (66 x 19-ft) video screens show the races in progress as well as all manner of bet-ting, racing forms and other relevant data. The total amount wagered every season is staggering – the highest of any racing establishment in the world – but most of the profits are donated to charity. If you can't make it to the actual races, visit the **Hong Kong Racing Museum** (open Tues–Sun 10am–5pm; free), which opened in 1996 at the Happy Valley Stand inside the racecourse. The museum has eight galleries and a video presentation that tell the history of horse-racing in the colony, providing background on the obsession that racing has become in Hong Kong.

Above the racecourse there are several places providing panoramic views of the area. One is the **Stubbs Road Lookout**, which offers vistas of the harbour, the Kowloon penin-sula and the Central Plaza building, with the racecourse just down to the right. Another is **Lovers' Rock** ⓭, at the hillside above Bowen Road near Shiu Fai Terrace. In addition to the tourists, local men and women flock to the site on the 6th, 12th and 26th days of each lunar month to light joss sticks, hang wine bottles on strings to the tree opposite the rock and pray for harmonious mar-riages. Bowen Road is around 4 kilometres (2½ miles) long, and one of Hong Kong's best urban strolls. Like Stubbs Road, nearby Wong Nai Chung Gap Road also offers superb views of the city. Also on this road, which leads to Repulse Bay Beach, is the Hong Kong Cricket Club, founded in 1851. The original club was located in what is now Chater Garden, Central (see page 86). Views of the harbour are also good from the former Wan Chai Gap Station, which now houses Hong Kong's **Police Museum** ⓮ (open Tues 2–5pm, Wed–Sun 9am–5pm; free). The museum traces the history of the Hong Kong police force, with an occasional oddity on display such as the stuffed head of a tiger that was shot in 1915 after it killed a policeman.

Causeway Bay

Down Tai Hang Road towards the harbour to King's Road is **Causeway Bay** (Tung Lo Wan), bounded on the

The Hong Kong Jockey Club has a race-day turnover in excess of HK\$1 bil-lion. Most of its earnings go to charity and civic projects.

BELOW: the Hong Kong Racing Museum at Happy Valley.

ORIENTATION
This chapter covers the area from Admiralty MTR Station and Pacific Place shopping mall in the west to Shau Kei Wan in the east.

BELOW: gridlock on Gloucester Road.

east by Victoria Park. The bay here was spanned by a causeway before it disappeared into a great land reclamation project in the 1950s; the former coastline is traced by Tung Lo Wan Road, while the present-day "bay" is occupied by the **Royal Hong Kong Yacht Club** on Kellett Island (another misnomer as the result of reclamation work) and the Typhoon Shelter. Members voted to keep the club's royal title, although the Chinese translation makes no allusion to the House of Windsor.

This part of Hong Kong's waterfront also features a unique genuflection to the musical genius of Noël Coward: the **Noon-Day Gun** . Nobody knows for sure why the gun is fired at noon every day, but according to legend, this ritual, began one day in the mid-19th century, when one of the Jardine's opium ships sailed into the harbour and a willing minion gave the vessel a 21-gun salute. The governor was incensed that a mere trader should receive the same greeting as himself, so, as penance, he ordered that the gun be fired at noon every

day in perpetuity. One would have assumed the gun would fire its last in July 1997, but despite the demise of the colonial era the Jardine-owned Noon-Day Gun tradition looks likely to continue just as long as Jardine keeps trading.

Causeway Bay's modern history began in 1972 when the **Cross-Harbour Tunnel** opened. This is one of the largest tunnels in Asia. Its four lanes cross 2 kilometres (1¼ miles) of harbour water between Hong Kong Island and Kowloon. There are now three cross-harbour tunnels, but this one is still the busiest.

This tunnel transformed Causeway Bay into a thriving urban area. Deluxe hotels such as the Park Lane and the Excelsior opened their doors. The World Trade Centre, next to the Excelsior, now holds 42 storeys of offices, restaurants, bars and shops. Causeway Bay is best known as a busy shopping district with large department stores, many of them Japanese. The streets are often crowded to the point of being uncomfortable, even by Hong Kong standards, and pollution levels are notoriously bad. **Times Square** , a few blocks south of the main crossroads of Causeway Bay, is a huge modern mall with restaurants, shops and a cinema.

Two blocks east is **Victoria Park** ⓱, named after Queen Victoria, whose statue can be seen surveying the activities of her former subjects. One of the less loyal daubed her with red paint, and traces are still visible despite the efforts of the park's cleaning staff. This welcome swathe of expansive parkland in the middle of Causeway Bay has a public swimming pool, jogging tracks and tennis courts and is very popular with tai chi devotees in the early morning. Tens of thousands of people gather here on special occasions, such as Chinese New Year and, notably, during the Mid-Autumn Festival, when the park is illuminated with lanterns – a beautiful sight. At the southernmost reach of Causeway Bay, the 40,000-seat **Hong Kong Stadium** ⓲ is the SAR's largest outdoor, multi-purpose venue, host to the annual Rugby Sevens – renowned as Asia's most

boisterous sporting tournament – and numerous smaller events.

Nearby, off Tai Hang Road, are the **Tiger Balm Gardens** (Aw Boon Haw) – a collection of surreal sculpture depicting Chinese mythological creatures, within the grounds of a lavish villa. Sadly the complex has been closed to the public since 2001 and is likely to be demolished, although the villa itself will probably survive.

Travelling by MTR (or tram) to the east leads past the old Shanghainese residential neighbourhood of **North Point** to the newly emerging bars and restaurants of Quarry Bay, the shopping extravaganza of Tai Koo Shing, and the well interpreted **Coastal Defence museum** ⓳ (open Fri–Weds, 10am–5pm; entrance fee) near Shau Kei Wan, which details the maritime military history of Hong Kong. The **Hong Kong Film Archive** near Sai Wan Ho MTR is also well worth a look, while the up-and-coming strip of bars and restaurants at **Lei King Wan** (aka SoHo East) is just around the corner. ❑

Map on pages 106-7

In Hong Kong They strike a gong And fire off a noon-day gun To reprimand each inmate who's in late.
– NOEL COWARD
MAD DOGS & ENGLISHMEN

BELOW: the Mid-Autumn Festival in Victoria Park.

RESTAURANTS

Cantonese
Dim Sum
63 Sing Woo Rd, Happy Valley. Tel: 2834 8893. Open: L and D daily. **$$**
Crowded little eatery in a sleepy neighbourhood that is widely appreciated for its well-above-average dim sum. A clean and efficient operation housed in a decadent Shanghai-style teahouse.

Dynasty
3/F Renaissance Harbour View Hotel, 1 Harbour Rd, Wan Chai. Tel: 2802 8888. Open: L and D daily. **$$$**
Dynasty's palatial dining hall with its tasteful décor and selected antiques forms the nightly backdrop for a recital of music played on traditional instruments. But don't let that detract from the food; the chef is a highly regarded barbecue expert, but the kitchen excels in all areas. Look for seasonal delicacies like snake soup.

Farmhouse
AIA Plaza, 18 Hysan Avenue, Causeway Bay. Tel: 2881 1331. Open: L and D daily. **$$$**
Farmhouse aims to resurrect 'home-style'

Cantonese cooking, which puts emphasis on natural flavours and textures. Specialities include stuffed chicken wings and simply steamed grouper.

Forum
485 Lockhart Rd, Wan Chai. Tel: 2891 2516. Open: L and D daily. **$$$$**
Celebrity owner Yeung Koon Yat is the Bao Yu king. Bao Yu are preserved abalone from northern Honshu in Japan, and Yeung is acknowledged as the undisputed master of their lengthy and complicated preparation. These dehydrated shellfish are bank-breakingly expensive, but other Cantonese dishes are, by contrast, surprisingly reasonable. The opulent kitsch décor features photos of Yeung pressing palms with an endless procession of dignitaries, celebrities and politicians.

Kung Tak Lam
31 Yee Wo St, Causeway Bay. Tel: 2890 3127. Open: L and D daily. **$**
This outstanding Chinese vegetarian restaurant features a menu of meat and fish substitutes like roast goose (actually braised rolled beancurd skin) and crispy deep-fried eel

(fashioned from preserved shiitake). The dining room has views over Victoria Park, service is knowledgeable and efficient, and the place is scrupulously clean. A very healthy option.

Lao Ching Hing
Basement, Century Hotel, 238 Jaffe Rd, Causeway Bay. Tel: 2598 6080. Open: L and D daily. **$$**
Neglected subterranean restaurant with ancient décor favoured by many old Shanghainese immigrants who moved to Hong Kong after the revolution. Resolutely authentic, with some intriguing menu selections.

Tai Woo
27 Percival St, Causeway Bay. Tel: 2893 0822. Open: L and D daily. **$$**
Little-known and well off the tourist trail, Tai Woo is very highly regarded by locals. With its exemplary service and its highly creative yet respectful menu, it is an example to restaurants everywhere. Check out the spare ribs in strawberry sauce or the hairy crab dumplings served in individual bamboo steamers.

Victoria City
2/F Sun Hung Kai Centre, 30 Harbour Rd, Wan Chai. Tel: 2827 9938. Open: D daily. **$$**

LEFT: Wasabisabi style.
RIGHT: vegetarian food at Kung Tak Lam restaurant.

Seafood heaven for local Cantonese. Seen as one of the best for daily dim sum and well worth the trip. The highlight is steamed garouper. The open bright room can get very noisy when busy.

Water Margin
12/F Times Sq, 1 Matheson St, Causeway Bay. Tel: 3102 0088. Open: L and D daily. **$$$**
An airy, wispy and delicate minimalist temple to nouvelle chinois. Water Margin is a design showcase that gives an insight into Eastern aesthetics. Trendy and not cheap, but with a range of unusually creative dishes.

Other Chinese

Chuen Cheung Kui
108–120 Percival St, Causeway Bay. Tel: 2577 3833. Open: L and D daily. **$$**
Long-standing Hakka cuisine specialists famous for chicken cooked in salt and served with a pungent garlic and scallion sauce. The ground floor dining room offers congee, noodles and snacks, but the main event is up the stairs on the first floor.

Pine and Bamboo (aka Chung Chuk Lau)
30 Leighton Road, Causeway Bay. Tel: 2577 4914. Open: L and D daily. **$$**
With its ugly, cramped and claustrophobic dining room, Pine and Bamboo has to have great food to make the trip worthwhile. And it does: mutton hotpot, spring-onion cake and

some of the best Peking Duck in town keep the customers coming back.

Quan Ju De Roast Duck Restaurant
4/F China Resources Building, 26 Harbour Rd, Wan Chai. Tel: 2884 9088. Open: L and D daily. **$$**
A Hong Kong branch of the legendary Peking Duck restaurant in Beijing. Pancakes, shredded scallions and dabs of hoi sin sauce. Highly organised and efficient with waitresses in cheong sams split to the thigh.

Ye Shanghai
L3 Pacific Place, Admiralty. Tel: 2918 9833. Open: L and D daily. **$$**
Cool and sophisticated with views over the hustle and bustle of Admiralty, this modern Shanghainese restaurant serves traditional dishes like xiao long bao

(steamed dumplings stuffed with pork), drunken chicken and steamed hairy crab to appreciative diners.

Japanese

Wasabisabi
13/F Times Sq, 1 Matheson St, Causeway Bay. Tel: 2506 0009. Open: L and D daily. **$$$**
One of the hippest joints in town, Wasabisabi has the feel of the catwalk and the ambiance of an exclusive nightclub – albeit one incongruously located within a rather pedestrian shopping mall. The ambitious Japanese menu has all the right ingredients. The bar is turned into a nightspot after-hours for its trendy clientele.

Middle Eastern

Zahra
409A Jaffe Rd, Wan Chai.

Tel: 2838 4597. Open: D daily. **$$**
This tiny family-run Lebanese oasis is extremely popular and booking is essential. Check out the kibbeh or the babaganoush, which are prepared fresh every day. Very friendly and very popular.

Burmese

Golden Myanmar
379–389 Jaffe Road, Wan Chai. Tel: 2838 9305. Open: L and D Mon-Fri, D Sat-Sun. **$**
A tiny hidden gem serving wonderful and very inexpensive Burmese cuisine. Stunning pickled tea salad or pork and preserved mango curry are to die for.

● *For a list of bars in Wan Chai and Causeway Bay, see pages 219–20*

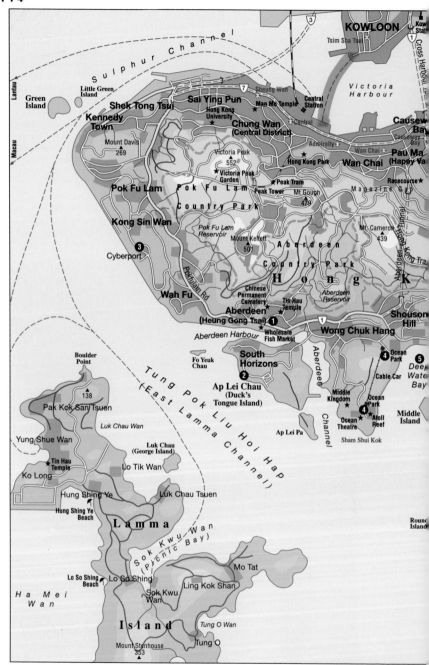

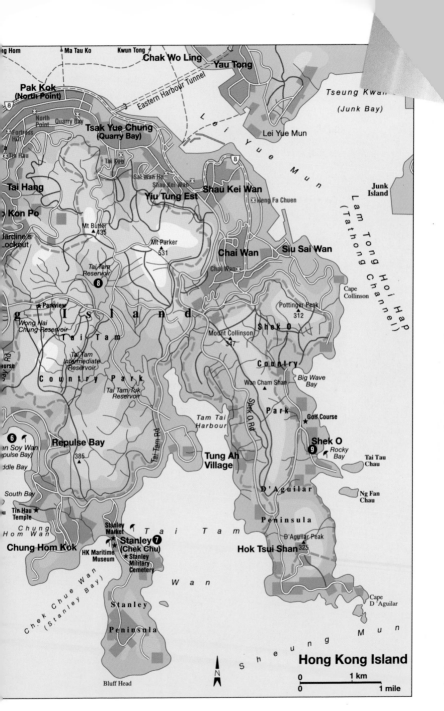

THE SOUTH SIDE

The southern part of Hong Kong Island acts as alter ego to the commercial north. Except for the busy spots of Aberdeen and Stanley, much of the coast here is relatively pristine and uncrowded

I n contrast to the northern coast of Hong Kong Island, which has changed almost beyond recognition in recent years with successive land reclamation projects, the rocky southern shore remains more or less as nature intended. The character of this relatively unspoilt part of Hong Kong provides a complete contrast to the heavily urbanised strip on the other side of the mountains. The rides and dolphins at Ocean Park are a major draw, while elsewhere there are some good beaches, challenging walks and pleasant villages.

Aberdeen and Ap Lei Chau

The harbour town of **Aberdeen** (Heung Gong Tsai) can be reached by road from Kennedy Town through the residential district of Pok Fu Lam and past the new Cyberport development. But most visitors take a more direct route south from Wan Chai through the Aberdeen Tunnel along Stubbs Road and Magazine Gap Road. There are buses or minibuses to Aberdeen from Exchange Square in Central District, or one can take a taxi. The tunnel route is generally the fastest, but you miss the sweeping views of Hong Kong Island from Stubbs Road.

Aberdeen, named after the earl who was Secretary of State for the Colonies in 1848, has a character unlike any other part of Hong Kong, with huge numbers of floating vessels bobbing in the water along its shoreline. This natural typhoon shelter is home to what remains of Hong Kong's "boat people" and their raggle-taggle collection of junks and sampans. They consist of two main groups: the Tanka (literally, the egg people, because they used to pay taxes with eggs rather than cash) and the Hoklo. Other Chinese have never accepted them (pre-Communist

Map on pages 114-5

LEFT: hiking on the central ridge of Hong Kong Island.
BELOW: the view across the Lamma Channel to Repulse Bay.

TIP

Buses from Central (Exchange Square) to the southern parts of Hong Kong Island include; nos. 6 and 260 which run to Stanley and Repulse Bay; no.66 to Repulse Bay; nos. 29R, 629 and 629S to Ocean Park, no. 309 to Shek O; bus no. 315 operates between the Peak, Ocean Park and Stanley. For Aberdeen take buses nos. 7, 71, 91 and 94.

BELOW: Aberdeen's famed floating restaurants.

China wouldn't even permit them to settle on land), but the Hong Kong government has encouraged most to leave their boats and settle on land reclaimed from the harbour. Many of the fishing people have been lured to work in factories. Romantics might bemoan this loss of traditional life, but these hot, metal-roofed boats are akin to floating slums, with unsanitary and unsafe living conditions.

At any rate, tourists are usually impressed by the colourful 30-minute ride through **Aberdeen Harbour** to the flamboyant floating restaurant moored in the "yacht basin" of **Shumwan**, across from the Aberdeen Marina. As one of the world's largest floating restaurants, with seats for over 4,000, the gaudy extravaganza captures the atmosphere of a traditional grand-scale Chinese restaurant, though its menus can hardly be described as gourmet.

Back on dry land, the **Tin Hau Temple** on Aberdeen Main Road is rather shabby for most of the year, but comes alive during April's Tin Hau Festival. Tin Hau is the goddess of the sea and traditionally impor-

tant to the fishing community. At festival time, thousands of boats converge on Aberdeen's shores and the temple is decorated with paper shrines and lanterns. Lion dances are performed outside – an event that's charged with atmosphere and highly photogenic. Along Aberdeen's main street is a cultural centre called the Warehouse (Po Wo), housed on the site of the former Aberdeen Police Station in an atmospheric tropical garden.

A bridge links Aberdeen to **Ap Lei Chau** (Duck's Tongue Island) ❷. Just two minutes away from Aberdeen, it houses Hong Kong's prolific boat-builders. They make ferries, sloops, cruisers, speedboats, yachts and steel lighters, as well as traditional sampans and junks. Ap Lei Chau is also the site of a huge residential complex called South Horizons and an extensive collection of "factory outlet" stores selling anything from furniture to fashion.

Towering above Aberdeen Harbour on the hillside is the quaintly named **Chinese Permanent Ceme-**

tery, which is entered through a pagoda-style gate. From the cemetery there is an excellent view of the town and shoreline below; higher still is the scenic **Aberdeen Reservoir**. Opposite the cemetery is the **Aberdeen Wholesale Fish Market**, which is set for redevelopment to make it a tourist attraction instead of the unsightly local market that it is now. Whatever the aspirations may be for transforming the market into a Fish Market Complex, with a Festival Marketplace for tourists, for now it remains a rather pedestrian, long tin shed full of fish and other seafoods, resounding in the early morning with the shouts of fishermen haggling for the best price for their night's catch.

A little further along the coast to the west at Telegraph Bay, work proceeds apace on the 24-hectare (60-acre) site of **Cyberport ❸**, a controversial commercial and residential project aimed at IT professionals – many people believe the idea to have been ill conceived, badly planned and a complete waste of money, a view borne out

by the lack of tenants. The project will be fully complete in 2007.

Ocean Park to Stanley

From Aberdeen, go east past the Police Training School at Wong Chuk Hang to one of Hong Kong's biggest home-grown attractions. Opened in 1977 at a cost of HK$150 million, **Ocean Park ❹** (open daily 10am–6pm; tel: 2552 0291; entrance fee) is a combination of theme park and oceanarium. The complex is divided into two sections, a lowland site and a headland site, linked by a 1.4-kilometre (1-mile) cable-car.

On the headland overlooking the South China Sea, Ocean Theatre is one of the largest marine-mammal theatres in the world, with a seating capacity of 4,000, a giant pool large enough for dolphins and occasional visiting diving shows. Wave Cove simulates a rocky coastline with a machine that generates waves up to a metre (3 ft) high. At two different levels, sea lions, seals, dolphins, penguins and sea birds may be seen diving or skimming along the cove's surface. There is also the Atoll Reef,

Map on pages 114-5

The Ocean Park cable-car connects the two sections of the site.

BELOW: the sea lion tank at Ocean Park.

Repulse Bay is one of Hong Kong's water-sports centres.

BELOW: large, prominently-displayed fish tanks at local seafood restaurants advertise the freshness of what's on the menu.

the largest aquarium in the world, with 2,000 sea creatures from 250 different species, including an 80-year-old, two-metre (seven-foot) grouper, on three different levels of viewing galleries. The park is also home to two giant pandas, An An and Jia Jia.

Also on the headland is an amusement park with various rides, including two gut-churning white-knuckle roller-coasters and the Abyss Turbo Drop that simulates falling from a 20-storey building.

In the lowland section, Film Fantasia is a hi-tech theatre containing 100 hydraulic seats that tilt forwards, backwards, left and right to make you feel part of a space voyage. It is advisable not to go right after a meal. Discovery of the Ancient World is an adventure trail with clever lighting, sound effects, interactive displays and artificial fog to recreate seven scenic zones of the primeval equatorial rainforests.

The underwater viewing tunnel at the Shark Aquarium allows you a sprat's-eye view of more than 200 sharks and rays from some 35 different species. Ocean Park also carries out its own in-house shark-breeding programme. Of course the opening of Disneyland on Lantau presents a major challenge for Ocean Park, which is already kept afloat by large groups of Asian tourists. Plans for an on-site luxury hotel and spa plus other improvements are on the drawing board, so it looks like local hero Whiskers the Seal is going to have to duke it out with Mickey Mouse in Park Wars.

Beyond Ocean Park to the east is a region of rocky coasts and smooth white sands – home to 14 of Hong Kong's 36 designated beaches. No office buildings or factories are anywhere in sight, but on summer weekends it can seem as if every office and factory worker in Hong Kong has made their way here. A few locations, such as Rocky Bay on the road to Shek O, have virtually no public facilities but offer unparalleled views and uncrowded stretches of sand and sea. Others, like Repulse Bay, attract bus loads of tourists, fast-food restaurants and, at weekends, about as much peace and quiet as a carnival. Repulse Bay and Stanley are also home to several residential developments that command some of the highest real-estate prices and rents in the world.

Deep Water Bay ❺, the first beach beyond Aberdeen and Ocean Park, has some beautiful mansions, and is reputed to enjoy some of the best feng shui in Hong Kong. It also has a nine-hole golf course managed by the Hong Kong Golf Club (open weekdays to the public). Further along the road is the exclusive Hong Kong Country Club. The long stretch of beach here offers a quiet place to soak in the sun or go for a swim.

A popular destination on the south side of Hong Kong Island is **Repulse Bay** (Cheen Soy Wan) ❻, named after the battleship HMS

Repulse, which took an active part in thwarting pirates who plundered here in the mid-19th century. Now widened to several times its original size and developed into a playground for tourists as well as urban Hong Kongers, Repulse Bay Beach has everything except peace and quiet. It once had one of the finest resort hotels in the East, the eponymous Repulse Bay, but the structure has been overshadowed by a large blue apartment building with a big square hole in the middle also called The Repulse Bay. Some say the hole is a passageway for the heavenly dragon to come down from the mountains; others say it was put there to generate good feng shui; still others say it was just the architect's attempt at being funky.

A replica of the old hotel stands in front of the apartment block, preserving a soupçon of grace from days gone by. The building houses a number of excellent restaurants and a very cool spa. On the waterfront, there are a beachside restaurant, hamburger and noodle stands, and luxurious high-rises.

The hills that rise steeply from the shoreline have a sombre history. It was here that invading Japanese troops came pouring down at the end of 1941 during World War II. The Repulse Bay Hotel was a military target because British and Canadian troops used it as a base to keep open the road between Stanley and Aberdeen. After three days of fighting, the hotel was taken, and Commonwealth prisoners were marched to Eucliffe Mansion (this folly has also been demolished and replaced by villas), about half a kilometre (⅓ mile) from the hotel. Most of the prisoners were executed, and survivors were incarcerated at the Stanley Internment Camp.

Just beyond Repulse Bay are two beaches that are a bit quieter. Middle Bay and South Bay are favourite hang-outs for the more serious beach bums eager to tan their toned bodies away from the crowds.

Fifteen minutes' drive further southwest is the popular tourist magnet of **Stanley** (Chek Chu) ❼. Named after Lord Stanley, a 19th-century Secretary of State for the

Map on pages 114-5

The Repulse Bay apartment building with its famous hole.

BELOW: the south side of Hong Kong Island has several good beaches.

Shopping for bargains at Stanley Market.

BELOW: the art of calligraphy.

Colonies, Stanley was the largest indigenous settlement in Hong Kong when the British first set foot here in 1841. In fact, a Tin Hau temple here documents that the town was founded in 1770 by the pirate Cheung Po Tsai, who had taken control of the island.

Stanley Market, the principal attraction on Stanley peninsula, draws thousands of visitors on weekends – locals in search of a bargain as well as tourists looking for souvenirs to take home. A few steps from New Street, where the buses stop, is an extensive area packed with shops selling clothes (factory over-runs or seconds), rattan, fresh food, ceramics, budget art, hardware, brass objects, Chinese crafts – almost anything.

Hong Kong residents come to Stanley for its restaurants and seaside feel. A modern shopping mall occupies a site at the end of Main Street, directly opposite one of the SAR's most amazing modern architectural projects. **Murray House**, a former British Army barracks built around 1848, was moved stone by stone from Central, and the stylish conversion now houses restaurants and boutiques. Next door, a new **maritime museum**, exploring the territory's long relationship with all things marine, is due to open its doors in 2006.

East of the bus station is the **Old Stanley Police Station**, one of only 30 protected historic buildings in Hong Kong. The early British settlers regarded a posting to Stanley Police Station (built in 1844) as highly dangerous. Only a dirt track connected the town to the city of Victoria (now Central), and pirates frequently attacked and robbed the garrison. Stanley was all but abandoned in the 1850s, until the original police station was replaced by the building which stands today. The station is also thought to have been the last point of resistance to the advancing Japanese forces in the battle for Hong Kong during World War II. On Christmas Day 1941, the town's commanding officer refused to believe that the British had surrendered, and so the town fought on for a day after troops elsewhere had laid down their arms. That this historic building is currently occupied by a supermarket says a great deal about the parlous state of Hong Kong's heritage.

Down the road is **Stanley Prison**, which is still in use, while the two-storey building topped with a mock guard tower next to its parade ground houses the quirky **Correctional Services Museum** (open Tues–Sun 10am–5pm; free). Its nine galleries chart the history of Hong Kong's penal system, with creepy exhibits like a mock gallows and fake cells. To the right of the prison is **Stanley Military Cemetery**, whose tombstones date back to early colonial times. It was also in Stanley – at both the prison and at nearby St Stephen's College – that the Japanese interned British prisoners of war.

Map on pages 114-5

Near the cemetery is St Stephen's Beach, cleaner and more pleasant than Stanley's main beach.

Beyond Stanley

The beaches past Stanley are a little less accessible and therefore less crowded. To reach them, head north along Tai Tam Road past the **Tai Tam Reservoir** ➑. Though this is the largest of the three reservoirs on Hong Kong Island, it can only meet Hong Kong's needs for three days. In fact, most of Hong Kong's water supply is piped from across the border in China. The area around the reservoir is hilly and picturesque, and includes **Tai Tam Country Park**, a popular picnic and hiking spot. The well-marked walk up and to the north leads past pretty woodland and waterfalls; during the week it's most likely to be deserted. At the top, a newly developed trail around Wong Nai Chung Gap traces the events of the battle for Hong Kong in 1941.

Tai Tam Road leads up to Chai Wan, or you can head back south along Shek O Road, skirting Mount Collinson on the left and Tai Tam Harbour to the right for Hong Kong's most southerly beaches, Shek O and Big Wave Bay.

The market place at **Shek O Village** ➒ is a modest collection of shops selling beach paraphernalia. There are also some restaurants with seats outdoors, and bike-rental shops. What the market and beach hide, though, are some truly luxurious homes. Shek O's larger houses were numbered in the order that they were built – not sequentially – and are some of the few in Hong Kong with gardeners as well as maids. The golf club here is one of the SAR's most exclusive – membership is by invitation only and exorbitantly expensive. Sporty types can take heart at **Big Wave Bay**, a little up the coast, with Hong Kong's best surf. Stroll out to Shek O Headland, facing the islands of Tai Tau Chau and Ng Fan Chau. To the right is the southernmost point of the island, **Cape d'Aguilar**. Up until the early 1990s, Vietnamese refugee boats could be seen around here as they drifted towards shore and what they hoped was freedom. ❏

Shek O main beach is one of the most pleasant on Hong Kong Island.

RESTAURANTS

Cantonese

Jumbo Floating Restaurant
Shum Wan Pier Drive, Wong Chuk Hang, Aberdeen.
Tel: 2553-0527.
Open: L & D daily. **$$**
This vast floating seafood emporium in a grubby inlet of Aberdeen waterfront is almost obligatory for package-deal travellers, and every night parties of tourists queue for tables. It is a great place for observing Cantonese culture, but the gaudy, glitzy, pseudo-imperial style doesn't guarantee good food; locals eat elsewhere.

Shek O Chinese and Thai Seafood Restaurant
303 Shek O Village. Tel: 2809 4426. Open: L & D daily. **$**
Popular, unpretentious open-air place serving Cantonese and Thai dishes on the crossroads in the centre of sleepy Shek O. Friendly staff serve steamed fish, tom yum soup and fishcakes.

International

The Boathouse
88 Stanley Main St, Stanley.
Tel: 2813 4467. Open: L & D daily. **$$**
The bright and breezy Boathouse makes the most of its shorefront location, while the uncomplicated menu has an emphasis on good quality, fresh seafood and a range of salads and mains.

The Verandah
Repulse Bay Hotel.
Tel: 2812 2722. Open: L & D daily. **$$$$**
Follow the sweeping drive through the well-tended tropical gardens and enter the delightful art deco dining room, with gorgeous views out across the South China Sea. The menu offers serious, highly professional European fine dining. It's expensive, but curious travellers could drop in for tea or drinks on the way to Stanley.

● ● ● ● ● ● ● ● ● ● ● ● ●
Prices are for a three-course meal with one beer or a glass of house wine.
$ = under HK$150
$$ = HK$150–300
$$$ = HK$300–500
$$$$ = over HK$500

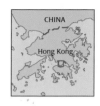

Always regarded as playing second fiddle to Hong Kong Island, the districts of Tsim Sha Tsui, Yau Ma Tei and Mong Kok in Kowloon nevertheless define the chaos and bustle of the SAR

Map on page 128

The Kowloon peninsula is just a few square kilometres in size, but it is one of the most crowded (500,000 per sq. km, or 200,000 per sq. mile, according to one count) and developed areas in the world. At the southern end is Tsim Sha Tsui (pronounced *chim-sa-choi*), once a sharp, sandy point and now a hyperactive shopping district. Further north are the more traditional districts of Yau Ma Tei and Mong Kok, where street markets and old buildings have escaped demolition.

Kowloon is in many ways very different from the glittering island across the harbour, more down to earth and more Chinese. Yet, somewhat paradoxically, Tsim Sha Tsui – its southern tip – is the location of the majority of Hong Kong's tourist hotels. Nathan Road is host to the quintessential Hong Kong image of gaudy neon signs and hundreds of small electronics shops. Save for the waterfront views, it is not an especially attractive place. But few can deny the electricity that charges life here, especially at night.

Lacking the steep mountainsides that hem in the north shore of Hong Kong Island, Kowloon sprawls. Until Kai Tak Airport closed in the late 1990s, regulations restricted its buildings to a modest height. Now, they shoot skywards as never before, a process most obvious above Kowloon Station on the West Kowloon Reclamation, where the Union Square development is to include a 484-metre (1,588-ft) skyscraper, set to be the city's tallest when it is completed in 2007. Also in West Kowloon the government has earmarked the land around the cross-harbour tunnel's mouth as the site of a new "cultural district", though details are still under discussion.

LEFT: Temple Street night market.
BELOW: plenty of designer watches are fakes.

The Kowloon Clock Tower is all that remains from the old railway terminus.

BELOW:
inside the Hong Kong Science Museum.

The district of most interest to travellers is principally Tsim Sha Tsui, although Yau Ma Tei and Mong Kok have a lot to offer, too.

Around the waterfront

The obvious place to start in Tsim Sha Tsui is the **Star Ferry Pier ❶**, where the ferries land from Central and Wan Chai. An obvious landmark is the adjacent **Railway Clock Tower**. Dating from 1921, the tower is the final vestige of the historic Kowloon-Canton Railway (KCR) Station, once the Asian terminus of a system that ran all the way (with a few changes en route) back to Europe. In the mid-1970s it was replaced by a new station to the east, at Hung Hom.

Immediately behind the tower is the unmistakeable **Hong Kong Cultural Centre ❷**, a minimalist structure with a sweeping concave roof covered in ugly pink tiles. Its construction caused a great deal of controversy in 1984, as it was designed without windows – thereby inexplicably turning its back on one of the world's most dramatic views.

Nonetheless, it is there to stay and to be used. During the Hong Kong Arts Festival in January and February, the centre stages local and international opera, classical music, theatre and dance.

This complex abuts the igloo-like **Hong Kong Space Museum ❸** (open Mon, Weds–Fri 1–9pm, Sat–Sun 10am–9pm; tel: 2721 0226; entrance fee, but free on Weds), with daily showings of IMAX movies on space travel and exhibitions of Chinese astronomical inventions. The **Hong Kong Museum of Art ❹** (open Fri–Weds 10am–6pm, closed Thurs; tel: 2721 0116; entrance fee, but free on Weds) displays traditional and contemporary calligraphy and painting, along with historic photographs, prints and artefacts of Hong Kong, Macau and Guangzhou. Other galleries exhibit Chinese antiquities and travelling exhibitions of fine art.

One of the unfortunate losers to suffer from the construction of the Cultural Centre was the venerable **Peninsula Hotel ❺**, directly across Salisbury Road. Its exquisite rooms lost their classic harbour views but

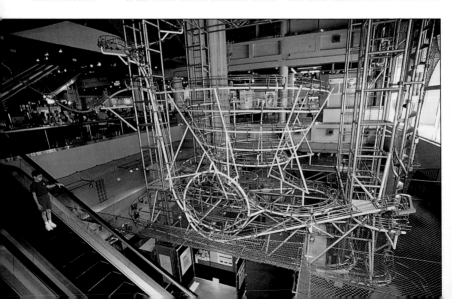

regained them with the addition of a tower grafted onto the original 1928 building. The Pen's sumptuous gilt-corniced lobby is accented by a string quartet on the balcony, and from rooftop helipad via swish restaurants, pool, spa and bars (the gents at the stylish Felix bar is the supreme loo with a view), this remains the acme of Hong Kong's accommodation, however hard the new kids on the block may try.

Situated immediately north of the Star Ferry Pier is **Star House ❻**, where *cheongsams*, porcelain, and what appears to be almost every conceivable kind of Chinese handicraft available, are on sale at the huge Chinese Arts and Crafts store. Adjoining Star House on Canton Road is the mammoth **Harbour City ❼** complex, encompassing **Ocean Terminal** and **Ocean Centre** and filled with hotels, antique stores and designer boutiques. The deep-water mooring means that cruise ships regularly tie up here, disgorging their passengers directly into the malls and other entertainments of downtown Tsim Sha Tsui.

From the Star Ferry Pier eastward along the harbour, a waterfront promenade extends past the Cultural Centre and InterContinental Hotel towards **Tsim Sha Tsui East** and **Hung Hom Bay**, a stretch of reclaimed land packed with hotels, offices and shops. This provides a great vantage point for viewing the north shore of Hong Kong Island, one of the most spectacular cityscapes in the world. The promenade – dubbed the **Avenue of Stars ❽** – is decorated with tributes to the famous and less so of Hong Kong and Chinese cinema, with Hollywood-style stars set in the pavement. Some of the monikers – Fung Bo Bo, Ivy Ling Po, Tso Tat Wah – will be familiar only to the more manic film buff, but many other characters are honoured here, including of course San Francisco-born Bruce Lee, Beijing native Jet Li and the first Asian 007 girl – Michelle Yeoh – who hails from Ipoh in Malaysia. The promenade is being extended to include more shopping and dining outlets, and work should be completed by the middle of 2006.

Map on page 128

As with most museums in Hong Kong, the Museum of Art has free admission every Wednesday.

BELOW:
the Peninsula Hotel is the height of luxury.

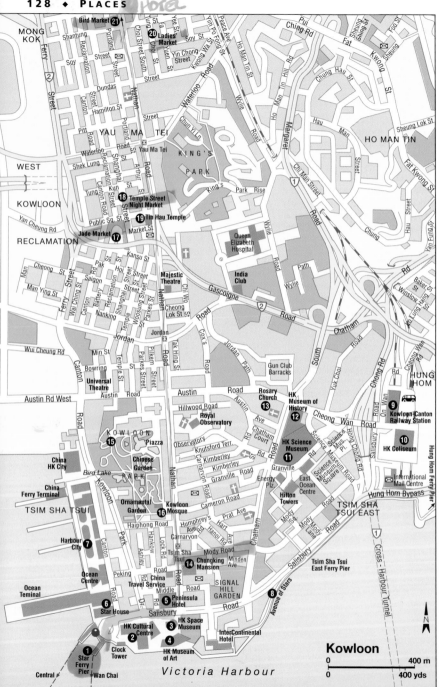

Kowloon

MONG KOK

Bird Market 21
Ladies' Market 20

YAU MA TEI

WEST
KOWLOON

RECLAMATION

Temple Street Night Market 18
Tin Hau Temple 19
Jade Market 17

Majestic Theatre

KING'S PARK

Queen Elizabeth Hospital

India Club

HO MAN TIN

Gun Club Barracks

Universal Theatre

Rosary Church 13
HK Museum of History 12

HUNG HOM

Kowloon-Canton Railway Station 9

HK Coliseum 10

Royal Observatory

Hillwood Road

HK Science Museum 11

International Mail Centre

China HK City 15

KOWLOON PARK

Chinese Garden

Piazza

Bird Lake

Ornamental Garden

Kowloon Mosque 16

Hilton Towers

East Ocean Centre

TSIM SHA TSUI

China Ferry Terminal

Harbour City 7

Ocean Centre

Chungking Mansion 14

TSIM SHA TSUI EAST

Hung Hom Bypass

Ocean Terminal

Star House 6

HK Cultural Centre 2

HK Space Museum 3

Peninsula Hotel 5

China Travel Service

SIGNAL HILL GARDEN

Tsim Sha Tsui East Ferry Pier

Avenue of Stars 8

InterContinental Hotel

Star Ferry Pier 1

Clock Tower

HK Museum of Art 4

Central

Wan Chai

Victoria Harbour

Kowloon

0   400 m
0   400 yds

N

Map on page 128

In Hung Hom, the **KCR Station** ❾, built in 1975, was the terminus for trains to the New Territories until the new extension to Tsim Sha Tsui East opened in 2005. However, this is still the place where through trains to China begin their journeys – every two or three days to Beijing and Shanghai, much more frequently to Guangzhou – and the forecourt feels more like mainland China than Hong Kong. The **Cross-Harbour Tunnel** between Hong Kong Island and Kowloon emerges immediately west of Hung Hom Station. The tunnel took three years to construct and by the time it opened in 1972 it had cost a total of US$427 million. Of the harbour's three tunnels, it remains the busiest, with more than 150,000 vehicles passing through it every day. Ten minutes' walk away is **Hung Hom Ferry Pier**, with services to Central, Wan Chai and North Point.

Behind Hung Hom Ferry Pier is **Whampoa Gardens**, a commercial and residential project built around the old Kowloon Dockyard, which operated from 1870 to 1984. With added landfill, the dock now holds a 100-metre (330-ft) concrete "ship" – one of the SAR's more quirky photo opportunities – filled with shops, restaurants and gardens.

The unusual-looking inverted pyramid situated on the harbour side of the railway station is the **Hong Kong Coliseum** ❿, a 12,000-seat indoor stadium that hosts sell-out concerts by Canto-pop idols and international stars. Millions of dollars are spent on staging spectacular floor shows with dancers, elaborate costume changes, and hi-tech lasers and lights. Attending one of these concerts could be one of the more fascinating sights a traveller might encounter in Hong Kong, giving a different perspective on the local lifestyle.

On the other side of the harbour tunnel approach road, in **Tsim Sha Tsui East**, are two of the best museums in Hong Kong. The **Hong Kong Science Museum** ⓫ (open Mon–Weds, Fri 1–9pm, Sat–Sun 10am–9pm; tel: 2732 3232; entrance fee, but free on Weds) displays more than 500 scientific and technological interactive

The Hong Kong Space Museum is best known for its impressive IMAX cinema.

BELOW: electronics shops on the Nathan Road "Golden Mile".

exhibits, including robotics, computers, phones, a miniature submarine and a DC-3 aeroplane.

Just opposite is the **Hong Kong Museum of History** ⑫ (open Mon, Weds–Sat 10am–6pm, Sun and public holidays 10am–7pm; tel: 2724 9042; entrance fee, but free on Weds), which documents the 6,000-year story of Hong Kong from neolithic times right up to the 1997 handover. There are some imaginative displays, including lifelike mock-ups of old-style teahouses, cinemas and a Cantonese opera stage, and many interesting old photographs. West of the Science Museum across Chatham Road, the **Rosary Church** ⑬, completed in 1888, is one of Hong Kong's most historic Catholic churches. Morning and evening masses are conducted in Cantonese and English.

The Tsim Sha Tsui East area contains a number of bars where wealthy types pay an extortionate sum for the company of a hostess. A network of underground walkways links the new KCR station with various points around Tsim Sha Tsui and the MTR.

Nathan Road and surrounding streets are ablaze with neon lights during the evening.

BELOW: Chungking Mansion houses the majority of Hong Kong's budget guesthouses.

The heart of Tsim Sha Tsui

Introductions to Tsim Sha Tsui always used to churn out the phrase "Golden Mile", the nickname for **Nathan Road**, its central axis. The main shopping and entertainment area extends from here along Peking, Hankow and Haiphong roads, as well as to Carnarvon and Kimberley roads on the eastern side. But things are changing, as an enormous construction project is sidelining Nathan's slightly outré strip of shops and their touts. The area around Mody Road, which links Nathan and Chatham roads, is being turned into a large shopping mall, and bars and restaurants are springing up nearby. From grubby to groovy (although a little of the former still exists) in one fell swoop: it's the Kowloon renaissance, and in and around Minden Avenue – promoted as a new challenger to Lan Kwai Fong – they're already partying every night.

There are hundreds of good restaurants hereabouts, ranging from haute cuisine in five-star hotels to inexpensive stands dishing out

noodles and rice. Try local delicacies such as *daan tart* (egg custard tarts), baked fresh daily, with a glass of iced soya milk for a typically Chinese afternoon snack.

Tsim Sha Tsui is also home to a series of run-down mansion blocks, oddly wedged in amongst the shops and luxurious hotels, the most infamous being **Chungking Mansion** ⓮, a teeming labyrinth of cheap guest houses (there are few alternatives in budget accommodation in Hong Kong), curry restaurants, sweat-shops and sari stores right in the middle of the most commercial stretch of Nathan Road. Reviled by many as a haven for lowlife, it is also the scourge of property developers, who are desperate to capitalise on the prime location but unable to buy out the numerous owners and powerless to evict the residents, many of whom come from Pakistan, India, Nepal and various African countries.

For a number of years, Chungking Mansion has also been the temporary abode of the most thrifty of budget travellers.

A few minutes further north along Nathan Road is the pleasant expanse of **Kowloon Park** ⓯, offering a Chinese garden with lotus ponds, a chess garden, and an aviary (open daily 6.30am–8pm) housing a colourful collection of rare birds. The Sculpture Walk displays work by local artists. while at the northern end of the park past the flamingos' pond a bridge leads over Kowloon Park Drive to the lurid gold **China HK City Building**, departure point for ferries to various Chinese cities.

The southeastern corner of the park is marked by **Kowloon Mosque** ⓰, with its four minarets and large, white-marble dome gracefully standing out from the clutter of shops and restaurants opposite. Built in 1984, it serves the territory's 50,000 Muslims, of whom about half are Chinese. The original mosque building, built in 1894, served the British army's Muslim troops. On the other side of Nathan Road, **Carnarvon** and **Kimberley** roads are both stuffed with clothing and electronics shops,

Map on page 128

Right in the heart of Tsim Sha Tsui, Kowloon Park is a welcome green space.

BELOW LEFT: items for sale at the Yau Ma Tei jade market.

Jade

Jade was formerly the preserve of China's elite. Belief in its powerful essence is nearly as old as Chinese civilisation itself, and its prominence in Chinese art and literature attests to its long-standing value. Jade was prized for the aesthetic beauty of the stone, the skill needed to carve it, and for the magical properties that it was believed to possess.

Most jewellery was made from jade, favoured over gems and precious metals, and some people held that the stone glowed with the vitality of the owner or became tarnished if the wearer fell ill. The Chinese have long believed that wearing jade ornaments imparts good health, good luck and protection from evil spirits.

There are two types of jade: jadeite and nephrite. Early jade objects were carved from nephrite, a softer form of jade that can be worked with primitive tools.

The best known single piece of jade is Jade Mountain of the Great Yu Taming the Flood. According to records, the uncut stone was discovered in Xinjiang province and weighed more than five tons, requiring more than three years to transport to Beijing and six years for a team of artisans to carve.

while nearby **Knutsford Terrace** hosts a couple of dozen bars and restaurants that are good value.

Yau Ma Tei

From Tsim Sha Tsui, Nathan Road slips into Yau Ma Tei. At the junction of Jordan and Canton roads there are several jade- and ivory-shops selling mah-jong sets. Shanghai Street still has shops selling red Chinese wedding dresses, embroidered pillowcases and other items for a Chinese bride's trousseau. At the corner of Shanghai and Saigon streets stands the Tak Sang Pawn Shop, a World War II-vintage building where for decades gamblers have hocked their worldly possessions to pay off loan sharks.

Ning Po Street and Reclamation Street are well known for paper models of houses, cars, and notes from Hell Bank that are burned at funerals, so as to assure that the deceased will be well-off in the afterlife. At the junction of Kansu and Battery streets the **jade market** ⓱ (open daily 9am–6pm) is packed with stalls. Dealers offer jade in every sculptable form, from large blocks of the raw material to tiny, ornately carved chips. Unless you are an expert, take along a Hong Kong Tourist Board (HKTB) information leaflet on jade, and spend wisely, as not all the artefacts on offer are genuine. The best time to go is in the morning.

Shanghai Street continues north into an area once famous for its temples, now renowned for the **Temple Street night market** ⓲ that lights up after dusk. Palmists, physiognomists, and a fortune-teller whose trained bird selects slips of paper to predict the future vie to reveal your destiny. This area has numerous open-air restaurants, where oysters, prawns, clams, lobsters and fish are laid out on beds of ice to tempt diners.

Over a century old, the **Tin Hau Temple** ⓳ complex (open daily 7am–5.30pm) is in Public Square Street. This is Hong Kong's main Tin Hau temple (there are scores throughout the territory), originally built closer to the harbour. Land reclamation forced it to move inland

BELOW:
the bird market.

to here. Locals still visit it regularly to worship Tin Hau, the protector of fisherfolk, whose image is draped in intricately embroidered scarlet robes. To the right of the altar are 60 identical deities that represent every year of the 60-year lunar calendar. Worshippers place Hell Bank notes under the god dedicated to the years of their birth. Another temple in the complex was built to honour Shing Wong, the local city god, and the Ten Judges of the Underworld, depicted with human torsos and animal heads. The Fook Tak Temple is dedicated to Fook Tak, an earth god, and Guanyin, the goddess of mercy. Shea Tan Temple is dedicated to a protector of the community.

Mong Kok

Mong Kok (properly Wong Kok in Cantonese: a long-dead sign writer got his letters mixed up) was for many years associated with sleaze. The area got a shock in 2004, when Langham Place, a glitzy combined office block, shopping mall and five-star hotel, opened next to the MTR station right in the heart of of what used to be the seediest part of town. The shoddy bars and one-room bordellos continue to operate in nearby side streets, but the writing is on the wall. Langham Place – whose developer spent a dozen years buying up the tenements from myriad different owners – is the future, soaring 255 metres (840 ft) to the heavens and currently the highest building in Kowloon.

On the east side of Nathan Road, on Tung Choi Street, the so-called **ladies' market** ❷⓿ (open daily noon–10.30pm) sells everything from fake designer accessories and clothing to cheap cosmetics and toys. It is also a popular area for late-night snacks; restaurants and take-away carts display delicious noodles, seafood and congee. Tai Wo Restaurant (No. 105) has desserts and herbal teas to revitalise health.

Hundreds of colourful song birds in beautifully crafted cages can be seen at the famous **bird market** ❷❶ (open daily 10am–6pm), on the other side of Nathan Road on Yuen Po Street, about ten minutes' walk from the Prince Edward MTR station. ❏

The new shopping mall at Langham Place in Mong Kok.

BELOW: silk outfits for children.

RESTAURANTS

Cantonese

Hoi King Heen

B2, Grand Stanford Inter-Continental Hotel, 70 Mody Rd, Tsim Sha Tsui East. Tel: 2731 2883. Open: L Mon-Sat, D daily. **$$$**

Hoi King Heen offers endlessly creative Cantonese fine dining for those in the know. Chef Leung is famous for his ability to adapt novel ingredients into classic Cantonese

PRICE CATEGORIES

Prices are for a three-course dinner per person with one beer or glass of house wine:
$ = under HK$150
$$ = HK$150–300
$$$ = HK$300–500
$$$$ = over HK$500

cooking. A classy, quality operation.

Royal Garden Chinese Restaurant

B2, The Royal Garden Hong Kong, 69 Mody Road, Tsim Sha Tsui. Tel: 2724 2666. Open: L and D daily. **$$**

A visit to this ornate hotel restaurant takes in fish ponds, an arched wooden bridge and tiled canopies. The kitchen serves top dim sum and ocean-fresh seafood.

Super Star Seafood Restaurant

1/F, Wah Yuen Building, 87 Nathan Road, Tsim Sha Tsui. Tel: 2366 0878. Open: L and D daily. **$$**

An authentic Cantonese experience that is loud and lavish, brash and bold. The dish in demand is the steamed grouper

picked from teeming fish tanks, but anything on the menu is going to be good.

T'ang Court

1/F, Langham Hotel, 8 Peking Rd, Tsim Sha Tsui. Tel: 2375 1333. Open: L and D daily. **$$$**

T'ang Court is among the most stylish Cantonese hotel restaurants in town. The lush interior brims with sumptuous opulence, but don't let that distract you from a menu that dotes on shark's fin, bird's nest and abalone.

Other Chinese

City ChiuChow

East Ocean Centre, 98 Granville Rd, Tsim Sha Tsui East. Tel: 2723 6226. Open: L and D daily. **$$**

Chiu Chow cuisine is a sub-division of the Cantonese school from the coast around Shandong. The 500-seat City ChiuChow is a great place to sample special-ties like cold crab, *e-fu* noodles or chicken in *chin jiu* sauce.

Hutong

28/F, 1 Peking Rd, Tsim Sha Tsui. Tel: 3428 8342. Open: L and D daily. **$$$**

Serious Sino-chic featur-ing an intoxicating mix of the antique and up-to-date. The menu offers classic Northern

Chinese cuisine with a contemporary twist.

Peking Restaurant

1/F, 227 Nathan Road, Jordan. Tel: 2730 1315. Open: L and D daily. **$**

The Peking restaurant is a nostalgic blast from the past, manned by white-gloved geriatrics with limited attention spans. The Peking menu features good-quality roast duck and traditional accom-paniments.

Sun Hung Cheung Hing

1/F, 45–47 Kimberley Road, Tsim Sha Tsui. Tel: 2369 3435. Open: L and D daily. **$**

Mongolian barbecue is the draw at this off-the-beaten-track eatery. A sociable ritual of dunking delicacies in boiling broth simmering in a fire kettle draws both locals and tour groups. Peking Duck, Beggar's Chicken and other northern high-lights are worthy, well-prepared alternatives.

Japanese

Aqua

29/F, 1 Peking Rd, Tsim Sha Tsui. Tel: 3427 2288. Open: L and D daily. **$$$**

Aqua's panoramic vista from the pinnacle of a Kowloon skyscraper is integral to its glamorous interior design, and it benefits from regular pyrotechnic displays over

LEFT: the stunning interior at Aqua.
RIGHT: a dim sum trolley.

the harbour. Japanese (Aqua Tokyo) and (Aqua Roma) Italian menus.

Hibiki
15 Knutsford Terrace, Tsim Sha Tsui. Tel: 2316 2884. Open: L and D daily. **$$**
Neo-Japanese temple to tempura, sushi, sashimi and Kobe beef. Dark wooden textures and subdued lighting promote a cozy and comfortable ambiance, complemented by a comprehensive sake list.

Nadaman
LL2, Kowloon Shangri-La Hotel, 64 Mody Road, Tsim Sha Tsui. Tel: 2733 8751. Open: L and D daily. **$$$**
This exceptionally stylish Japanese hot spot is a satellite of a Tokyo chain with a solid reputation, and is a showcase of authentic Japanese cuisine. Nadaman is where Hong Kong's discriminating Japanese community chooses to eat.

Korean

Arirang
25 Canton Rd, Tsim Sha Tsui. Tel: 2956 3288. Open: L and D daily. **$$**
This Korean stalwart, with its pale-wood and marble interior, is great for social occasions as diners grill slices of meat or fish on a barabecue brazier set into each table, accompanied by kimchee and a range of pickled accompaniments. The menu can be confusing, but a range of set meals eases the choice.

Indian

Branto
1/F, 9 Lock Rd, Tsim Sha Tsui. Tel: 2366 8171
Open: L and D daily. **$**
A lively Indian vegetarian retreat with thalis, idlis and dosas offering great value for money.

American

Gripps
6/F, Marco Polo Hotel, 3 Canton Rd, Tsim Sha Tsui. Tel: 2113 3902. Open: L and D daily. **$**
A standard hotel buffet that offers a good feed at a reasonable price. In keeping with the US sports bar theme the star-spangled menu offers generous steaks, ribs and wings. Good harbour views, too.

French

Gaddi's
The Peninsula, Salisbury Rd, Tsim Sha Tsui. Tel: 2315 3171. Open: L and D daily. **$$$$**
The historic Peninsula Hotel's French haute cuisine legend is a high-society magnet, serving flawless food in splendid surroundings. Jacket and tie required. The chandeliered dining room exudes antique opulence.

Spoon
InterContinental Hotel, 18 Salisbury Road, Tsim Sha Tsui. Tel: 2313 2256. Open: L and D daily. **$$$$**
Spoon is nine-Michelin-star man Alain Ducasse's Far East outpost, located smack on the waterfront in the upmarket InterContinental hotel. French quality, and prices, with a contemporary menu of all things good available on the market. Diners can get creative by choosing ingredients from the menu from which the chef will conjure some magic.

International

Oyster and Wine Bar
18/F, Sheraton Hotel, 20 Nathan Road, Tsim Sha Tsui. Tel: 2369 1111. Open: L and D daily. **$$$**
This seafood emporium offers wide-angle views across the harbour and serves a cosmopolitan and ever-changing collection of jet-fresh oysters. The wine list is well chosen and the staff know their Kuamamotos from their Sydney Rocks.

Salisbury
YMCA, 41 Salisbury Rd, Tsim Sha Tsui. Tel: 2268 7818. Open: L and D daily. **$**
An unpretentious canteen serving Chinese and Western dishes at very reasonable prices. A no-frills, cost-cutter's retreat from Tsim Sha Tsui's tourist traps. Packed with parsimonious locals and backpackers.

The Place
Langham Place Hotel, 555 Shanghai Street, Mongkok Tel: 3552 3388. Open: L and D daily. **$$**
Hong Kongers love generous buffets because they allow them to try as much as they want from a wide choice of food presented fresh and ready to eat. The terrace is a wonderful opportunity to observe the contrast between the disappearing old Hong Kong and high-tech, big-money new.

● For a list of recommended bars in Tsim Sha Tsui, see page 220.

NEW KOWLOON

Once anchored by Hong Kong's inner-city international airport, the districts at the upper end of Kowloon peninsula are off the beaten tourist track, but they are worth exploration

BELOW: apartment block in New Kowloon.

Kowloon proper ends at Boundary Street in Mong Kok, which originally defined the frontier between Hong Kong and China. Although officially part of the New Territories, the districts immediately north of this street are more commonly known as New Kowloon. Most of the area is crammed with densely populated housing estates and shopping malls, oddly juxtaposed with historic architecture, temples and archaeological ruins. Stuck on the harbour

at the eastern edge of this crowded part of the city is the forlorn site of Kai Tak, Hong Kong's former international airport. The runway was so close to the apartment blocks of Kowloon City and Lok Fu that nervous flyers were advised to avoid looking out of the window when coming into land. The airport site is slated for redevelopment, to include a cruise terminal, park and multipurpose stadium, but currently hosts a mildly incongruous golf driving range.

Beneath the old flight path, around Kowloon Tong KCR Station, Waterloo Road and Dorset Crescent are dotted with love motels, discreetly situated behind high walls and security cameras. Guests' cars are covered up to hide the licence plates. Tinted windows and curtains hide luxurious rooms rented by the hour, which are kitted out with circular beds, jacuzzis and twin tub baths. Various other places around Hong Kong (in particular Cheung Chau) play host to these idiosyncratic part-time inns, a by-product of cramped apartments – many newly-weds live with parents – rather than any particular licentiousness. They are rather eclipsed nowadays by **Festival Walk** (atop Kowloon Tong Station), one of Kowloon's more attractive malls, with its own skating rink.

Kowloon City

Kowloon City ❶ is best seen on foot, starting at Lok Fu MTR Station. Walk up Wang Tau Hom East Road as far as Junction Road, then turn left and continue west. Along Junction Road, the **Chinese Christian Cemetery** on the left is a stark reminder of the lack of space in Hong Kong, with graves stacked up like sardines on concrete terraces.

Next door to the cemetery is the tiny **Hau Wong Temple**, with traditional roof tiles and incense spirals hanging from the rafters. Built in 1730, the temple is dedicated to Yang Liang Jie, a loyal and courageous general of the exiled Song dynasty's (960–1279) boy-emperor Ping. The general's birthday is celebrated on the 16th day of the sixth month on the lunar calendar. The temple keeper acts as a medium interpreting the advice of Hau Wong by means of *kay fook* – praying for the god's blessing.

Continue past the temple for 10 minutes until the junction with Carpenter Road, then turn left and head past Kowloon City Plaza on the left towards **Kowloon City Walled Park ❷**. Before the British arrived in 1841, the **Walled City** was already governed by a Manchu magistrate, and was subsequently excluded from the treaty that granted Britain the New Territories on a 99-year lease in 1898. At first, Qing-dynasty officials continued to be posted in the City. In 1899, however, British troops were dispatched on a punitive expedition, and the officials were expelled.

Yet British law was never fully implemented in the confines of the City, and the area deteriorated into a semi-lawless enclave which was left to its own devices. After World War II, illegal low-rise blocks completely lacking proper foundations sprang up on the site, resulting in a multi-storey squatter area with

Chinese herbal-tea dispenser in a Kowloon City tea shop.

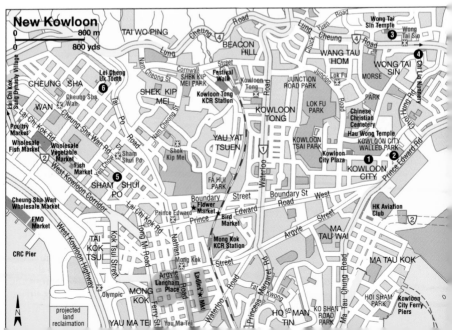

The old Walled City was dark, dirty and crowded.

BELOW: street life.

unauthorised electricity and water supplies. By the 1950s, the dank alleyways of the city had become a notorious haven for drug addicts, triad gangs, illegal immigrants and unlicensed doctors and dentists.

The Walled City remained a thorn in the side of the authorities. Beijing (and Taiwan) vehemently opposed plans for its demolition during the 1980s, as both countries regarded it as Chinese territory. Eventually, 35,000 residents were resettled in housing estates, with several tenants forcibly removed by the police, and the entire block was bulldozed to the ground, a process completed in 1992. Several remnants – the foundation of the former wall, the foundations of the south and east gates, and a flag-stone path next to the drainage ditch running along the foot of the inner wall – have been preserved in the Walled Park, which opened in 1996.

It's a beautiful space, modelled on the Jiangnan garden style of the early Qing dynasty, featuring a chess garden as well as the Mountain View Pavilion, from which **Lion Rock** (495 metres/1,624 ft)

can be seen looming in the distance to the north. Near the southern gate, an information centre houses a photographic exhibition detailing the history of the Walled City and the construction of the park, as well as many relics used or found within the Walled City. Two old cannons and a stone couplet from Longjin Free School are displayed outside.

Kowloon City is known for cheap, rough-and-ready restaurants that serve dishes within minutes of ordering. If you do not mind noise or sharing a table with strangers, then the area has an enormous range of inexpensive and highly-rated Chinese, Vietnamese, and especially Thai restaurants *(see page 141)*. There is a growing Thai community, mainly concentrated in the streets just to the south of the Walled City Park, which has opened up scores of supermarkets, restaurants, fast-food hole-in-the-walls and dodgy karaoke bars. Further east, enormous housing projects and the Lung Cheung Road contrast with the scenic hills leading up to Lion Rock.

A lucky temple

Probably the liveliest and most colourful place of worship in Hong Kong, and the most rewarding for outsiders to visit, is **Wong Tai Sin Temple ❸** (open daily 7am–6pm; free), which sits opposite the eponymous MTR station.

Wong Tai Sin, the Daoist god of healing, is said to have discovered the secret of transforming cinnabar (vermillion, a red mercuric sulphide) into an elixir for immortality. A painting of the god was brought to Hong Kong from China in 1915, and was first placed in a small temple in Wan Chai, before being moved to Wong Tai Sin. Backed by the formidable Lion Rock and facing the sea, geomancers agreed that this new site had feng shui in spades.

So much money was raised from donation boxes that the old site, built in 1921, was demolished and a new temple was constructed in 1973. The bright-yellow roof tiling is from China's Guangdong province, and the main temple's ceiling is panelled with pinewood from Burma, with bold red supporting pillars. The rear of the temple's main altar is carved to show, both pictorially and in calligraphy, the story of this great god. There are two gardens surrounding the temple and a Confucian hall next door.

Since Wong Tai Sin is also the god of good fortune, the Chinese, who are too cautious to rely solely on luck, flock to the temple to ask him for advice on all matters, including horse-racing and stock-market tips. The sound of rattling *chim* – a container holding dozens of fortune sticks – resounds all day long, as people shake them until a single bamboo stick falls out of the container. These sticks each have a number that is later interpreted, for a fee, by a fortune-teller at one of the rented stalls. English-speaking fortune-tellers will also provide chapter and verse on the future using a number of other methods. They are especially good (from a parental point of view) with children.

The optimum time to visit is during Chinese New Year, or at Wong Tai Sin's birthday on the 23rd day of the eighth lunar month (between

Map on page 137

Bamboo chim sticks at Wong Tai Sin Temple are used for fortune-telling.

BELOW: Wong Tai Sin Temple.

The Chi Lin Nunnery is reputedly the largest building in the world to have been constructed without the use of a single nail.

mid-September and mid-October), when thousands of worshippers crowd into the temple to light incense, burn paper money and rattle *chim* sticks.

One stop to the east on the MTR, the **Chi Lin Nunnery ❹** (open Thurs–Tues 9am–4pm; garden open 7am–7pm; free) is the largest Buddhist nunnery in Southeast Asia, bringing to life the artistic and architectural achievements of the Tang dynasty (618–907) from more than 1,000 years ago. Built on an expansive site close to Diamond Hill MTR station, the nunnery comprises a number of Buddhist halls serving various religious functions, and a tranquil garden with lotus ponds in front of the main entrance. There has been a great deal of restoration and rebuilding work in recent years.

The Hall of Celestial Kings houses a statue of the Maitreya Buddha (Milefo), the Buddha of the Future and a heavenly being who will descend to Earth to save humanity. Guardians of the Four Directions surround him. On the left is a hall commemorating the goddess of mercy, Guanyin, who sits inside a grotto. On the right is Baishiyaja Guru (Medicine Master), accompanied by the Sun and Moon Bodhisattvas, Buddhist redemption deities. The Sakyamuni Buddha rests on a lotus altar in the Main Hall. The Wan Fo Pagoda has a cast-bronze weather vane and wind chimes, and its seven tiers symbolise a gradual process of ascent in the eventual purification of the mind.

The complex includes a nursing home and clinic for the elderly, the nuns' living quarters, a Buddhist library and research centre, and a special school for students with learning difficulties. A souvenir shop sells Buddha images, charms, beads and books, and a dining hall, open on Sundays between 11am and 3pm, serves good vegetarian food.

Sham Shui Po and Cheung Sha Wan

The old districts of Sham Shui Po and Cheung Sha Wan are situated to the northwest of Mong Kok, well off the tourist trail but easily accessed by MTR.

Sham Shui Po ❺ showcases the development of Hong Kong's architecture from grim H-block resettlement estates hastily constructed in the 1950s to clean, modern apartment blocks erected in the 1980s. Sham Shui Po Police Station, at Lai Chi Kok Road and Yen Chow Street, is one of Kowloon's remaining colonial pre-war buildings. During World War II, the station was occupied and used by the Japanese to interrogate prisoners of war, and nowadays residents report a ghostly British soldier wandering around at night.

Sham Shui Po is undoubtedly the best place in Hong Kong for computers and related merchandise, and most arcades and stalls can be found on Yen Chow Street and Apliu Street. The police carry out frequent raids in these computer arcades to confiscate illegally made software and video games, but the next day, these pirated goods resurface and it's business as usual.

All along Apliu Street, there is an open-air market selling cheap electrical goods from secondhand stereos and computers to electric fans and clocks. Many of the latest gizmos, from I-Pods to DVD players, are *sui foh* – goods imported directly from Japan instead of through an agent and therefore available at much lower prices. Rip-offs do occur though, and it would be advisable to check all items carefully before parting with too much of your cash.

The nearby Lei Cheng Uk Housing Estate, near Cheung Sha Wan MTR station, is home to amazing archaeological discoveries made in 1955 by workers excavating the hillside. The **Lei Cheng Uk Tomb ❻** (museum open Fri–Weds 10am–1pm and 2–6pm, Sun 1–6pm; free) on Tonkin Street is a Han-dynasty burial vault over 2,000 years old. It dates back to between AD 100 and 200, when Kowloon was under the administrative control of the Wu Empire, which took control of southern China (including Hong Kong) in the period immediately following the collapse of the Han Empire. Four barrel-vaulted chambers form a cross under a domed vault, and there are a few funerary exhibits on show. ❑

A recent renovation has improved access and facilities for visitors to Lei Cheng Uk Tomb.

RESTAURANTS

Cantonese

Tso Choi Koon
17–19A Nga Tsin Wai Rd, Kowloon City. Tel: 2383-7170. Open: L & D daily. **$**
A true home-style Cantonese restaurant. Offal aficionados like to try the fried tripe or fried pig's brain; others opt for glutinous congee, fried chicken or fish.

General Chinese

Zen
Shop G24, G/F, Festival Walk, 80-88 Tat Chee Ave, Kowloon Tong. Tel: 2265 7328. Open: L & D daily. **$$$**
Modernist restaurant justly famous for its dim sum, although the whole menu stands up well to scrutiny. Influences from Shanghai, Beijing and Sichuan to Thailand and Singapore. Book ahead.

Chinese Muslim

Muslim Restaurant
1 Lung Kong Road, Kowloon City. Tel: 2382 2822. Open: L & D daily. **$**
Straightforward eatery catering to Chinese Muslim, with halal dishes typical of Xinjiang province. Specialities include mutton with scallions, a range of grilled kebabs and some very filling stuffed breads.

Thai

Golden Orchid
12 Lung Kong Road, Kowloon City. Tel: 2383 3076. Open: L & D daily. **$**
The area south of the Walled City Park is home to a large Thai community, with many excellent restaurants. The Golden Orchid is one of the best.

Other Southeast Asian

Mi
LG2, Festival Walk, 80 Tat Chee Ave, Kowloon Tong. Tel: 2265 8308. Open: L & D daily. **$**
One of the best food courts you are likely to come across anywhere. Food from all over Southeast Asia as well as Korea and Japan.

● ● ● ● ● ● ● ● ● ● ●
Prices are for a three-course meal with one beer or a glass of house wine.
$ = under HK$150
$$ = HK$150–300
$$$ = HK$300–500
$$$$ = over HK$500

THE NEW TERRITORIES

Hong Kong's northern hinterland is well off the tourist trail, which is surprising given its magnificent scenery. Some splendid beaches and ancient walled villages add to the appeal

CHINA

Hong Kong

The buffer between the urban area of Kowloon and the boundary with mainland China, the New Territories are an odd mixture. Nobody is ploughing with water buffalo any longer, but there are corners where time seems to have not so much stood still as gone into reverse. Conversely, other areas are as modern as anywhere else in the SAR, notably the New Towns such as Sha Tin and Yuen Long. A new rail line to the latter, a new spur to Ma On Shan in the east, and the main KCR track running straight up the middle to Lo Wu and mainland China mean that exploring the New Territories is rather easier than in previous years. And away from the electrified rails, there are calm beaches to seek out and lofty mountains to hike – after all, some four-tenths of the SAR is designated as country park.

Sha Tin and surroundings

Sha Tin ❶ is one of Hong Kong's largest New Towns, but it also offers plenty of recreation. Massive housing projects occupy what were once lush rice paddies whose produce was reserved for the Emperor, while the New Town Plaza, an extensive shopping and entertainment complex, offers cinemas, designer boutiques and a musical fountain that never fails to draw appreciative crowds.

The Sha Tin Valley has several places of worship. First and foremost is the **Temple of 10,000 Buddhas ❷** (open 9am–5pm daily; free), reached by climbing 431 steps flanked by gold-painted effigies of enlightened beings up the hillside above Sha Tin Station. The temple's main altar room actually has 12,800 Buddha statues along its walls. The temple is guarded by huge, fierce-looking statues of various gods, and by similarly ferocious watchdogs that are chained up in the daytime.

Maps
on pages
146, 153

PRECEDING PAGES:
farm workers in the
New Territories.
LEFT: Plover Cover
Country Park.
BELOW: statues at
the Temple of
10,000 Buddhas.

Public housing in New Towns such as Sha Tin accommodates a large proportion of the population.

The complex also contains an impressive nine-storey pagoda of Indian architectural design, commemorating a Buddha who was believed to be the ninth reincarnation of Prince Vishnu.

A further 69 steps up the hill is the **Temple of Man Fat**, containing the preserved remains of the man who created this temple-and-pagoda complex: Yuet Kai, a monk who spent a lifetime studying Buddhism and living a meditative life. His greatest concern was to achieve immortality. After his death he was buried, but, according to Chinese custom, his body was later moved to its final resting place. When the body was exhumed it was perfectly preserved and radiated a ghostly yellow glow. Since there was obviously something supernatural about Yuet Kai, it was decided to preserve his body in gold leaf for posterity.

From the Temple of 10,000 Buddhas, you can look across the valley at **Amah Rock**, which looks like an *amah*, or nanny, with a baby on her back. Legend has it that a local fisherman went to sea and did not return. His wife waited patiently for his return but he did not appear. After a

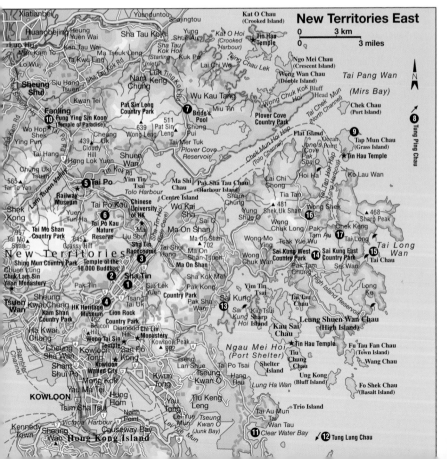

year the gods took pity on her and turned her into stone. Today the rock is a place of worship for Chinese women, and stands as a symbol of women's loyalty and fidelity.

A major destination in the valley is the Hong Kong Jockey Club's (HKJC) **Sha Tin Racecourse** ❸, which has its own station. Up to 75,000 punters flock here at the weekend race days.

Just south of Sha Tin, the KCR forks, with a new line (completed early in 2005) branching east to Ma On Shan and providing a possible alternative route round to the district of Sai Kung. A five-minute walk from the first station, Che Kung Temple, is the highly praised **Hong Kong Heritage Museum** ❹ (open Mon, Weds–Sat 10am–6pm, Sun 10am–7pm; tel: 2180 8188; entrance fee, but free on Weds), which opened in 2000. This is Hong Kong's largest museum, with 12 exhibition halls including a gallery of Chinese art, an exhibition entirely devoted to the development of the New Territories, one on the history of Cantonese opera

and another detailing the evolution of local toys. The displays are comprehensive and imaginative.

Further north (back on the main KCR East Rail line) past the **Chinese University of Hong Kong**, with its highly respected **art museum** (open Mon–Sat 10am–5pm, Sun 12.30–5.30pm; free), lies the market town of **Tai Po** ❺, which means "buying place". The old town is at the northeastern end of Tolo Harbour, where the highway crosses the Lower Lam Tsuen River. The **Hong Kong Railway Museum** (open Weds–Mon 9am–5pm; tel: 2653 3455; free), complete with vintage train carriages, is housed in the former station.

A short bus or taxi ride from Tai Po Market KCR station are the **Wishing Trees**, a pair of banyans which have become popular with locals for their alleged properties. The idea is to make a wish, write it down on the streamer provided and then hurl this into the tree. Unfortunately, a branch recently fell off one tree when it became overburdened, so the practice may be halted.

Map on page 146

Romer's tree frog, an endangered species found in the New Territories.

BELOW: natural shades at Tai Po Kau.

The chestnut bulbul is a resident at Tai Po Kau Nature Reserve.

BELOW: the empty hills of the New Territories are criss-crossed with hiking trails.

The call of the wild

One of the best places to escape from urban Hong Kong is the **Tai Po Kau Nature Reserve ❻**, a short taxi ride from Tai Po Market KCR station, or a 20-minute walk from the car park near the 14-milestone on Tai Po Road. The oldest of Hong Kong's reserves, planting began here in 1926 as part of the government's attempt to reforest the New Territories (much of the original forest cover had long since disappeared, and what was left was destroyed during the Japanese Occupation). Today, the forest shelters a good proportion of Hong Kong's flora and fauna.

Spread over 460 hectares (1,136 acres) are native tree species such as litsea, giant bean, sweet gum and *Castanopsis fissa*, which was once used to make agricultural implements, as well as the more exotic camphor, acacia and paperbark. The joss-stick tree (*Aquilania sinensis*) was used for making fans and joss sticks, and it is thought to be the reason behind Hong Kong's name, which means "fragrant harbour".

At least a dozen species of birds – including such exotica as rufous-capped babblers, scarlet-backed flowerpeckers and greater necklaced laughing thrushes, amongst an assortment of bulbuls and minivets – make the reserve their home. March, April and September are the best "birding" months. Mammals are also well represented, although mostly difficult to observe – the exception being the rhesus macaque monkeys, which can be quite aggressive, particularly if there is food around (avoid feeding them). Barking deer, civet cat, pangolin and porcupine are far more elusive.

To the northeast, the coast around **Tolo Harbour** has become more built up in recent years, but once past Shuen Wan, Ting Kok Road must rank among the most picturesque routes in Hong Kong, leading round to the Plover Cove Reservoir, Bride's Pool and Starling Inlet. At weekends and on public holidays, the roadside barbecue areas teem with noisy groups, but even then, a five-minute walk into the hills brings peace and solitude. The area around **Bride's Pool ❼**, with waterfalls and woodland glades, is especially beautiful, while the village of Luk Keng to the north still has several fine old houses inhabited by cackling ancients. The nearby village of Nam Chung marks the northern end of the **Wilson Trail**, a 78-kilometre (49-mile) walking route that runs from Stanley on Hong Kong Island to the northern end of the New Territories.

Mirs Bay islands

Out at Mirs Bay (Tai Pang Wan) in the far northeast of the SAR, **Tung Ping Chau ❽** (not to be confused with Peng Chau near Lantau) is one of Hong Kong's most remote isles. From its hilltops, you can get a panoramic view of the mainland's Bao An area. In former times, Ping

Chau had a population of 3,000, but most islanders have now moved to urban areas and only return on weekends and public holidays to run their restaurants. City people like to come to the island to have picnics and to enjoy the silence surrounded by long white beaches of smooth sand scattered with seashells, starfish and spiked sea urchins.

The island is made of what are known as "thousand-layer rocks" in different shapes and colours. There are other natural attractions as well, including caves and waterfalls with colourful names like Kang Lau Shek (Drum Tower Rock), Lung Lok Shui (Dragon Fall Water) and Nam Ki Shui (Hard-to-Get-over-Water). There are also old-fashioned stone houses with courtyards and winding passages. Because of its proximity to mainland China, Ping Chau is sometimes the first stopover for illegal immigrants from Guangdong.

At the northwestern end of Mirs Bay close to the Sai Kung peninsula is **Tap Mun Chau ❾** (also called Grass Island). The harbour is usually crowded with trawlers and other boats, as this is a central gathering point for fishermen from all over the region. **Tap Mun village** has a few seafood restaurants and shops, but many of the houses stand empty. A path winds through the village, up past the fortress-like police station, and onto a grassy plateau whose brisk winds make it very popular with kite-flyers young and old.

There are terrific views from the northern point of the island, particularly from the top of the hills next to the 100-year-old **Tin Hau Temple**. While there are dozens of Tin Hau temples all over Hong Kong, this one is special because it is the last one before the open sea. Traditionally, fishermen visit the temple to make offerings and pray for a safe return from their voyages. There is one odd thing about this particular location; when the east winds roar, their sounds can be heard in a crevice under the altar – this eerie howling is seen as a warning of storms to come. Former island residents who may have emigrated to all parts of the globe will make a special effort to come back to the temple for major festivals.

Map on page 146

TIP

The Tsui Wah Ferry Service (tel: 2272 2000 for information) operates ferries from Ma Liu Shui, near the University KCR station to Tung Ping Chau and Tap Mun Chau. There are two ferries each way on weekdays and three at weekends to Tap Mun Chau; Tung Ping Chau services only operate at weekends and public holidays.

BELOW: junks moored near Sai Kung.

The KCR's East Rail and West Rail, together with the new Ma On Shan Rail and the Light Rail, make getting around much of the New Territories quick and straightforward.

BELOW: Tsang Tai Uk, near Sha Tin, is a typical old village in the rural north of Hong Kong. Most of the younger residents have moved into the urban areas.

Parts of Tap Mun are covered with thick, impenetrable scrub, but in the upper reaches much of it is abandoned agricultural land. There are plenty of places to sit and relax over a picnic. The shore is rocky and what beaches there are lie covered in stones, but from here you can savour the views across the sea up to the China coast, which is gradually being filled with more and more construction projects.

The north

Fanling ❿ and its neighbour Sheung Shui are New Towns with over a quarter of a million residents. Nearby is **Luen Wo**, the region's traditional marketplace. While elsewhere in Hong Kong the mall and council-built marketplace are the norm, here (for now) shoppers make their way through a maze of stalls and side alleys, stepping around produce laid out on the ground, surrounded by the loud cries of merchants.

Fanling is also the site of one of the New Territories' least visited temples, **Fung Ying Sin Koon**, or Temple of Paradise. There is an intricate system of pathways and steps leading to the altar, and its grounds include many waterfalls and shady benches suitable for meditating. On a more earthly level, the Hong Kong Golf Club just outside Fanling has three exceptionally good 18-holers, known as the Old, the New and the Eden. It is the site of the Hong Kong Open Tournament every February.

The east

Sai Kung and **Clear Water Bay ⓫** are some of the most attractive areas in the New Territories. The road to the latter leads past the former **Shaw Brothers Movie Studio**, once a cornerstone of the local film industry. The studios, which once churned out the great classic Hong Kong movies in their hundreds, are now closed, and are to be converted into a HK$2 billion luxury residential project, while Shaw Brothers are moving their operation down the road to Movie City in the New Town of Tseung Kwan O.

At the far end of the road is the exclusive Clearwater Bay Golf &

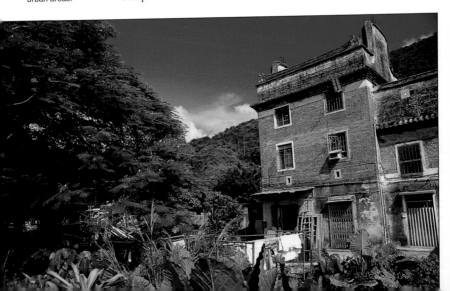

Country Club, easily recognised by its landmark pyramid-shaped clubhouse. Non-members can play here, but green fees are high. An indentation in the shoreline forms Joss House Bay, which comes to life once a year on the birthday of the sea goddess Tin Hau. Hundreds of fishing junks and sampans head for the **Tin Hau Temple** here to pay their respects to the Queen of Heaven and Goddess of the Sea. This temple was built by two brothers who allegedly were saved by Tin Hau after their junk was destroyed by a typhoon in the 11th century.

Also known as Nam Tong Island, **Tung Lung Chau** ⓬ is located off the southern tip of the Clear Water Bay peninsula. The island's biggest attraction is the **Buddhist Hall Fort** built about 300 years ago and renovated in recent years. To find the fort, follow the path from the hamlet at the ferry pier over the rolling, open landscape of northern Tung Lung. The fort, perched on a low headland in the northeast, was abandoned in 1810. But its interior is reasonably well preserved, with the

bases of the partitions between the rooms visible.

On the north shore of Tung Lung Chau are some rock carvings on the cliffs depicting the daily lives of people who lived in this area several hundred years ago. It is a perfect place to enjoy the beautiful sea view, with waves rushing to the shore and hiking trails lead along the cliffs and hills. Like most of the outlying islands, there is no regular ferry to Tung Lung, but *kaido* boats from Shau Kei Wan on Hong Kong Island operate on most weekends.

Hiram's Highway branches off Clear Water Bay Road just before the University of Science and Technology, and leads down to the town of **Sai Kung** ⓭. The road is named after a brand of sausage made by Hiram K. Potts that the highway's builder, John Wynne-Potts, devoured by the tin. While the fringes of Sai Kung have fallen prey to development, this town and its neighbouring villages still retain a strong seaside flavour. Along the seafront every imaginable and edible sea creature alive can be seen in the quayside

Map on page 146

Tin Hau, the goddess of the sea and protector of fishermen, is venerated throughout Hong Kong.

BELOW: traditional transport remains important in parts of the New Territories.

Island hopping from Sai Kung

Some of the most easily accessible outlying islands sit in the Inner Port Shelter (Ngau Mei Hoi) offshore from Sai Kung village, which at one time was a British military firing range. It's all peace and quiet nowadays though, and the harbour, home to more gin palaces than junks, makes a very photogenic start to the trip. Sampan owners will either make a one-hour tour for about HK$100 (bargain hard!), dropping you off for a short stroll at whichever island you desire, or charge around HK$300 to take you to your destination and then pick you up later. One of the nicest beaches is at Hap Mun Bay on Kiu Tsui Chau (Sharp Island), with fine sand and water that is usually clear. You can also camp overnight here, and there are barbecue pits for a cook-out. If recent visitors or perhaps a recent storm have left the beach in a mess, don't hesitate to move on round the harbour: there are other strands on Pak Sha Chau (White Sand Island) and tiny Cham Tau Chau (Pillow Island). Yim Tin Tsai (Little Salt Field) Island is remarkable for its Catholic chapel, which sees little use now as many of the islanders have moved away. Remember that whichever island you pick, you should take enough food and drink to keep you going, and sunscreen and mosquito repellent are also advisable.

Hakka women shield their faces with the black curtains around the brims of their wide hats. Theirs is a matriarchal society, and women think nothing of labouring alongside men at heavy manual jobs.

BELOW:
the fabulous white
sands at Tai Long Wan.

restaurants' tanks. Further east along the seafront you can catch the ferry to Kau Sai Chau golf course, the only public links in Hong Kong.

The road from town runs out to **Sai Kung Country Park** ⑭, the starting point of the **MacLehose Trail**. The trail stretches for 100 km (60 miles) through mostly open country, from one side of the New Territories to the other, across the beautiful grassy hills as far as Tuen Mun. The trail is well marked, and there are places to camp along the way. Some parts are extremely steep and hard going, but anyone who is used to hiking should have no problems tackling the shorter sections or any of the other walks in this area. At the very end of the road into the country park, **Hoi Ha** provides a small stretch of sand on the edge of a marine reserve.

The jewel in Sai Kung's crown is **Tai Long Wan** beach ⑮. Getting there involves an hour's trek, either around the High Island Reservoir or by cutting across the hills along the MacLehose Trail from the road at Pak Tam Au. Either way, it's more than worth it. There are two long

swathes of very pale and powdery sand, and enough surf to make it worth lugging a surfboard over the hill. There is also a café-cum-shop selling cold beer and hot noodles, and enough open space to romp far and wide. The one downside of Tai Long Wan is that there is a strong undertow, so don't swim out too far. A day of rest and relaxation here makes it extremely difficult to believe that this is part of Hong Kong.

Beyond the crest at Pak Tam Au, the road swoops down through woods and little villages to Wong Shek pier, but from just below the top it's worth pausing to admire the pristine views.

At **Wong Shek** ⑯ itself, the Jockey Club water-sports centre hires out dinghies and windsurfing boards. This is also a popular picnic and barbecue site – perhaps because it's seen as the "end of the line", just about as far away from the city as it's possible to get by road.

Further east, **Chek Keng** ⑰ is nearly deserted nowadays; one or two old black-clad crones run a shop selling soft drinks, but otherwise it's

fascinating to wander round the old buildings and paddy fields and imagine the time when the New Territories were a land apart, with inhabitants living on what they could earn from the land and the sea. You can walk on from here, using the MacLehose Trail to get over to Tai Long Wan or simply go back along the well-marked and maintained paths to Wong Shek. Either way, this remains a gloriously empty part of Hong Kong that even most locals know little about.

The west

For years, the Castle Peak side of the New Territories was cut off from the heart of Hong Kong. But the 30.5-km (20-mile) West Rail, linking urban Kowloon with Yuen Long and Tuen Mun, changed all that. A few years earlier, huge reclamation and construction projects changed the map almost daily as road and rail links were built for the new airport.

The most striking new arrival was the **Tsing Ma Bridge** ⑱, sometimes referred to as Hong Kong's "Golden Gate", linking Lantau and the airport to Tsing Yi Island, from where another shorter bridge crosses to Kowloon.

Some 2.2 kilometres (1.4 miles) long, Tsing Ma's 200-metre-high (650-ft) twin towers are visible along much of the highway that leads to Kwai Chung, an extensive complex of container terminals, and the industrial community of **Tsuen Wan** ⑲. This urban sprawl, one of the largest New Towns (population over one million), is at the end of the Tsuen Wan MTR line.

The Chinese presence here seems to have begun about the second century AD. In the 13th century, the Chinese empire stretched to this area because the emperor was being driven south by invading Mongols. In 1277, the emperor and his entourage arrived in Tsuen Wan.

Maps on p146 & below

A major new bridge, The Hong Kong–Shenzhen Western Corridor (HK-SWC), stretches for 5.5 kilometres (3½ miles) to link the northwestern New Territories with Shekou. The bridge is the fourth crossing between Hong Kong and Shenzhen.

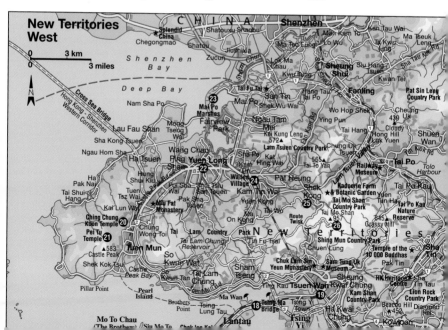

The Sam Tung Uk Museum provides a glimpse into the daily life of a New Territories walled village 100 years ago.

BELOW: the Tsing Ma Bridge, Hong Kong's "Golden Gate".

Later, in the mid-17th century when the Formosan pirate Koxinga was building his empire, the Manchu government ordered a mass evacuation of coastal areas to save the populace from the marauding buccaneer. Koxinga's forces demolished the vacated settlement of Tsuen Wan and it was not repopulated until the end of the 17th century.

These days, Tsuen Wan is worth the long MTR journey if only to poke around the **Sam Tung Uk Museum** (open Weds–Mon 9am–5pm; free), a beautifully restored Hakka walled village. The narrow alleyways trace a path past a central ancestral hall, an exhibition room and rows of tiny cubicles stocked with period furniture and farming tools.

Beyond Tsuen Wan, the Tuen Mun Highway passes another impressive airport-related bridge – **Tsing Long** – before reaching the sprawling New Town of **Tuen Mun**. Near **Castle Peak**, the large mountain west of Tuen Mun that is mostly occupied by army firing ranges, and adjacent to the Light Rail Transit (LRT) station, is a huge temple called **Ching Chung Koon ⑳**, which also serves as a home for the elderly who have no relatives or means of support. It is also a repository for many Chinese art treasures, including lanterns more than 200 years old and a jade seal that dates back 1,000 years. The library, which holds 4,000 books, documents the history of the Daoist religion. The temple is dedicated to Lui Tung Bun, one of the so-called Daoist Immortals.

On the slopes of Castle Peak stands a temple that is smaller but no less intriguing – **Pei Tu Temple ㉑**, dedicated to the eponymous monk, a famous figure in Chinese mythology.

Yuen Long ㉒ is another redevelopment project, greatly enhanced by the arrival of the KCR in 2003. It began as a traditional market town set in the middle of the largest flood plain in the New Territories. The population before development was around 40,000, but that figure is expected to grow to over one million when all the residential and commercial land in the area has been developed as planned.

North of Yuen Long, next to a low-rise housing estate called Fairview Park, lies **Mai Po Marshes ㉓** (open Mon–Fri 9am–5pm, Sat–Sun 9am–6pm; entrance fee; permits must be booked in advance, tel: 2526 4473). The easiest way to get there is to take a taxi from Yuen Long KCR station. The mangroves and mudflats here are a stopping point on the migratory routes of more than 400 different species of birds – best time to visit is spring and autumn. The Wetland Park, fully opened in December 2005, showcases the area's natural wonders via a 10,000-square metre (12,000-sq. yd) visitor centre containing extensive exhibits.

Until the 1980s, the view from the lookout point at Lok Ma Chau Police Station towards China was all rice paddies and villages. Nowa-

Map on page 153

days this has been replaced by the rapidly expanding city of Shenzhen.

Also a quick trip from Yuen Long are the walled villages of **Kam Tin** ㉔. The most popular for visitors is the Kat Hing Wai village, which stands rather incongruously across the road from a supermarket. Some 400 people live there, all with the same surname, Tang. Built in the 1600s, it is a fortified village with walls 6 metres (20 ft) thick, guard-houses on its four corners, arrow slits for fighting off attackers, and a moat. The authenticity may seem spoiled by some of the modern buildings inside, which peep over the old-time fortifications. There is still just one entrance, guarded by a heavy wrought-iron gate. Visitors can enter for a nominal admission fee.

From Kam Tin you can take a scenic route via **Shek Kong** ㉕, which used to be the British military garrison and airfield but is now home to a skeleton force of the Chinese People's Liberation Army. The far end of Shek Kong village marks the start of **Route Twisk** (Tsuen Wan–Shek Kong), one of the most panoramic drives in Hong Kong. Within minutes you are high up in forested mountains, seemingly far from all human habitation. The road zigzags for miles and then suddenly plunges right into the high-rise modernity of Tsuen Wan.

From the top of Route Twisk near Hong Kong's highest peak, **Tai Mo Shan** ㉖ (957 metres/3,140 ft), one can look over to China and down to Hong Kong Island. This is the only part of Hong Kong ever to have experienced frost.

Alternatively, continue on Lam Kam Road to Pak Ngau Shek in the Lam Tsuen Valley, and the **Kadoorie Farm and Botanic Garden** (open daily 9.30am–5pm; free). About as far from urban Hong Kong as it is possible to get, Kadoorie was set up in the 1950s to help local farmers, but has since evolved into a conservation centre. A wide range of local wildlife can be seen here; at the Raptor Sanctuary injured birds of prey are treated and released back into the wild, and there is also a breeding programme for various endangered species. ❏

To reach Kadoorie Farm take bus 64K from Tai Po Market KCR station (East Rail).

RESTAURANTS

Cantonese

Nang Kee Goose Restaurant
Sham Tseng Sun Tsuen, Sham Tseng. Tel: 2491 0392. Open: L & D daily. **$$**
Roasting goose is a serious business in Hong Kong, and wide consensus states that the Nang Kee has the number-one goose, despite its off-the-beaten-track location and a large number of similar restaurants nearby. Fork out for a taxi.

Indian

Dia
42–46 Fuk Man Rd, Sai Kung. Tel: 2791 4456. Open: L & D daily. **$$**
Modern Indian restaurant with sophisticated interior design. There is a large vegetarian element on the menu, and several vegan options.

Italian

Portofino
GF 1 Sai Kung Hi Pang Sq, Sai Kung. Tel: 2791 5818. Open: L & D daily. **$$**
Italian restaurant with a European menu and an emphasis on seafood. The dining room is popular with expatriate journalists, who lap up the laid-back atmosphere and the decent wine list. The food is always good, portions are generous and the service is professional.

Portuguese

Pousada
112 Pak Sha Wan, Hebe Haven, Sai Kung. Tel: 2335 5561. Open: L & D daily. **$$**
The expatriate enclave of Sai Kung has a number of good Western-style restaurants catering to the population, and Pousada is one of the best. Good-quality Portuguese food and wine served in an airy dining room tiled in terracotta and blue. A rooftop terrace offers great alfresco options.

● ● ● ● ● ● ● ● ● ● ● ● ●
Prices are for a three-course meal with one beer or a glass of house wine.
$ = under HK$150
$$ = HK$150–300
$$$ = HK$300–500
$$$$ = over HK$500

HONG KONG'S WILD SIDE

Somewhat surprisingly, country parks occupy over 40 percent of the SAR's land area, and offer easily accessible respite from this most stressful of cities

One of the many unusual aspects of Hong Kong is the contrast between some of the world's most densely populated urban areas and the utterly empty countryside that surrounds them. In parts of the New Territories and Outlying Islands it is possible to walk for mile after mile in dramatic mountain scenery, enjoy superb natural views, and see no-one for hours on end.

For its modest size, Hong Kong has some impressive mountains – at 957m (3,140ft) Tai Mo Shan is on a par with the highest mountain in England, and several others in the New Territories and Lantau are not far behind. A well-signposted network of hiking trails extends across all 22 country parks, with some longer distance routes such as the MacLehose, Wilson and Hong Kong Island trails.

Areas of woodland occur at lower and middle levels, sometimes as a result of reforestation, but most upland areas were deforested long ago by the agricultural needs of villagers. The higher areas are almost all grassland and shrubland, bright green in summer, brown in the dry winters.

ABOVE: this mountain stream, fed by run-off from Mount Kellett, is just a few hundred yards from the tower blocks and traffic of Aberdeen.

ABOVE: the convoluted coastline of the New Territories has some fine stretches of beach – nowhere more so than at Tai Long Wan on the eastern edge of Sai Kung Country Park.

LEFT: grass fires are common in Hong Kong during the dry months from October to January, sometimes ravaging entire hillsides. Warnings are displayed at country parks when the risk is high.

HONG KONG'S FAUNA AND FLORA: WHERE TROPICAL MEETS TEMPERATE

Located on the eastern edge of the Eurasian land-mass, Hong Kong lies in a transition zone between the cooler lands to the north and the tropical south. The cool winters brought by the northeast monsoon winds mean that the natural vegetation cover is not tropical 'jungle', but rather broad-leaved forest with temperate oaks and laurels as well as tropical species such as lianas, banyans and fan palms. The original forest cover disappeared centuries ago to be replaced either by agriculture or grass-land (on the hills), but some areas are now successfully reforested.

A wide variety of wildlife survives in Hong Kong. The Tai Po Kau Nature Reserve shelters rhesus macaques, pangolins, civet cats and barking deer as well as a large diversity of birds, amphibians and reptiles. The Mai Po Marshes are an important resting point for migratory birds. Marine life has been badly hit by pollution, but Chinese river dolphins can still be seen off the coast of Lantau.

BELOW: the MacLehose Trail (pictured at its eastern end with Sharp Peak in the background) is one of several long-distance hiking trails across the uplands of the New Territories, Hong Kong Island and Lantau.

TOP: the odd-looking litchi lantern bug.
MIDDLE: a rhesus macaque monkey at Tai Po Kau.
BOTTOM: the Burmese python is one of several poisonous snakes found in Hong Kong.

THE OUTLYING ISLANDS

Each of the three principal outlying islands, Lantau, Cheung Chau and Lamma, makes a rewarding day trip from the city. Attractions include sandy beaches, seafood restaurants, appealing villages, beautiful scenery and – on a different note – Lantau's new Disneyland theme park

A substantial majority of Hong Kong's visitors arrive at the state-of-the-art international airport on what used to be an "outlying island", but one which is now joined by road-and-rail suspension bridge to Kowloon. Within a short space of time they are being whisked into the city aboard the smooth Airport Express train, passing not towering skyscrapers but lofty mountains which are part of Lantau's country park. Such are the contrasts on Hong Kong's islands.

More changes are underway on Lantau: an all-singing-and-dancing Walt Disney theme park opened in September 2005; a major exhibition centre has been built next to the airport; and a new cable-car transports day-trippers up the steep mountainside to Po Lin Monastery.

Hong Kong's other large outlying islands, Lamma and Cheung Chau, are far less developed. There are no proper roads (just narrow concrete paths), and few structures are higher than three storeys. The remainder of the islands – more than 230 of them – are either uninhabited or support small rural communities.

This scattered archipelago provides a glimpse of Hong Kong through the looking glass, a portion of the South China coast that reflects both rapid change and timeless cohesion. Naturally, many young islanders have moved away into the city and left their homes to ageing parents. Until recently, fishing was the major means of earning a living for the remaining islanders, but times have changed and the most profitable businesses are now restaurants and tourism.

Lantau

Lantau ("broken head" in Cantonese) is by far the largest of Hong Kong's islands. Its north and east are

BELOW: rural islander.

dominated by the new airport, a four-lane highway, and double railway lines which thunder along the shore to the apartment blocks of Tung Chung, Tsing Ma Bridge and the new Disneyland theme park. The rest of the island is far less developed. In the south are long beaches and small townships such as Silvermine Bay (Mui Wo) linked by ferries and packet boats known as *kaido* to Peng Chau (pleasant though hardly a must-see) and Cheung Chau. In the west, Tai O and Fan Lau are favourite destinations for day-trippers, and there are good coastal and hill walks.

The centre of Lantau is dominated by lofty mountains, notably Lantau Peak (934 metres/3,064 ft) and Sunset Peak (869 metres/2,851 ft), criss-crossed with wandering pathways and dusty trails linking a number of Buddhist monasteries. The 70-kilometre (43-mile) Lantau Trail and other intersecting side routes are good for a short stroll, a day trip or overnight trek. A particularly good hike circles the 20,900-million-litre (5,500-million-gallon)

Shek Pik Reservoir, on the western slopes of Lantau Peak. Alternatively, a coastal path runs from Shek Pik round to Tai O.

Monastery in the clouds

Up on the mountainous central spine is Lantau's best-known attraction, the red, orange and gold **Po Lin Monastery** ❶ (Precious Lotus Monastery; open daily 10am–6pm; free). The large complex, which dates back to the 1920s, is busier and noisier than the average Buddhist retreat. Its canteen serves good vegetarian meals between 11.30am and 4.30pm. The real crowd-puller, however, is the **Big Buddha**, at 24 metres (79 ft) the world's largest outdoor bronze statue of a seated Buddha, completed here in 1990. A long flight of steps leads up to the statue, with fantastic views from the top. There is an exhibition in the base of the statue explaining how it was built.

A cable-car, named **Ngong Ping 360**, is due to open in early 2006 and will link Tung Chung with the monastery, but for the moment visitors

Map on page 161

TIP

Ferries operate from the Outlying Islands Ferry Piers in Central to Silvermine Bay (Mui Wo) on Lantau approximately every 30–50 minutes throughout the day on weekdays, and every 40–60 minutes at weekends. For information call First Ferry, tel: 2131 8181.

BELOW: the southwestern shore of Lamma Island.

After years of financial wrangling, and one of the largest infrastructure construction projects the world has ever seen, the airport at Chek Lap Kok was completed in 1998.

BELOW: the Big Buddha overlooking Po Lin Monastery.

arrive by road (no.2 bus from Mui Wo, bus nos. 11 or 23 from Tung Chung, or take a taxi).

Near the cable-car, on a hill overlooking Tung Chung, is a fort built in 1817. The fort's thick ramparts still stand, as do six old cannons, much as they did during the 19th century when they guarded the town and bay from smugglers, pirates, scoundrels and unexpected "outer barbarians".

West of Po Lin, in the direction of Tai O on Lantau's northern coast, is an excellent walking path that traverses mountain ridges, canyons and streams en route to Lantau's **Yin Hing Monastery ❷**, a haven rich with traditional Buddhist paintings and statues. The monastery sits on a slope and commands a fine view of the surrounding mountains, farmland and the South China Sea.

One of Lantau's older communities, **Tai O ❸** is located on the northwest coast, closer – as the crow flies – to Macau than to Central. Here, the island's Tanka "boat people", who traditionally lived on their boats near shore, have become semi-land dwellers. Some of their larger junks

have been turned into three-storey permanent living structures. Further up at Tai O Creek, they have also built rickety homes on stilts over parts of the creek where the water rises during tide changes. The ropeferry that was once a feature of Tai O has been replaced by a functional bridge. Immediately beneath its arch, boatmen with their eye on a fast buck offer trips out to see Hong Kong's pink dolphins, who somehow manage to exist in the polluted waters offshore; it is better to take a trip with the environmentally sensitive Hong Kong Dolphinwatch *(see page 227)*. Old women still hang around the bridge landings, offering short boat rides up and down the canals. A short stroll on both sides of the tidal creek is worthwhile for a look at the boat people and their unique way of life.

Hong Kong's most eccentric accommodation is **Lantau Mountain Camp**, located 770 metres (2,526 ft) up **Sunset Peak**. The camp consists of 20 small stone huts, built before World War II as a rest haven for Christian missionaries taking time off from their work in China.

The huts can also be rented by laymen who book in advance.

Lantau is understandably famed for the long, smooth and often empty beaches that line much of its southern coastline. The most popular and crowded beach (probably because it is the easiest to reach) is at **Silvermine Bay (Mui Wo) ❹**. A boom anchored permanently off the beach keeps sharks at bay (attacks in Hong Kong waters are rare) and lifeguards with reflector sunglasses permanently at the ready are on duty in the summer months. A clutch of bars and restaurants has opened in the village, roistering affairs that become extremely busy at weekends. There are also numerous Chinese restaurants – either cheap and moderately cheerful at the Mui Wo Cooked Food Market by the ferry pier, or slightly more pricey beneath the banyan tree set above the road on the way to the Silvermine Beach Hotel just before Five Cents Bridge.

Away from the rest of the island is a major real-estate development called **Discovery Bay ❺**, a well-planned and uncrowded, if rather soulless, housing/resort complex that includes a golf course. "DB", or "Disco Bay", is a magnet for expats with a hankering for suburbia, and has excited comparison with the movie *The Truman Show* as well as a considerable number of column inches in the (late lamented) satirical magazine *Spike*.

Disneyland

Hong Kong's eagerly awaited **Disneyland ❻** (open Mon–Fri 10am–7pm, Sat–Sun 10am–9pm; tel: 1 830 830; entrance fee – *see page 226*) opened its doors to the public in September 2005, complete with its own link to the MTR, two hotels, shops, restaurants and the sort of amusements that thrill at more-or-less similar venues in Paris, Tokyo and the United States. Learning from

Map below

Away from Po Lin, much of the central part of Lantau is dotted with small Buddhist monasteries.

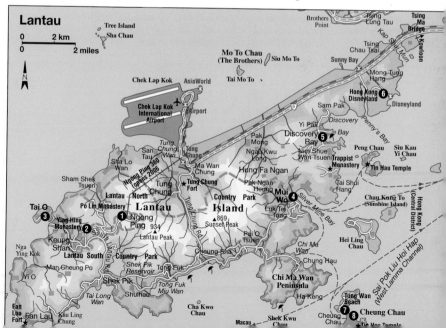

A Buddhist monk at Po Lin. The monastery has managed to retain a semblance of serenity despite the number of tourists who come here to see the Big Buddha, the proximity of the airport and the new Disneyland.

BELOW: the Sleeping Beauty Castle at Fantasyland, part of the Disneyland complex.

past mistakes, efforts have been made to reflect the local culture – feng shui experts were consulted on the layout of the 126-hectare (310-acre) site, while Chinese numerology was also taken into account: on-site hotels avoid the number four when numbering their floors because the four is considered bad luck to the Chinese, and one of the main ballrooms covers an area of 888 square metres, reflecting the perceived good fortune of the number eight. Following pressure from conservationists and animal rights groups, however, traditional Chinese shark's fin soup is not available in any of the park's restaurants.

Disneyland is divided into themed areas. Tickets give access to all. The nostalgic **Main Street USA** evokes a typical small town in the American mid-west from the early 1900s. There are marching bands, rides on old-time buses and other contraptions, plus the largest concentration of shops and restaurants on site. **Fantasyland** is set around a fairy-tale castle where stories and characters such as Winnie the Pooh, Dumbo and Snow White are brought vividly to life, much to the delight of small children. **Adventureland** is billed as "an exotic trek into unexplored regions", with attractions including a Jungle River Cruise and Tarzan's Treehouse. **Tomorrowland** focuses on space exploration, and features a dramatic roller-coaster, a Buzz Lightyear shoot-em-up extravaganza and other extraterrestrial thrills.

The Hong Kong government owns 57 percent of the US$1.8 billion project (Disney invested US$316 million for its 43 percent stake). Five to six million visitors are anticipated annually, and if all goes well it is likely that the park will expand to include a fifth themed area, thought to be either Frontierland or Mickey's Toontown.

Cheung Chau

Cheung Chau ("long island" in Cantonese) is the most densely populated of the outlying islands. The curving waterfront promenade, the *praya,* is one of the most pleasant places in Hong Kong, especially after sunset when its alfresco restaurants

burst into life only yards from the fishing vessels bobbing at anchor. Home to Hong Kong's first and so far only Olympic gold medallist (from Atlanta 1996), Lee Lai-shan, Cheung Chau has a strong windsurfing tradition, centered on Afternoon Beach (Kwun Yan Wan).

The village of **Cheung Chau ❼**, near the ferry dock, is a tangle of alleyways. There are no vehicles on the island apart from small motorised carts and an amusing bonsai-sized police car, fire engine and ambulance, a phenomenon that grants an automatic serenity. Head off in any direction from the ferry terminal and you will pass both modern and traditional shops and restaurants.

A short distance to the left of the ferry dock, up the main road, is **Pak Tai Temple**, built in 1783 and dedicated to the god Pak Tai, protector of fishermen and the island's saviour from plague during the late 1700s. Inside, in front of the altar, are statues of two generals, Thousand-Li Eye and Favourable Wind Ear, who were said to be able to see or hear anything at any distance.

Scattered about the island are several temples dedicated to Tin Hau, goddess of the sea. Cheung Chau was once the haunt of pirates, including the notorious Cheung Po Tsai. As on the other outlying islands, "Family Trail" walks are well-marked and lead to **Cheung Po Tsai Cave** as well as other scenic spots.

Each year the island hosts the four-day **Bun Festival**, usually in May. Known as *Ching Chiu* in Cantonese, it originated many years ago after the discovery of a nest of skeletons, believed to be the remains of people killed by pirates. The island was subsequently plagued by a series of misfortunes; to placate the restless spirits of the victims, offerings were made once a year. How pastry buns came into this story is anybody's guess.

During the festival, giant bamboo towers covered with edible buns are erected in the courtyard of Pak Tai Temple. In the past, the local men would climb up the towers to pluck their lucky buns – the higher the bun was, the more luck it would bring. The ritual ended in 1978 when one of the towers came

Map on page 161

TIP

Ferries operate from the Outlying Islands Ferry Piers in Central to Cheung Chau every 30 minutes daily. For information call First Ferry, tel: 2131 8181. Lamma ferries are run by Hong Kong and Kowloon Ferry Ltd (HKKF), tel: 2815 6063. Services run at 20–60 minute intervals to Yung Shue Wan, less frequently to Sok Kwu Wan.

BELOW: alfresco seafood restaurants are easy to find on the outlying islands.

The main outlying islands are linked to Central by frequent ferry services.

crashing down, bringing broken bones and bruises rather than luck. Now the buns are handed out in a less interesting but more orderly – and safer – manner to participants.

Another attraction during the festival are the colourfully-clad "floating children", who are hoisted up on stilts and paraded through the crowds. There are also performances of Chinese opera, lion dances and other festive events to entertain the hordes that descend from all over Hong Kong and overseas.

There are some excellent beaches on Cheung Chau. The main strand is **Tung Wan** ⑧, on the other, eastern, side of the narrow isthmus from the harbour. Below the Warwick Hotel at the southern end of the sands is a 3,000-year-old bronze age rock carving. Other good beaches are Afternoon Beach (Kwun Yam Wan), just past the rock carving, and Pak Tso at the island's southwestern tip.

Lamma

BELOW: the harbour at Yung Shue Wan.

The second largest of the outlying islands is **Lamma**. Rich in grassy hills and picturesque bays, the rugged terrain means that there is only a very small area of farmland. Archaeologists have associated Lamma with some of the earliest settlements in the region.

Lamma has a population of around 8,000, mostly concentrated in and around the village of Yung Shue Wan. Among them are a sizeable number of expatriates, who value the peace and quiet: despite a frequent ferry service to Central, this roadless island remains slow-paced, although it can get crowded with day-trippers at weekends.

Yung Shue Wan (Banyan Bay), at the northern end of Lamma, is one of two ferry gateways to the island. The village has a good supply of restaurants serving Japanese, Thai, Mediterranean and Indian cuisine, as well as several Chinese seafood establishments on the waterfront.

It is only a short stroll out into the countryside. On a side street just past the town's main intersection is Yung Shue Wan's **Tin Hau Temple**, dedicated to the queen of heaven and the goddess of the seas. The 100-year-old temple is guarded by a

pair of stone lions. Inside, behind a red spirit stand (to deflect evil spirits), is the main shrine with images of the beaded and veiled Tin Hau.

The most popular walk on Lamma is a well-maintained pathway running much of the length of the island to Sok Kwu Wan. The well-marked, hilly, concrete-paved track runs past neat vegetable plots and three-storey buildings (nothing higher is permitted, with the exception of the power station chimeys that loom behind the hill to the right of the path), then along **Hung Shing Ye Beach**, a pleasantly clean stretch of sand.

The walk treats hikers to views out across the sea. The contrast between bustling, crowded Hong Kong Island and empty Lamma could not be more startling. The walk from one end of Lamma to the other can be completed in an unhurried hour and a half, and should end with a fine seafood meal.

Sok Kwu Wan, which lies on the eastern shore of a long fjord-like inlet known as Picnic Bay, is the Lamma village closest to Aberdeen and a popular weekend pleasure-junk mooring. The bay brims with floating fish farms, all tended by a fleet of boats of various shapes and sizes, and is one of the main suppliers of Hong Kong's seafood restaurants. Not surprisingly, the village has a long string of seafood restaurants, beguiling in the evening with bright lighting displays and marvellous aromas.

A gentle trek from Sok Kwu Wan leads to **Mo Tat Wan**, a quiet bay with a solitary international restaurant (that punches well above its weight) and its own *kaido* service back to Aberdeen.

Po Toi

Po Toi is a group of islands located at the southernmost area of the SAR, southeast of Stanley, and inhabited by only a handful of people. Reached by *kaido* from Aberdeen or Stanley, the main island, Po Toi, is home to a large rock resembling a snail. Under the rock is a cave with carvings shaped by wind and rain. The open-air restaurants near the pier in the south serve excellent seafood. ❑

● *For details on the islands in Mirs Bay and the eastern New Territories, see pages 148–50.*

Map on pages 80-1

Lamma Island has a large population of expats keen to escape from the noise and pollution of the city.

RESTAURANTS

Cantonese

Han Lok Yuen (The Pigeon Restaurant)
16–17 Hung Shing Yeh, Lamma Island. Tel: 2982 0680. Open: L & D daily. **$$**
Overlooking the beach at Hung Shing Yeh, a 20-minute walk from Yung Shue Wan. The shaded terrace is scattered with round tables groaning with plump pigeons roasted a tempting golden brown.

Lamma Mandarin
8 First St, Sok Kwu Wan.

Lamma Island. Tel: 2982 8128. Open: L & D daily. **$$**
Wild and raucous when packed with seafood-crazy local and mainland tourists, but otherwise blissfully chilled. Choose your fish live from the tank and relax with a beer.

Lamcombe
47 Main Street, Yung Shue Wan, Lamma Island. Tel: 2982 0881.
Open: L & D daily. **$**
The Lamcombe is less crowded than its counterparts in Yung Shue Wan, but the seafood is just as good. Try the crispy deep-fried squid with sweet and sour sauce.

International

Deli Lamma
36 Main Street, Yung Shue Wan, Lamma Island.
Tel: 2982 1583.
Open: L & D daily. **$**
Quirky bar and restaurant serving an Indian and Western menu. The dark dining room attracts day-trippers and local residents, and there's a terrace out the back.

N.E.W.S Bistro
40 Cheung Sha Lower Village. Lantau Island.
Tel: 2984 0113. Open: L & D Weds–Mon (closed Tues). **$$**
Twenty minutes by cab from the ferry terminal at Mui Wo on Lantau, N.E.W.S Bistro serves an eclectic menu of Asian and Western favourites on the beachfront.

● ● ● ● ● ● ● ● ● ● ● ●
Prices are for a three-course meal with one beer or a glass of house wine.
$ = under HK$150
$$ = HK$150–300
$$$ = HK$300–500
$$$$ = over HK$500

HONG KONG'S FESTIVALS

The city is at its most colourful during one of the traditional Chinese festivals

Despite the brash modernity, Hong Kong is a city whose population remains close to its roots, where temple deities and ancestors are honoured with equal fervour. These traditions are at their most vibrant and visible during the colourful Chinese festivals.

Lunar New Year, in January or February, is the major annual event, a time for being with family, when most businesses shut down for at least a week. Children and the unmarried receive *lai see*, lucky red packets containing newly minted money. Employees get a bonus. Shops are decorated in fine style, and there are noisy dragon dances and processions. On the 15th day of the Lunar New Year the **Spring Lantern Festival** involves the hanging of colourful traditional lanterns in homes, restaurants and temples. Fishermen decorate their boats in bright colours and flock to Tin Hau temples around the territory on the **Birthday of Tin Hau**, the goddess of the sea, in April or May. At the Tin Hau Temple in Aberdeen and in the New Territories town of Yuen Long there are parades with lion dances and floats. The **Cheung Chau Bun Festival** in May is one of the most exciting local festivals; figures in historical costumes parade on stilts or ride on floats across the island. During the **Dragon Boat Festival** in June, elaborately decorated dragon boats race to the beat of loud drums. International dragon-boat races are held in the following week. Many people's favourite is the **Mid-Autumn Festival** (Moon Festival) in September. Paper lanterns of all shapes and sizes are illuminated and taken out to public parks – notably Victoria Park in Causeway Bay. People also eat special sweet cakes known as mooncakes.

ABOVE: the climax of the Chinese New Year celebrations is the awesome fireworks display over Victoria Harbour. Large buildings are lit up with stunning displays throughout the festive period.

BELOW: at Chinese New Year, dragon dances are performed to ward off evil spirits.

BELOW: handing out *lai see* at Chinese New Year. The standard good wish is *Kung Hei Fat Choy*, "May You Be Lucky and Get Rich."

LEFT: Hong Kong's Dragon Boat Festival (June), owes its existence to an event around 200 BC. Chu Yuan, a poet who had fallen out of political favour with the king, jumped into a river in protest and drowned. The frantic paddlers of today recreate the desperate actions of Yuan's friends as they tried to save him.

THE CHINESE ZODIAC

Chinese festivals operate using the lunar calendar. Beginning with Chinese New Year in late January or early February, the year is divided into 12 months of 29 days, with an extra month added in every two and a half years in the same way as Western calendars use leap years.

The calendar operates in 60-year cycles, divided up into five smaller cycles of 12 years. Each of these years is represented by an animal, and each of the five cycles by an element (wood, water, metal, earth and fire). As with Western astrology, the permutations are thought to provide clues into a person's character. The 12 animals are as follows:

Rat: (1948, 1960, 1972, 1984, 1996) charming, imaginative but quick-tempered.
Ox: (1949, 1961, 1973, 1985, 1997) a leader, conservative and patient.
Tiger: (1950, 1962, 1974, 1986, 1998) sensitive, emotional, stubborn.
Rabbit: (1951, 1963, 1975, 1987, 1999) popular, obliging, sentimental, cautious.
Dragon: (1952, 1964, 1976, 1988, 2000) charismatic, clever, prone to indiscretion.
Snake: (1953, 1965, 1977, 1989, 2001) wise, thoughtful, charming and intuitive.
Horse: (1954, 1966, 1978, 1990, 2002) hard-working, intelligent but egotistical.
Ram: (1955, 1967, 1979, 1991, 2003) artistic, pessimistic, generous.
Monkey: (1956, 1968, 1980, 1992, 2004) intelligent, witty, popular but distrustful.
Rooster: (1957, 1969, 1981, 1993, 2005) extravagant, brave, hard-working.
Dog: (1958, 1970, 1982, 1994, 2006) honest, faithful, dependable but a worrier.
Pig: (1959, 1971, 1983, 1995, 2007) clever, sincere, honest but prone to set difficult goals.

RIGHT: the Bun Festival on Cheung Chau placates the spirits of former residents of the island who were slain by pirates. It's a riot of colour and invention, albeit slightly toned down these days. *For full details see page 163.*

MACAU

Often perceived as existing in the shadow of its illustrious neighbour, Macau is in fact quite different to Hong Kong. A major economic boom has brought rapid change, but the unique Mediterranean ambience largely survives

I f ever the Pearl River Delta had "bling", it's now, and specifically in Macau. Established by the Portuguese in 1557 as the first European colony on China's shore, Macau was for much of recent history a sleepy outpost, playing second fiddle to its high-profile neighbour. Things have changed quickly, and nowadays Macau is a gambling Mecca, clocking up nearly 1½ million visitors a month. Returned to China by Lisbon in December 1999 when it became a Special Administrative Region like Hong Kong, reclamation projects have conjured an airport out of the sea, a score of new casinos are planned for what was previously a strip of waste land, and theme parks and shopping malls are filling in the gaps. Yet amidst all the pizzazz, sizeable areas of old Macau survive – graceful old buildings redolent of southern Europe, overlooking cobbled streets shaded by ancient banyan trees. Potter over to Coloane for lunch in one of the restaurants off the square and you could be on the Iberian peninsula rather than in the heart of the Orient. Bigger and bolder Macau may have become, but it still has acres of charm.

Fun, games and gambling

Macau's premier entertainment rumbles to the rattle of the roulette ball with the speed of a croupier shuffling a deck of cards. Gambling – or gaming as the industry would have it – is Macau's prime revenue-earner, fleecing the pockets of millions of mainland Chinese and other nationalities every year, but equally sending quite a few on their way with riches beyond the dreams of avarice. At present, the SAR's 18 casinos fall into two distinct classes. The first is epitomised by the Lisboa, owned by gazillionaire Stanley Ho, who for many years grew

Map on page 172

PRECEDING PAGES: the 17th-century light-house on Guia Hill.
LEFT: European ambience on Largo do Senado Square.
BELOW: the famous Lisboa Casino.

MACAU

Shenzhen

Hong Kong

Friendship Bridge

Macau-Taipa Bridge

Sai Van Bridge

TAIPA

Macau International Airport

★ Taipa House Museum

Macau Port Kao Ho

A-Ma Cultural Village ★

Macau Country Club ★

Hác Sá Beach

SEAC PAI VAN PARK

COLOANE

Baía Cheoc Van

Lotus Bridge

COTAI

27

28

Av. da Ponte da Amizade

Portas do Cerco

20

Av. da Ponte da Amizade

Estrada dos Cavaleiros

Istmo Ferreira do Amaral

R. A. Tamagnini Barbosa

Rua da Longuvada

R. Direita do Hipodromo

Av. A.

R. Central da da Areia Preta

de Maio

Rua do Nordeste

R. do Avenida 1° de Maio

Es. Mar. do Hipodromo

Av. Leste do Hipodromo

Rua Novo da Areia Preta

Estrada Marginal da Areia Preta

Lin Fung Miu (Lotus) Temple

19

Fortress of Mong-Ha

Lacerda

COLINA DE MONG-HA

Canidromo

Avenida do

Rampa dos Cavaleiros

Kun-Iam Temple

18

Av. de Venceslau de Morais

Rua dos Pescadores

Macau-Seac Tin Hau Temple

Reservatório de Água

Avenida de Horta e Costa

Fran- cisco Xavier Pereira

de Almirante

do Ouvidor Arriaga

e Costa

Mesquita

COLINA DA GUIA

Avenida da Amizade

Guia Cable Car

21

Dr Sun Yatsen Memorial House

Guia Fortress & Lighthouse

23

HK-Macau Ferry Pier

Casino de Macau (Floating Casino)

Hong Kong

Taipa

LOU LIM IOC GARDENS

22

Camões Grotto & Garden

8

Old Protestant Cemetery

St Michael's Cemetery

Museum of Macau

7

São Paulo (St Paul's Façade)

Fortaleza do Monte

São Domingos (St Dominic's)

Sta Casa da Misericórdia

Largo do Senado

Sé (Macau Cathedral)

Leal Senado

Santo Agostinho (St Augustine)

Dom Pedro V Theatre

St Joseph's Seminary

Governor's Residence

São Lourenço (St Lawrence)

Bishop's Palace

Portuguese Consulate

COLINA DA PENHA

Temple da Deusa A-Ma

Maritime Museum

Barra Hill

Pousada de São Tiago

Fortaleza da Barra

Friendship Monument

Avenida Dr. Sun Yat-Sen

Rua das Lorchas

Rua da Ribeira do Patane

Rua da Barca

R. Entre Campos

R. Coelho do Amaral

Estrada

Meira

Rue T.

Rua de B.

Rua da

Estalgens

Av. Almeida Ribeiro

Central

R. P. Antonio

Av. da Praia Grande

R. da Praia Grande

Calçada da Barra

Rua da Barra

R. da Barra

Av. de República

Rua do Dr. L. Pereira Marques

Rua do Almirante Sérgio

Porto Interior

Fonte Cibernética (Cybernetic Fountain)

Bahia da Praia Grande

Hotel Lisboa

Av. Infante D. Henrique

Avenida da Amizade

Macau Forum

Jai Alai Casino

Fisherman's Wharf

Sands Casino

24

Art Museum

26

Macau Cultural Centre

25

Dr. Rodrigo Rodrigues

Av. do Dr. Luis Gonzaga Gomes

Avenida da Amizade

Av. de Berlim

Av. do Dr. Carlos

Av. do Dr. Carlos

CR Silva Marques

Avenida Xian Xing Hai

Avenida de Roma

Rua Cidade de Sintra

Rua Cidade de Coimbra

Avenida Dr. Sun Yat Sen

NAPE

Kun Iam Statue

Macau-Taipa Bridge

Macau Tower Convention and Entertainment Centre

Taipa, Coloane

Macau

0 — 500 m

0 — 500 yds

N

(metaphorically) fat on a gaming monopoly. The Lisboa – an outsize wedding cake on the waterfront – could scarcely be described as classy, with milling hordes sweating and spitting round the tables and snatching at the handles of the Hungry Tigers, as fruit machines are called.

The second type of casino is very different. In 2002 it was finally agreed to open the industry up to some other players – to a certain amount of unrestrained glee in Nevada. The **Sands Casino** was the first of the new breed to start operations – a gilded edifice that rather blighted the view from the neighbouring Mandarin Oriental's pool. The Greek Mythology Casino gave a totally new face to the previously slightly humdrum island of Taipa, and American mogul Steve Wynn (who had some sensible things to say about the prevalence of loan sharking in Macau) has grand schemes for his own Asian casino. He's not the only one. It's proposed to add 20 more casinos on **Cotai** – a stretch of reclaimed land between Taipa and Coloane – as well as accompanying malls and hotels. Revenues have grown by more than 30 percent in the past three years. Las Vegas, currently considered the number one gaming city in the world, made US$5.3 billion in 2004, but Macau wasn't far behind with US$5 billion.

Other changes on the entertainment scene might not be such money-spinners but they are certainly impressive. In the Outer Harbour area, the HK$1.2 billion **Fisherman's Wharf** is an ambitious conglomeration of food courts, fun fair, convention centre, retail outlets, an amphitheatre and a marina. Meanwhile, the completion of **Ponte 16** – a cultural theme park in the Inner Harbour – is likely at some point in 2006.

The historic centre

The best place to start any foray into old Macau is the **Largo do Senado** ❶ (Senate Square), the old city's main square covering some 3,700 square metres (4,425 sq. yds), which has been repaved with a bold Portuguese wave-pattern mosaic. A handy **tourist information centre** is situated right on the square (open 9am–6pm daily).

Across the main road (Almeida Ribeiro) is the **Leal Senado** ❷ (Loyal Senate) building, regarded by most as the best example of Portuguese architecture in Macau. It now houses the Institute of Civil and Municipal Affairs. The Leal Senado was dedicated in 1784 and its facade completed in 1876. It was restored in 1939, with further internal restoration completed in the late 20th century. The title "Loyal" was bestowed on Macau's Senate in 1809 by Portuguese King John VI, who was Prince Regent at the time, as a reward for continuing to fly the Portuguese flag when the Spanish monarchy took over the Portuguese throne in the 17th century. An inscribed tablet

Map on page 172

Fast, frequent jetfoils link Macau with Hong Kong in just one hour.

BELOW: the facade of the Leal Senado.

The magnificent facade of São Paulo (St Paul's) is probably Macau's best-known landmark.

here, dating from 1654, grants Macau its sacred title: "City of the Name of God, Macau, There is None More Loyal." Head up the staircase to the fine wrought-iron doors and beyond to a small courtyard with *azulejos* tiles. Up more stairs, the library (open Mon–Fri 1–7pm) and council chamber show fine examples of Old World woodwork. Half the offices on the ground floor have been converted into a gallery for special exhibitions.

There are three churches of note in the vicinity. Back on the main square and opposite the tourist office is the white church of **Santa Casa da Misericórdia** ❸ with its small museum of religious artefacts. At the northern end of the square is **São Domingos** ❹ (St Dominic's), one of the oldest of Macau's churches. It dates from the 17th century, but the Spanish Dominicans built a chapel and convent on this site as early as 1588. At the back is another museum of ecclesiastical relics. Nearby to the north is the **Sé** ❺ (Macau Cathedral). It was declared the mother church of the Macau diocese in 1850, which then

included all of China, Japan and Korea. The stained-glass windows are the main attraction of this rather plain building.

From São Domingos follow the pavement north along one of Macau's main shopping streets before turning uphill to the ruins of **São Paulo** ❻ (St Paul's; open access). Its towering facade and impressive grand staircase are the most striking of all Macau's churches. Historians often cite it as the finest monument to Christianity in Asia. Unfortunately, the site must have bad feng shui. The first church on the site was destroyed by fire in 1601, and construction of a new one began the following year. The present classical facade was crafted by Japanese christians who had fled persecution in Nagasaki. In 1835 another fire destroyed São Paulo, the adjacent college and a library reputed to be the best east of Istanbul. In 1904, efforts were made to rebuild the church, but little progress was achieved. Still, today the grand facade of São Paulo remains as Macau's most enduring icon.

Map on page 172

Overlooking the facade of São Paulo are the massive stone walls of the **Fortaleza do Monte** ❼ (open Tues–Sun 10am–6pm; free), simply called **Monte Fort**, built in the early 1600s. When Dutch ships attacked and invaded Macau in 1622, the half-completed fortress was defended by 150 clerics and African slaves. A lucky cannon shot by an Italian Jesuit, Geronimo Rhu, hit the powder magazine of the Dutch fleet's flagship and saved the city. In 1998 the **Museum of Macau** (open Tues–Sun 10am–6pm; entrance fee, except on 15th of every month) was opened on the site of the fortress. The lively and well-captioned exhibits chart the history of the enclave and its citizens, from its first settlement through to the handover to the Chinese.

A short stroll to the west will take you to picturesque **Camões Grotto and Garden** ❽, where Luís de Camões, the celebrated Portuguese soldier-poet, is said to have composed part of the national epic, *Os Lusiadas* (The Lusiads). A bronze bust of Camões rests in the garden's grotto. Above the grotto is an observatory built by a French explorer, Count de La Pérouse.

South of Largo do Senado

Many of Macau's best historical sights lie south of Largo do Senado, across Avenida de Almeida Ribeiro, in a string all the way to the southern tip of the peninsula. The first of these is **Santo Agostinho** ❾ (St Augustine). The baroque-style church of St Augustine is the largest in the region. Spanish Augustinians founded a church here in 1586, but the present structure dates from 1814, and its ornate facade from 1875. Across the small picturesque square (Largo de Santo Agostinho) sits the exquisite **Dom Pedro V Theatre** ❿. The renovated 18th-century building is now closed to the public, but it was once the residence of the president of the select committee of the East India Company, that for centuries wielded enormous power from India to the South China Sea. The fully restored theatre has 350 seats.

St Joseph's Seminary ⓫ was dedicated in 1728, and its sole

17th-century cannons overlook the city from the battlements of the Fortaleza do Monte.

BELOW: Portuguese youth at play.

purpose was to establish Jesuit missions in China, a task it performed with gusto. Today its vast halls, classrooms and living quarters have mostly disappeared, but its architecture and sculptures are worth viewing, and its beautiful chapel is open to the public. The mid-18th-century church of St Joseph's is reached through the seminary, or through the street if the front door is open. The church protects a sacred relic – a 13-centimetre-long (6-in) piece of bone from the left arm of St Francis (some ardent Catholics believe this protects the city from natural disasters). The statues in the lovely chapel were salvaged from São Paulo in 1835.

A little further south, the imposing pale-yellow church of **São Lourenço** ⓬ (St Lawrence's) is raised up above street level and surrounded by a small garden. The church was originally built in the 1560s of wood, rebuilt in 1618 and finally reconstructed with stone in 1803. It was later rebuilt in 1846, and then again in 1892. It is one of the most elegant of Macau's reli-gious edifices and is open to the public. The grand double staircase leading up from the street, iron gates, towers and crystal chandeliers are European, but the roof is made of Chinese tiles. It overlooks the pastel-pink government buildings.

The steep hill near the southern end of the peninsula is **Colina da Penha** ⓭ (Penha Hill), topped by the magnificent **Bishop's Palace** ⓮, unoccupied for many years now but partly open to the public. From one vantage point, it's still possible to see across the old city to Macau's Inner Harbour (Porto Interior), and less than a kilometre further, mainland China. The Palace – larger than anything similar in the Far East outside the Philippines – was, at one stage in early Eurasian history, the seat of Roman Catholicism in Asia. Macau was also the training and publishing centre for Roman Catholic missionary work in this part of the world.

One of Macau's favourite old haunts, the Bela Vista ("nice view") Hotel, closed in 1999 to make way for the new Portuguese consulate. Completely rebuilt in the early 1990s, the eight-suite inn, a gem of colonial architecture, was considered to be one of Asia's finest.

No sojourn to Macau would be complete without a visit to **Temple da Deusa A-Ma** ⓯ (A-Ma Temple). The temple squats beneath Barra Hill, at the entrance to Macau's Inner Harbour. It is the oldest temple in the territory, said to date back 600 years to the Ming dynasty. It was certainly there in 1557, when Macau was ceded to Portugal. The original temple was believed to have been erected by fishermen from southeast China and dedicated to Tin Hau, the patron goddess of fishermen and called A-Ma in Macau. It was then called Ma Kok Miu (Ma Point Temple). The Chinese named the area A-Ma-Gao,

TIP

Macau's churches, temples and parks are generally open to the public with no entrance fee.

BELOW: typical colonial architecture.

or the Bay of A-Ma. The oldest surviving part of this temple is a lower pavilion to the right of its entrance. There is a coloured, bas-relief stone carving here said to be a rendering of a Chinese junk that carried the goddess A-Ma from Fujian province through typhoon-ravaged seas to Macau, where she walked to the top of Barra Hill and ascended to heaven. Near the Temple is the **Maritime Museum** ⓰ (open Weds–Mon 10am–5.30pm; entrance fee, but free on Sun), with displays tracing the history of shipping in the South China Sea. Next to the museum you can jump on a motorised Chinese junk for half-hourly tours of Macau's Inner and Outer harbours.

The impressive walls of the old **Fortaleza da Barra** ⓱ (Fortress of Barra) rise far above the avenue guarding the entrance to Macau's Inner Harbour. At a gap in the rampart, a cannon and crimson awning mark the entrance to the Pousada de São Tiago, a luxury hotel nestled within the walls of the old fortress. Furnishings and fixtures imported from Portugal grace this desirable 22-room inn.

To get up to the Pousada, pass through large hand-carved wooden doors into a cave-like staircase chiselled out of the thick stone walls. Water cascading down the back wall adds to its mystery as you turn up a second flight of stairs. A picturesque café and bar with a tree-shaded open-air terrace rim the top of the old fort walls and complete the panorama. The Pousada's white stucco walls and red tiled roofs are terraced into the hillside and rise up another two levels. Even the fort's chapel has been preserved much as it was when Portuguese defenders were fighting off the Dutch.

Macau's most prominent tourist attraction, at odds with its history-steeped churches and temples, is the

338-metre (1,110-ft) **Macau Tower**, a concrete totem on the tip of the artificial lakes. Take the lift to the **observation deck** (open daily 10am–9pm; entrance fee) for 360-degree views of Macau, and look through its glass floors (not recommended for vertigo sufferers). Thrill-seekers can "skywalk" around the edge of the platform, or ascend all the way to the top of the mast. Next door's Convention and Entertainment Centre houses some souvenir shops, nice restaurants and a 500-seat cinema/theatre.

North and east Macau

Near the southern foot of Colina de Mong-Ha sits **Kun Iam Temple** ⓲, dedicated to Guanyin, the Buddhist Goddess of Mercy. Some small temples in this complex are dedicated to A-Ma. The present temple dates back to 1627 and was built on the site of an earlier 14th-century temple. Foreign visitors, particularly Americans, will be interested to know that on a table in this temple's courtyard the first Sino-American Treaty was signed in 1844 by Ki Ying, China's

Map on page 172

The Macau Grand Prix race is the biggest event in Macau. The race starts in front of the Lisboa Hotel and winds its way through 6 kilometres (4 miles) of city streets. The two-day event is on the third weekend in November.

BELOW: old-fashioned barber shop.

The bronze Kun Iam statue on the NAPE waterfront.

BELOW:
Stanley Ho (fourth from left) has for years been the main figure in Macau's lucrative gambling industry.

viceroy in Guangzhou, and Caleb Cushing, who was the United States' "Commissioner and Envoy Extraordinary and Minister Plenipotentiary" to China.

On the other side of the hills is the quaint **Lin Fung Miu** ⑲ (Lotus Temple), built in 1592. In the old days it served as a guest house for mandarins travelling between Macau and Guangzhou. Its most recent restoration was in 1980, and it is an excellent example of classical Buddhist architecture. Clay friezes over its entrances are some of the best examples of Buddhist art in the region. Beautifully garbed in silk robes and an opulent headdress, an image of the sea goddess Tin Hau stands tall over the main altar.

The Macau Special Administrative Region's border gate with mainland China, **Portas do Cerco** ⑳, was built in 1870. Not many years ago, the gate was closed to all foreigners (though Chinese passed through it in both directions daily) and visitors were forbidden to photograph it. Today the gate is open from early morning to mid-

night, accommodating people going between Macau and Zhuhai *(see page 193)*. Protecting the other approach to the city is the Fortress of Mong-Ha, on Colina de Mong-Ha, constructed to provide a defence vantage to guard the Portas do Cerco. Built in 1849, the fort's barracks now hold a 24-room *pousada* for official visitors, as well as a hotel-and-tourism training school.

Most tours make a quick visit to the **Dr Sun Yat-sen Memorial House** ㉑ (open Weds–Mon 10am– 5pm; free). Sun Yat-sen, the father of modern China, is revered in both Beijing and Taipei. The memorial is near the Kiang Vu Hospital where he practised medicine. (He was one of the first Western-trained Chinese doctors in this area. His birthplace is across the Chinese border, in Zhongshan.) The memorial is not as old as you might expect – in the 1930s it was used as an explosives depot until it accidentally blew up. The present structure was built near the original monument site. Close by is one of the best gardens in Macau:

Lou Lim Ioc ㉒, beautifully built in the Suzhou style. Its walks twist amid miniature ornamental mountains, resembling a classical landscape painting.

Colina da Guia rises east of the Sun Yat-sen memorial and Lou Lim Ioc, and is home to the **Guia Fortress and Lighthouse** ㉓ (open daily 9am–5pm; free), which is one of Macau's landmarks. This 17th century Western-style lighthouse – the oldest on the Chinese coast – stands atop Colina da Guia and used to guard coastal approaches. It is the highest point in Macau. Besides the views, there is a small art gallery. A **cable-car** links the hilltop with Flora Garden below (7am–6pm).

To the south of the Avenida da Amizade lies a rectangle of reclaimed land that is one of the most up-and-coming areas in Macau. Known as the NAPE, the area is home to the huge **Sands Casino** ㉔, the new development of Fisherman's Wharf, and a growing number of restaurants and bars. The state-of-the-art **Macau Cultural Centre** ㉕ is located at the junction

of Avenida Man Sing Hai and Avenida Dr Sun Yat-sen. It comprises the Auditorium Building, several gallery spaces, a conference hall, dance and music studios, a restaurant and a five-storey **Art Museum** ㉖ (open Tues–Sun 10am–5pm; entrance fee), which houses a permanent collection of over 3,000 works. Along the seafront towards the Macau–Taipa Bridge is one of Macau's nightlife zones, with a range of close-knit bars, cafés and restaurants where you can drink, dance and eat till the wee hours. The waterfront nearby is marked by the beautiful bronze **statue of Kun Iam**, designed and crafted by Portuguese artist, Christina Reiria. The dome under her feet holds a small meditation centre and Buddhist library.

Taipa and Coloane

The "other" Macau is not on the peninsula that is generally regarded as Macau, but consists of the two outlying islands of Taipa and Coloane. Many years ago, access to these islands was by small ferry

TIP

The casinos of Macau maintain a dress code that is more permissive for women than for men. For example, men may not wear shorts, while women are allowed to do so. Neither sex, however, can wear flip-flops.

BELOW: the new Macau–Taipa Bridge, with the Macau Tower in the background.

Map
on page
172

The swimming pool at the Grand Hyatt Hotel on Taipa.

BELOW:
Coloane Village.

boats that, in the case of Coloane, could only approach at high tide. Today, both are connected to Macau proper by a series of bridges and causeways, served by lumbering buses and taxis that are not quite in sync with Macau's much-vaunted up-and-coming modernity.

Taipa ㉗ has a number of high-rises, relieving some of the pressure on congested Macau. The island has historically been a centre for junk-building and firecracker manufacture, and in the early 1700s became the busy centre for Western trade with China when an imperial edict banned English and French ships from Guangzhou, insisting they moor at Taipa instead.

The Portuguese ambience persists in a few places today, notably along the **Avenida da Praia**, the former (pre-reclamation) waterfront, which rivals its larger and more famous predecessor on the Macau peninsula for beauty. Five old houses, painted mint-green, have been beautifully restored and converted to a string of three museums, a small art gallery and a civic

meeting hall. You can poke around the **Taipa House Museum** (open Tues–Sun 9.30am–5pm; entrance fee), the best of the museums, stocked with period furniture.

New casinos on Taipa have already given the economy a substantial boost, and in time the island is set to become a major entertainment hub. A large reclamation project around the old causeway linking Taipa and Coloane is being developed. Known as Cotai, it will eventually house numerous casinos and other "entertainment centres".

Coloane ㉘ is almost twice as big as Taipa, and is popular for its beaches, golf course (next to the Westin Hotel) and restaurants, including the superb *Fernando's* on **Hac Sa beach**, where lunches rarely finish before dusk. The island's hilltops have been given over to a Qing-dynasty-style cultural complex called **A-Ma Village**, devoted to the goddess A-Ma (aka Tin Hau) and complete with drum and bell towers, museum and carved marble altar, which are approached via a staircase carved with auspicious mythical beasts. The complex is surrounded by a park complete with picnic areas, fishing zones and a hiking trail.

One of Coloane's beaches, **Kao Ho**, is the site for Macau's deep-water port. Situated on the northern end of the island, Kao Ho was once a traditional haven for South China Sea pirates. Most of the islanders supported piracy, a major source of livelihood. But one day the pirates overstepped their watery bounds. After a mass kidnapping of Chinese children from Guangzhou, and a subsequent refusal of outrageous ransom demands by Coloane's buccaneers, Portuguese authorities went after the pirates and defeated them in a two-day battle, in 1910. A memorial to this incident is set into a tiny square in front of the **Chapel of St Francis Xavier**. ❏

RESTAURANTS

Portuguese

A Lorcha
289 Rua Almirante Sérgio,
Macau. Tel: 313 193. Open:
L & D Weds–Mon. **$**
One of the best of
Macau's Portuguese
restaurants serving pork
with clams, *feijoda* (pork-
and-bean stew) and
seafood rice.

Bolo de Arroz
11 Travessa de Sao
Domingos, Macau. Tel: 339
089. Open: L & D daily. **$**
Small pastry shop with a
mezzanine dining area
serving moreish straight-
from-the-oven custard
tarts, well-made
espresso and a range of
European cakes and pas-
tries. Well worth seeking
out as a refuge from the
heat and the crowds in
Leal Senado and around
the ruins of St Paul's.

Clube Militar de Macau
Avenida de Praia Grande
975, Macau. Tel: 714 009
Open: L & D daily. **$$**
Set in an attractive build-
ing dating from 1870,
when it functioned as an
officer's mess, the Clube
Militar is graciously
decorated, furnished with
authenticity,and conserv-
atively managed. It still
attracts the cream of the
city's Portuguese and
Macanese society. The
food is truly Portuguese,
as is the chef, and the
wine list is above
average. Terrific value.

Fernando's
9 Praia Hac Sa, Coloane
Tel: 882 531. Open: L & D
daily. **$$**
Every weekend, and on
many weekdays, scores
of diners queue for
tables at this beachfront
institution on the south-
ern tip of Coloane Island.
Crispy African chicken,
prawns in clam sauce
and casseroled crab are
all excellent, and even
the salad is exceptional.
Portuguese wine is rea-
sonably priced.

Flamingo
Hyatt Regency Hotel, 2
Estrada Almirante Marques
Esparteiro, Taipa Island.
Tel: 831 234 ext. 1874.
Open: L & D daily. **$$$**
The monolithic facade of
the Hyatt Regency Hotel
hides this verdant jewel of
a restaurant with
eyebrow-arching design
and a dining room that
seems to hang in a tropi-
cal jungle. The menu fea-
tures great African
chicken, *bacalhao* (salt
cod) and tamarind duck.

Nga Tim Café
Rua Caetano No. 8, Coloane
Village, Coloane. Tel: 882
086. Open: L & D daily. **$$**
A charming alfresco café
on the corner, Nga Tim
fills up fast and satisfies
its many regular cus-
tomers with a straightforward menu of
Portuguese and
Macanese classics.

French

Robuchon A Galera
3/F Hotel Lisboa, 2 Avenida
de Lisboa, Macau. Tel: 577
666. Open: **$$$$**
Joel Robuchon, lauded by
the Parisian media as
"chef of the century",
rather eccentrically
chose the Lisboa Hotel
as the location for his
only establishment out-
side France. Regarded as
among the best restau-
rants in Asia. Fiendishly
expensive for dinner;
good value for lunch.

Italian

Pizzeria Toscana
1/F Grand Prix Stand,
Avenida da Amizade. Tel: 726
637. Open: L & D daily. **$$**
Located in an unprepos-
sessing low-rise block
within walking distance of

the Macau–Hong Kong
ferry pier, Pizzeria
Toscana is a surprise
because the food is so
good. Many of the Italian
ingredients are flown in,
and the chef knows how
to deal with them cor-
rectly. Great for coffee
and a snack or an
impromptu lunch.

● *For recommended bars
in Macau, see page 220.*

PRICE CATEGORIES

Prices are for a three-
course dinner per person
with one beer or glass of
house wine:
$ = under MOP$150
$$ = MOP$150–300
$$$ = MOP$300–500
$$$$ = over MOP$500

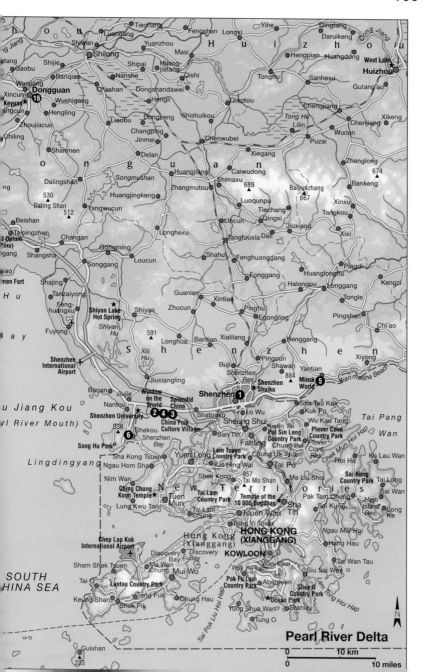

Pearl River Delta

Shenzhen and the Pearl River Delta

Just over the border from Hong Kong, the booming city of Shenzhen and the Pearl River Delta region are spearheading China's remarkable economic growth

The past decade's stupendous growth in the Pearl River Delta – with the Special Economic Zone (SEZ) of Shenzhen playing poster boy – is only the beginning of the story. It's just going to go on getting bigger. Some commentators are already speaking of the Pearl River Super Zone, comparing it to Chicago and Manchester in their manufacturing heyday.

Occupying around 40,000 square kilometres (15,500 sq. miles) from Jiangmen along the coast to Huizhou and running inland as far as Guangzhou and Zhaoqing, the Delta is home to more than 40 million people, with population levels forecast to rise as high as 70 million in the next 15 years. In 2002 the region, including Macau and Hong Kong, recorded a GDP of US$281 billion, compared with US$1,265 billion for the whole of China.

The Delta's transfiguration from paddy fields to stocks and shares deals, described by *The Economist* magazine as "so huge as to transform global trading patterns and investment flows", started in 1992. The then paramount leader Deng Xiaoping toured China's southern provinces, passing on the message that to get rich was glorious. SEZs with looser regulations and taxation started up in Shenzhen and Zhuhai shortly after. Investors from Taiwan and Hong Kong hurtled in, putting their international marketing savvy to prime use, to be swiftly imitated by their mainland counterparts. By 2002 the Delta's gross industrial output had reached US$194 billion annually, while exports had topped US$314 billion every year.

Shenzhen and environs

Shenzhen ❶, slap bang next to the Hong Kong border, was always going to do well. This is the new

Map on pages 184–5

PRECEDING PAGES: in the heart of Shenzhen's shopping district.
LEFT: the city is growing at an incredible rate.
BELOW: Deng Xiaoping made Shenzhen China's first Special Economic Zone.

TIP

The new Shenzhen subway links the city centre with the theme parks. Tickets are cheap, with fares ranging from rmb 2 to 5. Trains, however, are infrequent – roughly every 15 mins. There are also plenty of taxis, as well as buses, either from the bus station past Lo Wu Commercial City shopping mall at the border, or from a stop along Jianhe Lu, the main street leading north from Lo Wu.

BELOW: sightseeing at the Window on the World theme park.

face of the PRC, where capitalism has been given pretty much a free hand after decades of communism. Nowadays its Mission Hills Golf Club, which embraces ten 18-hole championship courses (designed with help from the likes of Jack Nicklaus, Nick Faldo and Vijay Singh) stands in the *Guinness World Records* as the world's largest. Shun Hing Square, some 384 metres (1,260 ft) tall, is the eighth highest building in the world. Yet at the end of the 1980s, there was little here except for a farming community.

Shenzhen airport now handles an increasing number of international and domestic flights, migrant workers flock here by the thousand, construction proceeds nearly everywhere you look. And as a firm indicator of the way the winds of change are blowing, a 2005 survey by Global Entrepreneurship Monitor of the world's most progressive cities ranked Shenzhen 10th in the elite 35, with Hong Kong back in 33rd place.

Even resident Hong Kongers make regular trips across the border here, in search of inexpensive nightlife and recreation, not to mention the shopping bargains at the emporia where the goods are "inspired by" major fashion companies like Prada and Chanel.

In fact, it's tempting to regard Shenzhen as one enormous wacky theme park, and there's certainly no shortage of the real thing. The three main parks are clustered together in the Nanshan District, about 12 km (8 miles) west of the downtown area. There are combination tickets available should you wish to see more than one park. **Window on the World ❷** (open daily 9am–10.30pm; entrance fee) showcases facsimiles of everything from Thai palaces to Japanese teahouses – to say nothing of the Eiffel Tower.

In a rather similar vein, **Splendid China ❸** (open daily 9am–9.30pm; entrance fee) packs the whole country into one park, while the **China Folk Culture Village ❹** (open daily 9am–9.30pm; entrance fee) presents 56 different ethnic perspectives; and – from the sublime to the incredulous – **Minsk World ❺**

SHENZHEN AND THE PEARL RIVER DELTA ♦ 189

(open daily 9am–7.30pm; entrance fee), on the other side of Shenzhen, is a 40,000-tonne former Soviet aircraft carrier.

However, most people head to Shenzhen to shop. One of the most extensive retail romper rooms is the exhausting **Lo Wu Commercial City Ⓐ**, on the right after you exit the customs hall. Jewellery, clothes, leather goods, knick-knacks and a cornucopia of other merchandise are packed one atop the other here – although shops selling the same sort of items tend to cluster together. The cardinal rule is to bargain fiercely. Offer less than half of the asking price and settle for no more than half. Although everyone will take Hong Kong dollars at par, they are worth marginally more than Reminbi, so pay in Chinese currency.

Shenzhen's other main shopping areas are **Dongmen Ⓑ**, with a wide range of shops and some good tailors, and at **Huaqiang Lu Ⓒ**, where

electronics goods stores can be found. There is little difference in price compared to Hong Kong as far as mainstream electronics brands are concerned, but the bargains lie in domestically manufactured items. (For more details on Shenzhen shopping, see page 224.)

Even half a day's shopping in Shenzhen is likely to take it out of you, which is why some sort of spa treatment is a good half-time diversion. Many of the malls include massage parlours and beauty salons – painting intricate designs on toe- and finger-nails is a speciality – and they usually have a bow-tied waiter on hand to supply refreshments.

If Shenzhen appears to be pretty wild during the day, wait until the evening, when the city reverberates with cheap, raw fun. Note that this is not a place for women to party alone. There are two main areas – **Lo Wu**, near the railway station, and **Shekou Ⓒ**, a satellite town about 45 minutes

Minsk World, a former Soviet aircraft carrier turned fun day out.

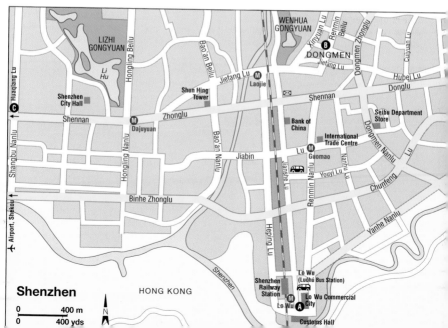

Shenzhen

HONG KONG

Shenzhen's nightlife is lively and raucous, with plenty of bars to choose from.

away by cab. Don't expect anything in the way of intimate little clubs – everything here is wild, glitzy, Las Vegas-style neon. In Shekou, there are a lot of girlie bars, but regular nightlife is also available. A new bridge is soon to link the city with Hong Kong *(see page 153).*

Around the Delta

Away from Shenzhen, there are many other burgeoning cities and townships in the Pearl River Delta. The busy city of **Foshan** ❼ lies southwest of Guangzhou, though the countryside between is fast filling up with new developments. Its smaller streets are reminiscent of an older city, home to merchants and bankers in the 19th century.

The main sight in Foshan is the **Zu Miao** ❽ (Ancestor Temple), a Daoist temple whose history dates back to the Song dynasty. Renovated in 1372, the temple houses a 2-tonne bronze statue of the northern emperor Zhenwu, the so-called water god who watched over the Zhu Jiang, which was prone to frequent flooding. The temple itself is well-pre-

served, with many finely sculptured friezes made from limestone, ash of shells, paper, rice, straw and sand. The once colourfully painted friezes depict fables and scenes of Foshan's history. Many of the friezes have faded to an antique tone, which adds to the temple's charm.

The grounds of Zu Miao are fairly spacious, with courtyards and halls displaying antique weapons, iron bells and porcelain figures. In the main courtyard, the city has set up an exhibit of old carved-stone street markers from the Qing dynasty, when the streets were so narrow that the addresses were carved horizontally into the buildings.

There are shops selling handmade crafts and porcelain souvenirs all the way to **Shiwan** ❾, about 2 kilometres (1¼ miles) to the southwest of downtown Foshan. In Shiwan there are many porcelain factories that welcome tour groups.

Southwest of Guangzhou lies **Xiqiao Shan** ❿, a hilly area with villages that have retained some of their 19th-century ambiance. Xiqiao is one of the more charming towns

BELOW:
market porcelain.

outside Guangzhou that still thrives on its local produce and river trade. From the town, one can travel by cable-car up to the crest of the nearby hills to walk along stone paths that wind through even smaller villages, rocky plateaus and waterfalls, including Feiliutian Chi which is reckoned to be the most picturesque.

Because of its proximity to the waterfalls and lakes, the eastern area of Xiqiao Shan has been built up for tourism. Further down the path from the hotel are caves and a lake at Baiyun, and a route back to the main road into Xiqiao.

To the east

In 1995, Guangdong province opened the **Grand World Scenic Park** ⓫ (open daily 9.30am–8.30pm; entrance fee) in an effort to spark local tourism. The park occupies a 480,000 square-metre (575,000 sq. yd) site to the east of Guangzhou, and seems to have been built to rival nearby Shenzhen's theme park of world sites in both scale and investment. The park features six theatres that were built as replicas of opera and music houses around the world, including examples from such disparate countries as Japan, France, England, Saudi Arabia, Greece and New York. The park strives to present festivities representing the eclecticism of 98 countries and the "landscapes of 26 countries". There are well-landscaped gardens and displays of Guangdong's horticulture within the park, as well as a variety of tacky souvenir stands and restaurants. The entrance fee is a bit steep.

Further east lies the original site of the **Huangpu Junxiao** ⓬ (Huangpu Military Academy). Zhou Enlai and other Communist Party officials were trained here; several prominent buildings constructed during the 1940s still stand. Today, the academy is a museum where one can learn about the history of the Communist Party. Unfortunately, little of the history is conveyed in English. The academy has become a must-see for mainlanders. A short distance to the south, **Yuying Shanfang** ⓭ was founded in the Qing dynasty by the successful Imperial

Map on pages 184-5

BELOW: park bench slumber.

It's possible to eat out well for just a couple of (US) dollars.

BELOW: the Pearl River Delta is a major centre for China's toy industry.

Examination candidate, Wu Yantian. It is no longer quite as bucolic as when it was first landscaped.

Accessible by both bus and boat, **Lianhua Shan** ⓮ (Lotus Mountain) lies about an hour southeast of Guangzhou on the Zhu Jiang. The mountain area was an important quarry 2,000 years ago, and today the mining caves and carved rock formations have eroded enough to take on a natural look. Lianhua Shan is officially deemed a "tourist resort", with its fair share of theme-park amusements, including a driving range, water slide, bumper cars and pricey restaurants. Fortunately, these new additions inhabit just one side of the mountain. Motorcycles will take you past this area to the top, which is capped by a pagoda built during the Ming dynasty.

Nearby, a statue erected in 1994 of Guanyin, the goddess of mercy, is made of 120 tons of bronze with pure gold plating and stands 41 metres (135 ft) high. The view from this spot takes in the extensive paddies of rice spread out below and the Zhu Jiang, or Pearl River, below that.

From the Guanyin statue, descend a long flight of steps to the mining area. Sturdy paths have been added that weave through the rocks and ponds, while Qing-dynasty inscriptions mark the various mining spots. The path will finally lead out to the original and now remote district of Lianhua, where an active temple is nestled in the lush greenery. Bamboo huts and additional cave formations give this area a truly magical feel. Exiting the park here and walking back to the boat dock you pass through a market area selling dried fish and snakes, as well as a variety of other seafood delicacies. There are many restaurants along the main road as well.

Panyu, a district to the southeast of Guangzhou, is home to the Nanhai Temple, built during the Sui dynasty (AD 580–618). Today it sits among some spacious grounds, with cultural relics housed within its walls. The city of **Nanhai** ⓯ itself is more like a Guangzhou suburb, easily reached by taxi. Excavations of Nanhai show that merchants from the Qin and Han dynasties used the

Map on pages 184-5

area as the starting point of China's emerging maritime trade, which eventually replaced the overland Silk Road in importance. Indeed, people from Guangzhou often brag about how their home town was a trading centre some 2,000 years ago, with silk, ceramics and tea as the three biggest exports for the region.

Most people who travel to **Dongguan** ⑯ do so for business reasons. Still, for those of an entrepreneurial bent, it is considered the factory headquarters of China. Indeed, Dongguan is home to one of the world's largest shoe factories, and stands as a city that has made a name for itself in the world.

Two decades ago you could have driven – assuming the road was passable – past Dongguan without realising it was there. Today the agglomeration of information technology firms clustered around the city is one of the largest on the planet. The motor industry has also descended on the region in force, with Honda, Nissan and Toyota picking Guangzhou as a base for their factories, and with a stampede

of auto-parts manufacturers from Japan following in their wake. In early 1998 it was announced that a US$25 billion, 29-km (18-mile) bridge would be built from Hong Kong across the open water to the mainland on the Macau side, no small feat. Such a bridge would open up communication considerably, and may well be up and running by 2009.

Shunde ⑰, on the road from Guangzhou to Zhuhai, is renowned for its Qing garden, and has some photogenic back lanes and canals. Further south, the large town of **Jiangmen** is eminently missable, although the Ming era villages in the surrounding countryside – centred round a two-storey watch tower – are a pleasant reminder of architectural whim in former days. Closer to Zhuhai, and on the coast, the memorial garden at **Cuiheng** pays tribute to its best-known son, Dr Sun Yat-sen, China's first republican president. **Zhuhai** ⑱ itself is the last major city before Macau, and is steadily growing in importance as a Special Economic Zone. ❏

RESTAURANTS

Cantonese

Laurel Restaurant
Shop 5010, Lo Wu Commercial City. Tel: 8232 3668. Open: L & D daily. **$**
The aim is to deliver innovative Cantonese food, and Shenzhen's dining public obviously approves. Try the marbled beef or the drunken chicken hotpot.

Other Chinese

Furong King
7 Youyi Road, Luohu District. Tel: 8217 8483.

Open: L & D daily. **$$**
Spicy, intensely flavoured cooking from Hunan province with spiced, smoked and air-dried meats.

Guo Bo Li Restaurant
Jianshu Rd (opposite Century Plaza Hotel). Tel: 8225 2827. Open: L & D daily. **$$**
The Guo Bo Li has Peking Duck plus a range of expertly prepared northern-style food on offer, with prices well below its Hong Kong counterparts.

Zhujia Zhuang
Jinbi Hotel, 3002 Chunfeng Rd, Luohu District. Tel: 2252 888. Open: L & D daily. **$$**
Yunnanese cuisine, featuring an abundance of mushrooms and "Crossing the Bridge noodles".

International

360° Restaurant
Shangri-La Hotel, 1002 Jianshe Road, Luohu District. Tel: 8396 1380.
Open: L & D daily. **$$$**
Perched on top of the Shangri-La hotel, the menu features light Western cuisine with Asian influences.

Muslim

Muslim Restaurant
2001, South Wenjing Rd, Luohu District. Tel: 8223 5466. Open: L & D daily. **$**
Good, authentic cuisine from Xinjiang province in northwest China.

● *For recommended bars, see page 220.*

● ● ● ● ● ● ● ● ● ● ● ● ●
Prices are for a typical dinner for one, with one beer or a glass of house wine.
$ = under 50 Rmb
$$ = 50–100 Rmb
$$$ = 100–150 Rmb
$$$$ = over 150 Rmb

GUANGZHOU

One of the first Chinese cities open to the outside world, Guangzhou has long had economic modernisation as its goal. Still, despite the usual urban bustle, some of old Canton remains

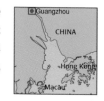

The mythical origins of booming Guangzhou (Canton) are not the most auspicious. As legend has it, five celestial beings, riding on the backs of five flying goats, landed in the southeastern coastal regions of China and founded Guangzhou.

But goats are spunky and independent, and in Guangzhou, there is a palpable sense of China's energy and of its breakneck pace in transforming itself into an international player. Guangzhou is a boisterous urban centre – one of China's most prosperous for many years now – with all the blemishes one equates with modern cities: air pollution, traffic jams, blocks of cramped housing overflowing with people, and an invigorating chaos. Around six million people live in the greater metropolitan area (the sixth largest in China).

Guangzhou ⓭ lies on the lower reaches of the **Zhu Jiang** (Pearl River). Flying goats notwithstanding, the city was probably founded in 214 BC as an encampment by the armies of the Qin emperor, Qin Shi Huangdi (221–210 BC). Initially it was called Panyu; the name Guangzhou first appeared during the period of the Three Kingdoms (222–280). During the Tang dynasty (618–906), the city was already an international port, but remained sec-

ond to Quanzhou – Marco Polo's Zaytun – for centuries. In 1514, a Portuguese flotilla reached the area. From 1757 to 1842, Guangzhou was the only Chinese port open to foreigners, and it was at the centre of the build-up to the First Opium War *(see pages 18–19)*.

The personality of Guangzhou differs significantly from that of northern China. While a visitor can stand in the middle of Tiananmen Square in Beijing and feel the solidity and backbone of Chinese author-

Map on page 196

LEFT: going shopping in Guangzhou.
BELOW: high-rise development.

River cruises along the Zhu Jiang provide alternative views of the city and its several islands. Most cruises operate in the evenings, departing from Xidi Wharf, just to the east of Shamian Island.

ity, in Guangzhou, the lack of order in the traffic and commotion is far more apparent.

Old Guangzhou

The island of **Shamian Ⓐ**, in the southwest of the city on the northern bank of the Zhu Jiang, is a preserved relic of the colonial past. Originally a sandbar, the small island was reclaimed and expanded, then divided in 1859 into several foreign concessions, primarily French and British. A canal was dug, and after ten o'clock in the evening, two iron gates and narrow bridges kept the Chinese off the island.

Shamian is compact and feels very much like a resort area, in sharp contrast to the hustle of the rest of the city. A programme of gentrification has renovated a number of old colonial buildings and nurtured restaurants and cafés, whilst former Catholic and Anglican churches have been reopened for worship. Many of the brightly painted former trade and consular buildings, most of which were constructed by the French, are now used as government offices.

To the north of Shamian Island, on the mainland along Qingping Lu, is **Qingping Shichang Ⓑ**, a market area that spills out into the side alleys around the main roads of Renmin Nan Lu and Nuren Jie. This was one of the first places to develop under China's gradual adoption of market economics and, as such, it was for a long time something of an oddity with its carnival-like atmosphere and crowds of shoppers. Today, Qingping is best known for selling every imaginable animal for food, including dogs, cats, owls and a variety of insects. Stalls lining Dishipu Lu and Daihe Lu sell jade, jewellery, old time-pieces, Mao paraphernalia and reproductions of antique porcelain.

To the east of the market is **Wenhua Gongyuan Ⓒ** (Culture

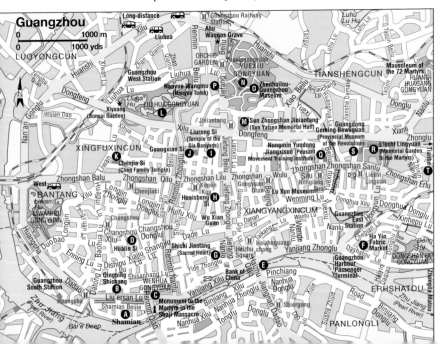

Park), with roller-skating rinks, an open-air theatre, theatre halls, art exhibitions and performances by the School of Acrobats. Nearby is the state-run Department Store of the South (sometimes called Nanfang Department Store), on the corner of Renmin Nan Lu.

To the north of this area, follow **Xiajiu Lu**, which together with **Changshou Lu** forms the centre of a lively shopping and restaurant area. Behind the Guangdong Restaurant, find a narrow side alley called Shangxia Jie that leads to **Hualin Si ❶**. This temple is said to have been founded by an Indian monk in 526, although the existing buildings date from the Qing dynasty. There are 500 statues of *luohan*, pupils of the Buddha, in the main hall.

The **Bund** (Yanjiang Lu) runs eastward along the waterfront from Shamian to **Haizhu ❸**, built in 1933 and the oldest steel bridge across the Zhu Jiang. Further along, a little way north from the Hai Yin bridge, is the **Hai Yin Fabric Market ❻** on Dong Hu Lu, one of the largest fabric mar-

kets in China. Over a thousand stalls in hundreds of rows sell wool, fine silk and locally made fabric at bargain prices.

To the northwest of Haizhu, the 50-metre (160-ft) double towers of the Catholic cathedral, **Shishi Jiaotang ❼** (Sacred Heart), are plainly visible. Built in the early 1860s, the cathedral was left to decay after 1949 before being restored in the 1980s. It now holds services under the auspices of the Patriotic Catholic Church, which the government has prohibited from contacting the Vatican.

Further north is the onion-shaped dome of **Huaisheng Si ❽**, a mosque dating back to 627 and founded by a trader who was said to be an uncle of the Prophet Mohammed. Arab traders were frequent visitors to China at the time, so the legend may well have some truth to it, although it does not give sufficient evidence for an exact date of the foundation. The 25-metre (82-ft) minaret, **Guang Ta** (Naked Pagoda), dominates the area, although high-rises are competing

A typical Chinese restaurant in Guangzhou.

BELOW: colonial architecture on Shamian Island.

Guangzhou was formerly known to Westerners as Canton. From the provincial name "Guangdong", the Portuguese somehow derived the name of Cantão. From Cantão came Canton.

to capture the skyline. Huaisheng Si is a cultural centre for Guangzhou's 5,000 Muslims.

Beyond Zhongshan Lu, a narrow street leads to **Liurong Si**  (Temple of the Six Banyan Trees; open daily 8.30am–5pm; entrance fee), with its **Hua Ta** (Flower Pagoda), built in 1097. It appears from the outside to consist of nine storeys, each storey with doorways and encircling balcony, but inside the pagoda there are actually 17 levels. Visitors can climb to the top for a view of Guangzhou's sprawling streets. The main hall contains three brass statues of the Buddha, eight *luohan* figures, statues of the god of medicine, and an image cast in 1663 of the goddess of mercy, Guanyin. Today, the temple is the local headquarters of the Chinese Buddhist Association.

Guangxiao Si (Temple of Bright Filial Piety; open daily 8.30am–5pm; entrance fee), a temple preserved during the Cultural Revolution on orders from Premier Zhou Enlai, lies a short distance to the west. The temple is believed to date back to sometime around AD 400, making it older than the city itself. Some of the present buildings were, however, built after a fire in 1629, and most probably only after 1832. The entrance is marked by a brightly painted laughing Buddha, and in the main courtyard a huge bronze incense burner fills the air with smoke. The main hall is notable for its ceiling of red-lacquered timber, and the back courtyard has some of the oldest iron pagodas in China.

The **Dongtie Ta** and **Xitie Ta** (Western and Eastern Iron Pagodas) date back to the city's earliest beginnings. There is a 7-metre (23-ft) stone pagoda behind the main hall with sculptures of the Buddha placed in eight niches. It is thought to date back to 967, but was only put in its present location at the beginning of Mongolian rule in the Yuan dynasty.

Chenjia Si (Chen Family Temple; open daily 8.30am–5.30pm; entrance fee), located on the western end of Zhongshan Lu close to the eponymous subway station, is one of China's more

whimsical temples, built in 1894 and restored after the Cultural Revolution. The temple has six courtyards and a classical Chinese layout, and is decorated with friezes crafted in Shiwan, near Foshan to the west. The largest frieze depicts scenes from the epic *Romance of Three Kingdoms*, with thousands of intricate figures against a backdrop of ornate houses, grandiose gates and pagodas. There is a giant altar of gold-leaf plating and additional wood, brick and stone friezes along the rooftops. The name recalls the descendants of the Chen clan, one of the most common family names in Guangdong province, who provided the funds to build the temple.

Chenjia Si is also home to the **Guangdong Folk Arts Museum**, which was established in 1959. The museum displays arts and crafts from all over China but especially Guangdong province. The collection includes embroidery, traditional dress of China's minority groups, porcelain figures and jade carvings. The displays are showcased in the temple's halls.

On Liu Hua Lu is **Liu Hua Gongyuan** Ⓛ (Liuhua Park), which features Guangzhou's largest artificial lake. Built as part of the government's Great Leap Forward Campaign in 1958, the park provides rowboats that take passengers around the lake to view the spacious grounds surrounding it.

Sun Yat-sen memorials

The **Sun Zhongshan Jiniantang** Ⓜ (Sun Yat-sen Memorial Hall; open daily 8am–6pm; entrance fee) is easy to spot with its eye-catching blue roof tiles. The hall, built shortly after the death of Sun Yat-sen in 1925 and completed in 1931, now houses a large theatre and lecture hall with seating for 5,000 people. The octagonal hall is made of steel and reinforced concrete, and sits in a lush 6-hectare (15-acre) park.

Guangzhou's largest park, **Yuexiu Gongyuan** Ⓝ is beautifully landscaped with three artificial lakes, rolling hills, rock sculptures and lush greenery. Its centrepiece is **Zhenhailou** Ⓞ (Tower Overlooking the Sea), built in 1380 and a

Map on page 196

Hua Ta (Flower Pagoda) at the Liurong Si (Temple of the Six Banyan Trees).

BELOW: the Sun Yat-sen Memorial Hall.

There are twelve daily trains between Guangzhou and Hung Hom Station in Kowloon. Journey time is just under two hours.

memorial to the seven great sea journeys undertaken by the eunuch admiral Zheng He to East Africa, the Persian Gulf and Java between 1405 and 1433. Today, the tower houses a **municipal museum** showcasing the history of Guangzhou (open Tues–Sun 9am–4pm; entrance fee).

Nearby is the marble and granite **Sun Yat-sen Monument**, which sits on a hill above Sun Yat-sen Hall. Visitors can climb to the top for a great view of the city. Also in Yuexiu Park is the Sculpture of Five Rams, which tells the story of five heavenly creatures who flew over the city on rams – or goats – and relieved the people of famine. Yuexiu Park has a golf driving range, bowling alley and swimming pool.

On the other side of Jiefang Bei Lu from Yuexiu Park is the **Nanyue Wangmu** **ⓟ** (Nanyue Tomb; open daily 9.30am–5pm; entrance fee), the tomb of the Nanyu emperor. In 1983, bulldozers clearing the ground for construction of the China Hotel dug up the tomb of the emperor Wen Di, who ruled southern China from 137 to 122 BC. The

spot where the tomb was found is now the site of a museum, housing the skeletons of the emperor and 15 courtiers, including concubines, guards, cooks and a musician, who were buried alive with the emperor.

The museum recreates the setting of the tomb, so that visitors can walk down stairs into the actual chambers. Archaeologists found that the tomb walls were built from sandstone carved out of Lianhua Shan, about an hour east along the Zhu Jiang. Thousands of funeral objects from jade armour to bronze music chimes are displayed in adjoining rooms. The museum also features a rare collection of porcelain pillows from the Tang and Yuan dynasties, donated by a Hong Kong collector.

Eastern districts

Guangzhou sprawls eastwards from Yuexiu Lu, a busy street which forms the approximate eastern boundary of the older part of the city.

Close to the junction of Yuexiu and Zhongshan Lu is the former Kongzi Miao, or Confucius Temple,

BELOW: unemployed at the railway station.

which lost its religious function during the "bourgeois revolution" in 1912. In 1924, **Nongmin Yundong Jiangxisuo ⓠ** (Peasant Movement Training Institute; open daily 8.30–11.30am, 2–5pm; entrance fee) was opened here as the first school of the Chinese Communist Party. The elite of the Communist Party taught here: Mao Zedong (his work and bedroom are on show), Zhou Enlai, Qu Qiubai, Deng Zhong, Guo Moruo and several others. This is also where Mao developed his original theory of peasant revolution.

After the collapse of a workers' uprising in 1927, the Communists were forced to retreat from the cities. A park and memorial, **Lieshi Lingyuan ⓡ** (Memorial Garden to the Martyrs) was created in 1957 in memory of the uprising and its nearly 6,000 victims. Nearby is the **Guangdong Geming Bowuguan ⓢ** (Provincial Museum of the Revolution; open daily 9am–5pm), a reminder of the role of the Guomintang (Nationalist Party) and its predecessors since the First Opium War.

South of Zhongshan San Lu are the old buildings of Guangdong University, where China's first modern and highly respected author, Lu Xun, lectured in 1927. A **museum** (open daily 9am–5pm; entrance fee) is dedicated to him.

In the northeast, near the zoo on Xianlie Lu, is the **Huang Huagang memorial park**, built in 1918 for the 72 victims of an uprising in 1911. The large park features monuments symbolising democracy and peace.

Guangzhou's new financial and shopping centre, **Tianhe ⓣ** lies further east. The giant Tianhe Sports Centre takes up at least five city blocks and features basketball courts, Olympic-size swimming pools, running tracks, football pitches and other sports facilities. Across the street is Team Plaza, a six-storey shopping mall that features a Japanese department store on the bottom level and expensive shops spiralling upward. Just north of the stadium is Times Square; it doesn't really compare to its namesakes in New York or even Hong Kong, but there are some good

Map on page 196

TIP

An efficient underground metro system connects most of Guangzhou's major sites of interest – look out for the red signs with the Y-shaped symbol. Tickets are inexpensive, but travellers might find it simpler and faster to take a taxi; fares are low.

BELOW: tthe Zhu Jiang (Pearl River) flows through the heart of Guangzhou

restaurants inside. High-rises, hotels and expensive restaurants continue to expand the city eastward.

Outside Guangzhou

After a few days in Guangzhou, most visitors want to escape the city for some fresh air, peace and quiet. An easy half-day trip to the north of the city leads to **Baiyun Shan** ⑳ (White Cloud Hills), a series of hills overlooking Guangzhou. To get there take a taxi or, if you feel up to it, bus no. 24 from the south side of Renmin Park – journey time is 30 minutes. A cable-car ascends to the top, where you can walk to several other peaks. Souvenir stands and teahouses are found at various peaks and precipices in the area, ideal places to sit back and take in the surrounding hills.

If you want to walk up to the peak, there is a paved road as well as stone paths that wind up through the trees. Nengren, an active Buddhist temple where many Chinese come to light incense and pray, is found half way up to the peak of **Baiyun Wanwang** (White Cloud

Evening View). There is also an old swimming pool nestled among the trees where locals escape during the summer heat.

At the base of Baiyun Shan is the garden of **Yun Tai**, with well-manicured flower beds, rock sculptures, fountains and greenhouses. If approaching Baiyun Shan from central Guangzhou, you will pass **Lu Hu**, a lake that previously supplied water for the city. Today it is better known for an expensive golf course and restaurant, although it is a nice place for a walk along the water and to relax under the cooling trees.

Two to three hours northeast of Guangzhou by long-distance bus is the town of **Conghua** ㉑ and **Conghua Wenguan**, a hot spring that has become a popular tourist destination for local and overseas Chinese. In addition to the hot spring, the area is known for its clean air and serene setting. Many long-term expats living in Guangzhou travel to Conghua to escape the city bustle and play golf. Unfortunately, expensive hotels have claimed as private property the area around the hot springs north of the

BELOW: images of rural China – paddy fields and red chillies.

city itself, so it is difficult for the traveller to meander around the aqua-green hot springs.

The land surrounding Conghua is known for its production of lychees and tea. Tour groups visit during summer and autumn, when lychees are in season. The Conghua Tea Farm also organises tours from Guangzhou.

Around 110 kilometres (70 miles) west of Guangzhou, **Zhaoqing ㉒** is known as "Little Guilin", with the same type of limestone karst formations found in Guilin, but on a much smaller scale. From Guangzhou there is a good rail service, as well as frequent air-conditioned buses from the city's long-distance bus station on Huanshi Xilu. Journey time is around 90 minutes, slightly longer by train. Minibuses operate from the west bus station on Zhongshan Balu. There are also jetfoils direct to Hong Kong (four hours).

South of the city, overlooking the river stands **Chongxi Ta**, a Ming-dynasty pagoda (open daily 8am–5pm; entrance fee). The main attraction in Zhaoqing, however, is

Qixing Yan (Seven Stars Crag), which lies to the north of the city and has been made into a large park (open daily 8am–5pm; entrance fee). The crags take their name from the legend that the small hills are actually stars that fell from the heavens. The limestone hills are fairly low, covered by greenery and surrounded by artificial lakes and modern pagodas that float over the water. There are stone paths that lead through the park and make for a pleasant walk. Each of the crags is named after what its shape symbolises – a toad, a stone house, a jade curtain. There are plenty of souvenir and refreshment stands scattered throughout the park.

Dinghu Shan, 20 kilometres (12 miles) east of Zhaoqing, is famous for a Ming-era Buddhist temple as well as many villages scattered over the mountain. Less touristy than its neighbour, Dinghu Shan offers scenic walks through lush subtropical forests, complete with babbling streams and waterfalls. To get there take a taxi or bus no. 21 from Xin Hu in Zhaoxing. ❏

Map on page 184-5

The beautiful scenery at Zhaoqing is reminiscent of Guilin

RESTAURANTS

Cantonese

Banxi
151 Long Jin Xi Lu. Tel: 8181 5777. Open: L & D daily. **$** One of three garden-style restaurants remaining in Guangzhou, the Banxi (or Panxi) consists of several linked dining rooms of differing ages with views overlooking Liwan Lake. The 100-year-old institution claims to serve over 1,000 varieties of dim sum.

Guangzhou Restaurant
2 Wen Chang Nan Road, Shangxiajiu Lu. Tel: 8138

0388. Open: L & D daily. **$$** Bustling and busy all day long. Specialities include double-boiled shark's fin soup with black chicken (much better than it sounds). Very popular with local residents for dim sum.

Snake Restaurant
41–45 Jiang Nan Lu. Tel: 8188 4498, 8188 2517. Open: L & D daily. **$$** The ground floor is a menagerie of slithering snakes corralled into cages. Upstairs, a dark dining room offers a

menu packed with lost-in-translation implausibles like "boiled snake shin with vegetable" or "fresh snake with unicorn".

Ying Hua
G/F, Victory Hotel, 53 Shamian North Street, Shamian Island. Tel: 8121 6688. Open: L & D daily. **$$** Dim sum aficionados queue early in the morning outside this highly-rated hotel restaurant.

Italian

Di Mateo
1/F, Westside, 175–181 Tianhe North Road. Tel: 8525 1300. Open: L & D daily. **$$**

Flashy Italian job, where the management has ambitions to introduce real European cuisine to the city. The menu features Italian restaurant staples like carpaccio, frittata and a range of well-prepared pasta. The dessert list features chocolate delice washed down with real espresso.

• • • • • • • • • • • •
Prices are for a typical dinner for one, with one beer or a glass of house wine.
$ = under 50 Rmb
$$ = 50–100 Rmb
$$$ = 100–150 Rmb
$$$$ = over 150 Rmb

TRANSPORT

GETTING THERE AND GETTING AROUND

GETTING THERE

By Air

Hong Kong

Hong Kong is a major international air-traffic hub for the region, handling over 35 million passengers a year. The impressive Hong Kong International Airport (HKIA) is located at Chek Lap Kok, on the northern shore of Lantau and about 34 kilometres (21 miles) from Central. The Y-shaped terminal is highly efficient. Aircraft are received at a plethora of gates; moving walkways and an Automated People Mover speed arrivals to Immigration where queues are dealt with swiftly. Suitcases are usually circling the carousel when you reach the baggage hall, and there is a large shopping mall, left-luggage office, post office, an adjacent 1,100-room hotel plus plenty of food and beverage outlets. The terminal is also dotted with other facilities, such as smoking rooms, ATMs and international communications embracing phone, fax and the Internet. Enquiry hotline: 2181 0000; www.hkairport.com.

The **Airport Express** (tel: 2881 8888) railway, which runs from right inside the terminal building, is the easiest and quickest way to get into town – trains reach Hong Kong Island in just 23 minutes, with stops at Tsing Yi and Kowloon stations. Single fares cost HK$90–100, returns HK$160–180. (Free shuttle buses operate between Airport Express stations and nearby hotels.)

Numerous **buses** link the airport with the city. Airbus services (prefixed "A") run at regular intervals to Hong Kong Island, Kowloon and the New Territories, and most run from 6am to midnight. The fare to Central is around HK$35. Slower "commuter" buses (prefixed "E") also run at similar times. There are also night buses, and shuttle buses to Tung Chung MTR station.

The **taxi fare** to Kowloon will work out at about HK$270, and about HK$340 to Hong Kong Island. There are direct **ferry services** from the airport to Macau and Shenzhen, as well as a fleet of **buses to destinations in Guangdong**.

Other airports

Macau International Airport (for enquiries tel: 598 8888, or see www.macau-airport.gov.mo) provides a convenient gateway for travellers from many points in Asia. The airport is on the east side of Taipa Island and is linked by bridges to the downtown area. It takes less than 30 minutes to get from the airport to anywhere in Macau. Taxi fares are about 40 Patacas (written as MOP$40). The regular AP1 bus, which serves major hotels, the Ferry Terminal and the border gate. The fare is MOP$3.30.

Shenzhen also has an airport, Shenzhen Baoan International Airport (www.szairport.com/eng), but it is not (yet) a major port of entry into China. If you are planning onward travel to other mainland cities, it is cheaper to fly from Shenzhen than from Hong Kong. The airport is linked to Hong Kong by a ferry and bus service, and is situated north-west of the city on the Delta coast.

Guangzhou's new Baiyun International Airport, which opened in August 2004, is 28 kilometres (18 miles) and a 45-minute drive from downtown. There are international flights from Guangzhou to various Asian cities as well as Los Angeles, Melbourne and Sydney, and domestic flights to most large Chinese cities. For flight information, tel: 020-3606 6999, www.gahco.com.cn/index_e.htm. Buses and taxis shuttle passengers to and from the airport. Expect to pay around RMB110 by taxi.

See page 208 for details on public transport in Macau, Shenzhen and Guangzhou.

AIRLINE OFFICES IN HONG KONG

Air Canada
Rm 1612, Tower 1, New World Tower, 18 Queen's Rd Central. Tel: 2867 8111. www.aircanada.ca

Air China
2/F CNAC Group Building, 10 Queen's Rd Central. tel: 3102 3030. www.airchina.com.cn/en/

Air New Zealand
17/F Jardine House, 1 Connaught Rd, Central. Tel: 2862 8988. www.airnz.co.nz

American Airlines
10/F Peninsula Office Tower, 18 Middle Rd, Tsim Sha Tsui. Tel: 2826 9269. www.aa.com

Asiana Airlines
34/F The Landmark, Central. Tel: 2523 8585. www.flyasiana.com

British Airways
24/F Jardine House, Central. Tel: 2822 9000. www.ba.com

Cathay Pacific Airways
10/F Peninsula Office Tower, 18 Middle Rd, Tsim Sha Tsui. Tel: 2747 1888. www.cathaypacific.com

Delta
25/F Caroline Centre, 28 Yun Ping Rd, Causeway Bay.

Tel: 2526 5875. www.delta-air.com

Dragonair
46/F Cosco Tower, 183 Queen's Rd, Sheung Wan. Tel: 3193 3888. www.dragonair.com

Emirates
11/F Henley Building, 5 Queen's Rd Central. Tel: 2526 7171. www.emirates.com

Garuda Indonesia
15/F Dah Sing Financial Centre, 108 Gloucester Rd, Causeway Bay. Tel: 2840 0000. www.garuda-indonesia.com

Gulf Air
2508 Caroline Centre, Yun Ping Rd, Causeway Bay, tel: 2769 8337. www.gulfairco.com

KLM Royal Dutch
22/F World Trade Centre, 280 Gloucester Rd, Causeway Bay. Tel: 2808 2111. www.klm.com

Korean Air
11/F Tower Two, South Seas Centre, Tsim Sha Tsui East. Tel: 2733 7111. www.koreanair.com

Lufthansa
11/F Nan Fung Tower, 173 Des Voeux Rd, Sheung Wan. Tel: 2868 2313. www.lufthansa.com

Malaysia Airlines
23/F Central Tower, 28 Queen's Rd Central. Tel: 2521 8181. www.malaysia-airlines.com

Northwest Airlines
18/F Cosco Tower, 183 Queen's Rd, Sheung Wan. Tel: 2810 4288. www.nwa.com

Qantas Airways
24/F Jardine House, Central. Tel: 2842 1438. www.qantas.com

Singapore Airlines
17/F United Centre, 95 Queensway, Admiralty. Tel: 2520 2233 (res.); 2216 1088 (flight info.). www.singaporeair.com

Sri Lankan Airlines
27/F Tower One, Lippo Centre, Admiralty. Tel: 2521 0708. www.srilankan.lk

Thai Airways International
24/F United Centre, Admiralty. Tel: 2876 6888 (res.); 2769 7421 (flight info.). www.thaiair.com

Virgin Atlantic Airways
18/F Alexander House, 15–20 Chater Rd, Central. Tel: 2532 3030. www.virgin-atlantic.com

GETTING AROUND

Although the dense high-rise jungles of Hong Kong and the bright neon signs exploding in electrified Chinese may at first all look daunting to the visitor, this is actually quite an easy city to get around. The highly efficient public transport system certainly helps matters.

Be aware, however, that since Hong Kong is extremely crowded, trying to navigate your way around in the rush hour may prove unpleasant – even impossible at times – for the uninitiated. Travelling at this time of day may also make you feel less than charitable towards the local population – necessity has dictated that people push in to get onto buses, trains and trams.

If you are waiting for a taxi, don't be surprised if a nimble local resident jumps in ahead of you when one appears, even if you have been waiting on the street corner for 10 minutes. If possible, avoid taking taxis at rush hours.

Public Transport

Rail

Hong Kong has a network of fast and efficient rail systems. Tourists are most likely to use the Airport Express, MTR and KCR East Rail. All are air-conditioned and operate from around 6am until just after midnight. *For details on the Airport Express see previous page.*

The **MTR** (tel: 2881 8888) network of five interlinked lines covers the main urban areas – the north shore of Hong Kong Island, the Kowloon peninsula

and the airport link along the north shore of Lantau Island. Adult single fares range from HK$4–26.

The MTR has a direct interchange with the KCR at Kowloon Tong, although you can also walk between Mong Kok MTR and KCR stations, and the new East Tsim Sha Tsui KCR station and Tsim Sha Tsui MTR— though both require a 10-minute walk.

The **KCR** (tel: 2929 3399) runs four lines – the East Rail, West Rail, Light Rail and Ma On Shan Rail. The **East Rail** – still known simply as "the KCR" – operates from East Tsim Sha Tsui in Kowloon, past Hung Hom to the boundary with the mainland at Lo Wu. Hung Hom is also the starting point for rail journeys to mainland China. KCR fares start from HK$4.50 for an adult in ordinary class.

The **West Rail** links Nam Cheong (near Sham Shui Po) in north Kowloon with the western New Territories through Yuen Long and ending in Tuen Mun. There are interchange stations linking the line with the LRT and MTR. Adult single fares start from HK$4.

The **Light Rail** (LRT) runs between Yuen Long and Tuen Mun. Fares start at HK$4.50. The new **Ma On Shan Rail** (tel: 2929 3399) branches out from the East Rail at Tai Wai (just south of Shatin) and runs to Wu Kai Sha facing Tolo Harbour in the eastern New Territories. Fares start at HK$3.50.

Ferries

The 12-strong Star Ferry fleet crosses the harbour between Central and Wan Chai on Hong Kong Island and Kowloon side from 6.30am–11.30pm every day. There are also routes from Hung Hom to both Central and Wan Chai. As fares for the upper deck on the main Central to Tsui Sha

Tsui route are only HK$2.20 (lower HK$1.70), this ranks as one of the world's great sightseeing bargains. Departures are every 6–12 minutes depending on the time of day, and the journey takes about eight minutes Central–Tsim Sha Tsui, and around 15 minutes Wan Chai–Tsim Sha Tsui.

Both fast and ordinary ferries to the outlying islands – Lamma, Lantau (including a 24-hour service to Discovery Bay), Cheung Chau and Peng Chau – leave from the piers to the north of the Airport Express station on Hong Kong Island. Fares start from HK$11. Fast ferries cost more. For more information on Hong Kong's ferries, contact the HKTB, tel: 2508 1234.

Buses

Six different bus companies provide services in Hong Kong, covering all the major areas as well as speedy connections to and from the airport. Routes are reduced at night. Fares range

from HK$1.20 for short journeys in the city to HK$45 for longer trips into the New Territories. Final destinations are marked in English and Chinese on the front top panel. Drivers rarely speak much English, but timetables and route maps are posted at bus stops. Exact change is needed, or use an Octopus Card (see panel below).

Enquiries: Citybus (tel: 2873 0818) and New World First Bus (tel: 2136 8888), which run on Hong Kong Island, Kowloon and the New Territories; Kowloon Motor Bus (KMB; tel: 2745 4466); Long Win Bus Co. (tel: 2261 2791), which serves the airport; Discovery Bay Transportation Services (tel: 2987 0208) and the New Lantao Bus Co. (tel: 2984 9848) on Lantau island.

Minibuses/Maxicabs

These 16-seater passenger vans, coloured cream with either a red or green side-stripe, run on fixed routes but will stop anywhere except on double yellow lines. They are usually faster than regular buses, but not as cheap. Destinations are usually written in English at the front of the van. Call out clearly when you want the driver to stop. Fares vary from HK$1.50–20. Vans with a green stripe (maxicabs) take Octopus Cards or exact change only. Those with a red stripe do not take Octopus Cards but will give change.

Taxis

It is usually easy to hail a taxi on the street, although at busy times you may need to join a queue at a taxi rank – best at a hotel. Taxis in Hong Kong and Kowloon are coloured red and in theory can take you anywhere in the territory apart from non-airport destinations on Lantau. However, sometimes you will come across taxis on Hong Kong Island which are so-called "Kowloon taxis": otherwise identical, these will only take passengers across to Kowloon. Green taxis operate in the New Territories, and blue cabs on

Lantau Island. All taxis can carry passengers between the airport and the rest of Hong Kong.

Initial fare in red taxis is HK$15, HK$12.50 for green, and HK$12 for blue cabs. There are additional charges for heavy luggage, animals and travelling via tunnels, which are all posted inside the taxi. Passengers must wear a seat-belt (when available) whether sitting in the front or rear.

Many taxi drivers can speak some English and know the main hotels and tourist spots in Hong Kong, but can at times become linguistically and geographically challenged. To avoid problems, take your destination written down in Chinese. If you encounter difficulties, all cabs are equipped with a radio telephone and somebody at the control centre should be able to translate.

Taking foreigners for a ride by a circuitous route is not unknown, and drivers will sometimes refuse a fare, usually if the journey will take them out of their way as they are about to finish

STREET SIGNS

All street signs are in both English and Chinese. Hong Kong street maps usually have both English- and Chinese-language sections in the back to make it easier to find your destination. Be aware that while sometimes the English name of a street or district is a transliteration of the Chinese, at other times the Chinese name is totally different and seemingly bears no relation to the English name.

work. You may call a police officer or phone the complaint hotline, tel: 2527 7177, but to save time it is probably better to walk off and find another taxi. If you lose something in a taxi you can call 1872 920 to try and trace it. You will need to pay a charge for them to search for you whether or not you get your belongings back.

REGIONAL TRANSPORT

By Rail

Guangzhou–Hong Kong

Twelve daily trains link Guangzhou's East Railway Station and Hunghom station in Kowloon. Travelling time is just under 2 hours. There is also a daily train between Foshan and Hong Kong via Guangzhou, with a traveling time of just over 2 hours.

In Guangzhou, away from the station itself, most hotels and the CTS (China Travel Service) office can help with train tickets. In Hong Kong, tickets can be purchased through travel agents, hotels, CTS offices and at Hunghom railway station (tel: 2947 7888). If tickets to Guangzhou are sold out, take the Kowloon–Canton Railway (KCR) to the border terminus of Lo Wu (a short 40-minute journey, with departures roughly every 10 minutes). The Shenzhen station is a few minutes walk across the border.

There are dozens of trains daily between Shenzhen and Guangzhou. Travelling time is two hours. Trains arrive in Guangzhou either at the central station or at Guangzhou East Railway Station (Guangzhou Dong), in Tianhe, a 30-minute taxi ride from the city centre.

All trains between Kowloon and Guangzhou are air-conditioned, but not all between Shenzhen and Guangzhou offer this service. Ask for the air-con class when buying a ticket – this will probably prove worth the extra money when temperatures soar in summer.

By Boat

Hong Kong–Macau

There are numerous ways to travel from Hong Kong to Macau by sea. Fares for sea crossings vary between services and the

TRAMS

A picturesque and extremely inexpensive way to get around on Hong Kong Island is by tram. Trams run across the north of Hong Kong Island west and east. Tram stops are frequent and you can simply hop on and off as you please. The flat fare is HK$2, or $1 for under-12s and over 65s (exact change required or use an Octopus Card), and the service operates between 6am and 1am. Sit on the top deck for the best views (see also page 97).

The **Peak Tram** is actually a funicular railway and has been running since 1888. It takes eight minutes to reach the upper terminus from the terminus on Garden Road, Central.

Trams run every 15 minutes, between 7am and midnight daily. The fare is $20 one-way, $30 return (Octopus Cards valid).

class of ticket, the time of the day, and the day of the week you travel. First Ferry runs its high-speed catamarans from the China Ferry Terminal in Tsim Sha Tsui. Turbojet services are slightly more expensive and more frequent, and they leave from the Macau Ferry Terminal in Sheung Wan. Tickets generally cost between HK$135 and HK$175 for economy class one-way. For the most up-to-date information on fares, check with the company providing the service or the Hong Kong offices of the Macau Government Tourist Office, tel: 2857 2287; www.macautourism.gov.mo

It is wise to buy your return ticket in advance, especially if you are travelling at the weekend or during a public holiday as tickets can get sold out. Baggage is limited to 9 kg (20 lb), and there is not much space on board for large suitcases.

Turbojets carry the largest percentage of passengers between Hong Kong and Macau, and take about an hour. Refreshments are provided on board, with complimentary newspapers, coffee and tea on the first-class top deck. Departures are every 15 minutes from 7am until 1am, and then roughly one an hour. Contact Turbojet on tel: 2859 3333.

The New World First Ferry "flying cats" are two-deck catamarans that carry 400 passengers. They leave every half-hour between 7am and midnight. Contact First Ferry on tel: 2131 8181.

Hong Kong–Guangdong

Ferries ply between Hong Kong and several Guangdong cities including Zhuhai, Shekou (for Shenzhen airport) and even all the way to Zhaoqing, but there is no longer a Guangzhou service. Most leave from Hong Kong's China Ferry Terminal in Tsim Sha Tsui. Tickets can be bought from the ferry pier or CTS offices.

By Helicopter

East Asia Airways and HeliExpress (www.helihongkong.com; in HK, tel: 2108 9898; in Macau, tel: 727 288) operate a **helicopter** service between Hong Kong and Macau. There are flights every 30 minutes from 9am until 10.30pm. The flights use helipads on the Macau Ferry Terminal in the Shun Tak Centre in Hong Kong and the Macau Ferry Terminal in Macau. One-way fares are HK$1,700 on weekdays, and HK$1,800 on weekends and Fridays. Journey time is around 20 minutes. There is also a less frequent helicopter service between Macau and Shenzhen.

Macau Transport

Buses

Buses and minibuses are also easy to use in Macau, with the English destination written on the front along with the Chinese. Bus stops have routes and numbers clearly marked. Exact change is needed. A battalion of buses wait

at the jetty terminal and stop at most major hotels, casinos and tourist sites. Fares are cheap, ranging from MOP$2.50 for anywhere on Macau peninsula to MOP$5 for Hac Sa on Coloane. Traffic jams are not usually too bad in Macau.

Taxis

The former Portuguese colony has a fleet of black or yellow taxis. The initial fare is MOP$10. Drivers are more friendly here than in Hong Kong and carry a list of tourist sites written in English and Chinese in their cab. There is a small surcharge for large luggage and crossing the causeway from Taipa into Coloane.

Pedicabs

As an echo of its former colonial past, there are a small gaggle of pedicab drivers who wait for custom at the jetty terminal and around the Hotel Lisboa. You will need to bargain with the driver – a typical price is around MOP$150 per hour, but note that a lot of Macau is hilly and unsuitable for these two-seater bicycle cabs.

Shenzhen Transport

Metro

Shenzhen has a brand spanking new metro system, with two lines. You can hop on the train at Luohu (Lo Wu) just outside the main border point with Hong Kong, and travel to Window on the World theme park. Tickets are cheap, with fares ranging from RMB2 to RMB5. Trains, however, are infrequent – roughly every 15 minutes.

Taxis

Red taxis are ubiquitous around the city and can be hailed almost anywhere. The initial fare is HK$12.50, and a typical journey across town will cost around RMB20–30. Fares are subject to a surcharge at night. Again, cabbies are unlikely to speak

English, so best to have your destination written down in Chinese characters. Also be careful of fake notes in your change (usually limited to RMB100 and 50 notes). The only way to avoid this is to make sure you have a good supply of small change (RMB20, 10 and 5 notes). Some drivers will also try to bump up their fare by taking you a long circuitous route, but unless you speak Chinese and know the city there is nothing you can do about this. Note Shenzhen's traffic grinds to a halt around rush hour.

Guangzhou Transport

Metro

Guangzhou also has a very efficient metro system with two lines. The network links Guangzhou East Train station (entry point from Hong Kong) with the city centre and many of the tourist sites. Tickets are small plastic discs which gain you entry through a turnstile – use coins to buy them from computerised vending machines. Fares are cheap, usually around RMB3 per journey. Destinations are written in *pinyin*, and announcements are also in English.

Buses

Buses are even cheaper but difficult to use if you don't know the city or speak Chinese, and also grindingly slow.

Taxis

The easiest way to travel about town is by taxi. Flagfall varies between different cabs (they are colour-coded), but an average in-town journey should cost no more than about RMB20. It is best to have your destination written in Chinese characters as cabbies are unlikely to speak English. Many cabs have a metal grill or thick plastic screen dividing the back seats and the driver, which is a bit disconcerting when you first hop in.

A CCOMMODATION

SOME THINGS TO CONSIDER BEFORE YOU BOOK A ROOM

Choosing a Hotel

Hong Kong has some of the world's best hotels, but they are also among the most expensive. Throughout the city's hotels service standards are high, and while the rooms, restaurants and ambience at the city's five stars are hard to beat, there are some excellent mid-range hotels too. Budget accommodation, on the other hand, is very limited.

Tourist arrivals are up in Hong Kong, largely due to a massive increase in visitors from the mainland. The hotel industry is enjoying high occupancy rates, and several new hotels have opened in recent years.

For more information about hotels in Hong Kong, check with the Hong Kong Hotels Association (tel: 2375 3838) or try the Hong Kong Tourist Board's website, www.discoverhongkong.com

Hotel Areas

Hong Kong's relatively small size means that you are never much more than an hour from the city centre and harbour. Most hotels are suitable bases for business or sightseeing. The majority of tourists stay in Tsim Sha Tsui, although Wan Chai and Causeway Bay are increasingly

making headway into this lucrative market.

Business travellers' choice of hotel is determined by the purpose of their trip. There are plenty of top hotels close to the main financial and business districts on Hong Kong Island. If an event at the Hong Kong Convention and Exhibition Centre is the focus of the trip then a hotel within walking distance in Wan Chai is useful. For business people using Hong Kong as a base for travel to southern China travellers hotels in Kowloon and the New Territories may be best.

The low level of personal crime in Hong Kong means that there are no districts to avoid. If you would like to escape the more dense urban areas it is perhaps worth investigating the handful of hotels located in the New Territories and the Outlying Islands; travel times into Central will be between 30 minutes to an hour.

Prices and Booking

Prices are generally high. In the following listings pages, hotels are grouped according to the maximum "rack rate" published by the hotel for a standard double room in peak season – ie during trade fairs and local public holidays. At these times booking

ahead is essential. If you plan to stay for a week or more, it's worth enquiring about longer-stay packages.

Rooms at the best hotels start at more than US$200 but significant reductions are often available. Good hotels in the moderate to expensive category are often reduced by 50 percent. Check with the hotel's own website, travel agents or hotel-booking websites for the best time to take advantage of bargain rates – reliable hotel-booking websites with good selection of hotels include Asia Travel, www.asiatravel.com, and Asia Hotels www.asiahotels.com.

Visitors arriving at the airport without hotel bookings can make reservations at a booth operated by the Hong Kong Hotels Association (open 6am and 1am) in the arrivals area.

There is no sales tax in Hong Kong; however, all hotels add a 3 percent government tax and a 10 percent service charge to bills.

In Macau, prices are significantly lower on weekdays, whereas in Shenzhen and Guangzhou you can usually get a double room in a five-star hotel for around US$60 (less than 50 percent of the official maximum price) unless there is a trade fair on at the time.

HONG KONG ISLAND

HOTELS

Luxury

Conrad Hong Kong
Pacific Place
88 Queensway, Admiralty
Tel: 2521 3838. Fax: 2521 3888
www.conrad.com.hk
Towering above the
Pacific Place complex in
Admiralty, this elegant,
modern business hotel
is located on floors 40
to 61. Its luxurious
rooms are some of the
most spacious in this
class. 510 rooms.

**Four Seasons Hotel
Hong Kong**
8 Finance St, Central
Tel: 3196 8888. Fax: 3196 8050
www.fourseasons.com
Scheduled to open in
the second half of
2005, this brand-new
hotel commands a dra-
matic presence on the
Hong Kong waterfront
next to the International
Finance Centre. 399
rooms.

Grand Hyatt
1 Harbour Rd, Wan Chai
Tel: 2261 0222. Fax: 2802 0677
www.hongkong.grand.hyatt.com
The high-rollers' hotel of
choice on Hong Kong
Island. This glitzy five-
star hotel is adjacent to
the convention centre
and is hence popular
with businesspeople
and delegates. The
luxury factor is even
higher since it opened
The Plateau, an amaz-
ing 7,000-square metre
(80,000-sq. ft) spa.
556 rooms.

Island Shangri-La
Pacific Place
Supreme Court Rd, Central
Tel: 2877 3838. Fax: 2521 8742
www.shangri-la.com/island
Regularly acclaimed as
one of the best hotels
in Hong Kong, this hotel
is a glamorous retreat
from the bustle of the
city. Exceptional restau-
rants add to the hotel's
deserved reputation.
565 rooms.

J.W. Marriott Hotel
1 Pacific Place
88 Queensway, Admiralty
Tel: 2810 8366. Fax: 2845 0737
www.marriotthotels.com/hkgdt
Classic modern luxury
hotel with Marriott's
signature clear in high
standards of service and
smart decor. 602 rooms.

Mandarin Oriental
5 Connaught Rd, Central
Tel: 2522 0111. Fax: 2810 6190
www.mandarinoriental.com
A Hong Kong institution
for the last four
decades, the Mandarin
holds its own in the face
of competition from
newer properties. Won-

derful combination of
impeccable service,
grand atmosphere and
plenty of classy chinois-
erie. Major renovation
2005–6. 541 rooms.

Ritz-Carlton
3 Connaught Rd, Central
Tel: 2877 6666. Fax: 2877 6778
www.ritzcarlton.com
Stylish five-star hotel in
Central with Old-World
ambience and exquisite
service. 216 rooms.

Expensive

Excelsior
281 Gloucester Rd,
Causeway Bay
Tel: 2894 8888. Fax: 2895 6459
www.mandarinoriental.com/
excelsior
A very popular hotel
managed by Mandarin
Oriental. Great location
in Causeway Bay over-
looking the yacht club
and harbour. Still the
best four-star hotel in
Hong Kong. 883 rooms.

**Harbour Plaza North
Point**
665 King's Rd, Quarry Bay
Tel: 2187 8888. Fax: 2187 8899
www.harbour-plaza.com/hpnp
Fresh modern de luxe
hotel located away from
the main tourist areas,
but close to Quarry Bay
and MTR station. Suit-
able for long-stay
guests. 566 rooms.

Le Meridien Cyberport
100 Cyberport Rd, Pok Fu Lam
Tel: 2980 7788. Fax: 2980 7888
www.lemeridien.com
Located in the new
Cyberport development
near Aberdeen, with
good amenities and styl-
ish use of technology.

173 rooms.

Park Lane Hong Kong
310 Gloucester Rd,
Causeway Bay
Tel: 2293 8888. Fax: 2576 7853
www.parklane.com.hk
A tourist favourite near
Victoria Park and right in
the thick of the shop-
ping district. 802
rooms.

**Renaissance Harbour
View Hotel**
1 Harbour Rd, Wan Chai
Tel: 2802 8888. Fax: 2802 8833
www.renaissancehotels.com/hkghv
A road bridge connects
this luxury hotel to the
Hong Kong Conference
and Exhibition Centre.
860 rooms.

Moderate

**Bishop Lei Interna-
tional House**
4 Robinson Rd, Mid-Levels
Tel: 2868 0828. Fax: 2868 1551
www.bishopleihtl.com.hk
Small hospitable hotel

PRICE CATEGORIES

Luxury: over US$200
Expensive: US$120–200
Moderate: US$60–120
Budget: under US$60
Prices are for a standard
double room at peak
season. Price reductions
are possible at off-peak
times *(see page 209).*

whose Mid-Levels location is extremely convenient. The best rooms have views of skyscrapers and harbour. Budget rate is offered for the most basic rooms. 215 rooms.

Charterhouse
209–219 Wan Chai Rd
Tel: 2833 5566, Fax: 2833 5888
www.charterhouse.com
Middle-of-the-road three-star hotel located on the border of Wan Chai and Causeway Bay. Compact but pleasant rooms furnished in a neo-classical style. 277 rooms.

Cosmopolitan Hotel
387–397 Queen's Rd East, Wan Chai
Tel: 3552 1111. Fax: 3552 1122
www.cosmopolitanhotel.com.hk
Opened in 2004, the Cosmopolitan is a 20-storey four-star hotel with a contemporary feel. Guests booking with the hotel are guaranteed a full 24 hours for their money, regardless of check-in time. 454 rooms.

Emperor (Happy Valley)
1 Wang Tak St, Happy Valley
Tel: 2893 3693. Fax: 2834 6700
www.emperorhotel.com.hk
Tucked away in a residential part of Happy Valley, close to the race-course. Good value – if

you can bear to be more than five minutes from the city centre. 150 rooms.

Novotel Century Harbourview
508 Queen's Rd West, Western
Tel: 2974 1234. Fax: 2974 0333
www.accorhotels-asia.com
In the heart of Western District, the Novotel is comfortable, bright and modern. Rooftop pool with interesting views. 274 rooms.

Novotel Century Hong Kong
238 Jaffe Rd, Wan Chai
Tel: 2598 8888. Fax: 2598 8866
www.accorhotels-asia.com
A good-value choice in this price bracket. Undistinguished, but a convenient good-quality hotel midway between Wan Chai and Causeway Bay. 512 rooms.

The Wesley
22 Hennessy Rd, Wan Chai
Tel: 2866 6688. Fax: 2866 6633
www.hanglung.com
A location between the shopping centres of Admiralty and the Wan Chai nightlife is a big plus for this hotel. Bright welcoming lobby, limited dining facilities. 251 rooms.

Wharney Guangdong Hotel
57–73 Lockhart Rd, Wan Chai
Tel: 2861 1000. Fax: 2865 1010

www.gdhhotels.com
Good-value business hotel located in the heart of the Wan Chai entertainment district. 358 rooms.

Budget

Alisan Guest House
5/F Flat A Hoito Court, 275 Gloucester Rd, Causeway Bay
Tel: 2838 0762. Fax: 2838 4351
Small guest house with clean, basic accommodation on three floors of a commercial building. All rooms include toilet and shower. Free Internet access. 21 rooms.

Ibis North Point
138 Java Road, North Point
Tel: 2588 1111. Fax: 2204 6677
www.accorhotels-asia.com/
This neat, clean, no-frills modern hotel has proved popular with tourists and business travellers. 275 rooms.

Mount Davis Youth Hostel
Mount Davis, Western District
Tel: 2788 3105. Fax: 2788 1638
www.yha.org.hk
Basic frugal accommodation with a beautiful hilltop location and wonderful harbour views. Free shuttle bus to/from Central (Shun Tak Centre; runs approximately every 2 hours).

Dormitory accommodation for 171 and self-catering facilities. A few family rooms plus triples, twins and just three double rooms.

APARTMENTS

Luxury

Jia
1–5 Irving St, Causeway Bay
Tel: 3196 9000. Fax: 3196 9001
www.jiahongkong.com
Sleek Philippe Starck-designed serviced apartments in Causeway Bay for one night or long stays. 54 apartments.

Ovolo
2 Arbuthnot Rd, Central
Tel: 2165 1080. Fax: 2868 6717
www.ovolo.com.hk
Smart and spacious one-bedroom serviced apartments just above Central. 20 apartments.

Moderate

Ice House
38 Ice House St, Central
Tel: 2836 7333. Fax: 2836 7000
www.icehouse.com.hk
Modern boutique studio apartments in a useful Central location next to Foreign Correspondents' Club, close to Lan Kwai Fong. 64 apartments.

KOWLOON

HOTELS

Luxury

InterContinental
18 Salisbury Rd, Tsim Sha Tsui
Tel: 2721 1211. Fax: 2739 4546
www.interconti.com
Formerly the Regent,

this is the most glamorous modern hotel on the Tsim Sha Tsui waterfront. Delightful rooms, wonderful harbour views, exceptional restaurants and superb spa. 495 rooms.

Harbour Plaza
20 Tak Fung St, Hung Hom
Tel: 2621 3188. Fax: 2621 3311

www.harbour-plaza.com/hphk
Hotel of choice for China's political and business leaders, located away from downtown Kowloon. Contemporary decor with the odd ostentatious touch. 411 rooms.

Kowloon Hotel
19–21 Nathan Rd,

Tsim Sha Tsui
Tel: 2929 2888. Fax: 2739 9811

www.thekowloonhotel.com
Across the road from
The Peninsula, this is a
good hotel in an excel-
lent location. 736
rooms.

Kowloon Shangri-La
64 Mody Rd, Tsim Sha Tsui East
Tel: 2721 2111. Fax: 2723 8686
www.shangri-la.com/kowloon
Superb luxury hotel on
Tsim Sha Tsui water-
front. Excellent restau-
rants and views. Short
walk to KCR and MTR
stations and Star Ferry.
700 rooms.

Langham Hotel
8 Peking Rd, Tsim Sha Tsui
Tel: 2375 1133. Fax: 2375 6611
www.langhamhotels.com
Solid five-star hotel with
handy location close to
Star Ferry, China Ferry
and cruise terminal. Five
minutes from railway
stations. 490 rooms.

Langham Place Hotel
555 Shanghai St, Mong Kok
Tel: 3552 3388. Fax: 2384 3670
www.langhamhotels.com/
langhamplace/
This glamorous new
hotel is leading the
revival of Mong Kok with
five-star class. Plush
rooms feature the latest
technology, which con-
trasts with striking art,
sculpture and architec-
ture reflecting Chinese
tradition. 665 rooms.

The Peninsula
Salisbury Rd, Tsim Sha Tsui
Tel: 2920 2888. Fax: 2722 4170
www.peninsula.com
Established in the
1920s, the Pen is Hong
Kong's only historic hotel
and arguably the best.
Potted palms and string
quartets in the lobby;
world-class restaurants
and bars, plus a Clarins
spa – this place oozes
class and elegance. If
money is no object this
is the ultimate choice.
300 rooms.

**Sheraton Hong Kong
Hotel & Towers**
20 Nathan Rd, Tsim Sha Tsui
Tel: 2369 1111. Fax: 2739 8707
www.sheraton.com/hongkong
Lively five-star hotel
close to Star Ferry,
KCR, MTR and Nathan
Road shopping areas.
Great restaurants and
bars, popular with
locals, tourists and
business travellers.
782 rooms.

Expensive

Holiday Inn Golden Mile
50 Nathan Rd, Tsim Sha Tsui
Tel: 2369 3111, Fax: 2369 8016
www.goldenmile.com
Ever-popular tourist
hotel in the middle of
Nathan Road – the
tourist golden mile of
Tsim Sha Tsui. 585
rooms.

**Hong Kong Gold Coast
Hotel**
1 Castle Peak Rd, Castle Peak
Bay, New Territories
Tel: 2452 8888. Fax: 2440 7368
www.goldcoasthotel.com.hk
Located on the west
coast of the New
Territories beside a
marina and a realistic
man-made beach. Five-
star luxury and extra
space are to be relished
if your trip to Hong Kong
is not centred on the
main island, and you
have time to spend
beside the large lagoon
pool or enjoying sports
facilities. 450 rooms.

**InterContinental Grand
Stanford**
70 Mody Rd,
Tsim Sha Tsui East
Tel: 2721 5161. Fax: 2732 2233
www.hongkong.interconti.com
Luxurious and fully
equipped five-star busi-
ness hotel in Tsim Sha
Tsui East. 579 rooms.

Marco Polo Gateway
Harbour City, 13 Canton Rd,

Tsim Sha Tsui
Tel: 2113 0888. Fax: 2113 0022
www.marcopolohotels.com
A good-quality tourist
hotel, part of the
Harbour City shopping
centre and cruise
terminal. 433 rooms.

**Marco Polo Hong
Kong Hotel**
Harbour City, 3 Canton Rd,
Tsim Sha Tsui
Tel: 2113 0088. Fax: 2113 0026
www.marcopolohotels.com
Largest of the three
Marco Polo hotels on
Canton Road. Recently
renovated, many of its
spacious rooms enjoy
harbour views. 644
rooms.

Marco Polo Prince
Harbour City, 23 Canton Rd,
Tsim Sha Tsui
Tel: 2113 1888. Fax: 2113 0066
www.marcopolohotels.com
Proximity to the China
Ferry Terminal and
relaxed restaurants dis-
tinguishes this Marco
Polo from its sibling
hotels. 394 rooms.

Miramar
118–130 Nathan Rd,
Tsim Sha Tsui
Tel: 2368 1111. Fax: 2369 1788
www.miramarhk.com
An unpretentious and
friendly hotel with an
indoor pool, a stone's
throw away from Tsim
Sha Tsui's best bars
and restaurants. 525
rooms.

**New World
Renaissance Hotel**
22 Salisbury Rd, Tsim Sha Tsui
Tel: 2369 4111. Fax: 2721 2105
www.renaissancehotels.com/hkgnw
A modern and efficient
hotel on the Tsim Sha
Tsui waterfront man-
aged by Marriott. 549
rooms.

Moderate

BP International House
8 Austin Rd, Tsim Sha Tsui

Tel: 2376 1111. Fax: 2376 1333
www.bpih.com.hk
Owned by the Boy
Scouts Association, but
operated by hotel man-
agement company, this
is a modest mid-range
hotel. Great location on
the edge of Kowloon
Park compensates for
unexciting interiors.
529 rooms.

Hotel Nikko Hongkong
72 Mody Rd, Tsim Sha Tsui East
Tel: 2739 1111. Fax: 2311 3122
www.hotelnikko.com.hk
A four-star hotel that is
especially popular with
Japanese tour groups.
462 rooms.

Hotel Concourse
22 Lai Chi Kok Rd, Mong Kok
Tel: 2397 6683. Fax: 2397 6440
www.hotelconcourse.com.hk
Large moderately priced
hotel in gritty, vibrant
Mong Kok. 430 rooms.

Kimberley Hotel
28 Kimberley Rd, Tsim Sha Tsui
Tel: 2723 3888. Fax: 2723 1318
www.kimberleyhotel.com.hk
Reliable three-star
hotel, two minutes from
bustling Nathan Road.
There's a good choice
of restaurants and bars
in nearby Knutsford
Terrace. 546 rooms.

Majestic Hotel
348 Nathan Rd, Yau Ma Tei
Tel: 2781 1333. Fax: 2781 1773
www.majestichotel.com.hk
Good-value three-star
hotel that offers guests
larger rooms than most.
380 rooms.

PRICE CATEGORIES

Luxury: over US$200
Expensive: US$120–200
Moderate: US$60–120
Budget: under US$60
Prices are for a standard
double room at peak
season. Price reductions
are possible at off-peak
times (see page 209).

TRANSPORT

ACCOMMODATION

ACTIVITIES

A – Z

LANGUAGE

The Minden
7 Minden Ave, Tsim Sha Tsui
Tel: 2739 7777. Fax: 2739 3777
www.theminden.com
Small, friendly boutique hotel, opened in 2005, in the heart of Tsim Sha Tsui's newest nightlife district. The European feel is enhanced by a terrace bar-restaurant. Functional and comfortable accommodation. Quality fabrics and original art add a luxurious touch. 60 rooms.

Nathan Hotel
378 Nathan Rd, Jordan
Tel: 2388 5141. Fax: 2770 4262
www.nathanhotel.com
Close to night markets and shopping district, Nathan Hotel is a mid-range hotel with 30 years of experience.192 rooms.

The Salisbury YMCA
41 Salisbury Rd, Tsim Sha Tsui
Tel: 2268 7000. Fax: 2739 9315
www.ymcahk.org.hk
Book ahead at this upmarket YMCA. Rooms are hotel-style and many enjoy panoramic views of the harbour. Large indoor pool, good restaurant and a range of sports and child-friendly facilities. 363 rooms.

Stanford Hillview Hotel
13–17 Observatory Rd, Tsim Sha Tsui
Tel: 2722 7822. Fax: 2723 3718
www.stanfordhillview.com
High-quality three-star hotel tucked away from the hustle of Nathan Road. 163 rooms.

Budget

Anne Black Guest House (YWCA)
5 Man Fuk Road, Ho Man Tin
Tel: 2713 9211. Fax: 2761 1269
www.ywca.org.hk
Clean, simple rooms. Ten minutes' walk from the Ladies' Market and Mong Kok KCR and MTR stations. A safe and inexpensive option. 169 rooms.

Chungking House
4&5/F Block A, Chungking Mansions, 40 Nathan Road, Tsim Sha Tsui
Tel: 2366 5362. Fax: 2721 3570
There are cheaper deals in the area, but in the dark corridors and grim stairwells of Chungking Mansions this is the only establishment approved by the HKTB. 75 rooms.

New Garden Hostel
13/F Mirador Mansions, 58 Nathan Road, Tsim Sha Tsui
Tel: 2311 2523. Fax: 2368 5241
One of the better Tsim Sha Tsui hostels, but still strictly backpacker accommodation, with choice of dormitories or private rooms. 60 rooms.

Rent-A-Room
Flat A 2/F Knight Garden, 7–8 Tak Hing Street, Jordan
Tel: 2366 3011 Fax: 2366 3588.
www.rentaroomhk.com
Popular budget hostel in Jordan, just north of Tsim Sha Tsui. Doubles and singles available. 28 rooms.

NEW TERRITORIES AND OUTLYING ISLANDS

HOTELS

Expensive

Regal Airport Hotel
9 Cheong Tat Rd, Chek Lap Kok, Lantau
Tel: 2286 8888. Fax: 2286 8686
www.regalhotel.com
Award-winning airport hotel connected to Hong Kong's Chek Lap Kok by an air-conditioned footbridge. Short- and long-stay rates available. 1,103 rooms.

Moderate

Concerto Hotel
28 Hung Sing Yeh, Lamma Island
Tel: 2982 1668. Fax: 2982 0022
www.concertoinn.com.hk
Small guest house, a 15-minute walk from the ferry pier, with a beachside location. 8 rooms.

Harbour Plaza Resort City
18 Tin Yan Rd, Tin Shui Wai, New Territories
Tel: 2180 6688. Fax: 2180 6333
www.harbour-plaza.com
A good value option for longer stays if you don't mind the location in a rather bland residential centre in the northwest New Territories. 1,102 rooms.

Panda Hotel
3 Tsuen Wah St, Tsuen Wan, New Territories
Tel: 2409 1111. Fax: 2409 1818
reservations@pandahotel.com.hk
The Panda tries hard to overcome its unlikely location in the large New Territories new town of Tsuen Wan. Convenient for airport and sea port. Large number of rooms assures availability and prices are always reasonable. 1,026 rooms.

Silvermine Beach Hotel
DD2 Lot 648, Silvermine Bay, Lantau
Tel: 2984 8295. Fax: 2984 1907
www.resort.com.hk
Close to the ferry pier on Lantau Island, this low-key beach hotel offers an alternative to the city. Outdoor swimming pool and adequate accommodation. 128 rooms.

APARTMENTS

Budget

Horizon Suite Hotel
29 On Chun Street, Ma On Shan, Sha Tin
Tel: 3157 8888. Fax: 2123 2128
www.horizonsuitehotel.com
Competitively priced New Territories complex of serviced apartments with easy access to country parks. Facilities

include 65-metre (213-ft) pool. For longer stays, rates start under US$1,000 per month. 831 apartments.

Sunrise Holiday Resort
Jackson Property Agents, 15 Main Street, Yung Shue Wan
Tel: 2982 2626. Fax: 2982 0636
www.lammaresort.com
Experience village life in a self-contained holiday apartment on Lamma Island. Five minutes from the ferry pier, this is a pleasant alternative to cramped city-centre budget accommodation. Surcharges on Saturdays and public holidays. 10 apartments.

MACAU

HOTELS

Luxury

Mandarin Oriental Macau
956–1110 Avda Amizade
Tel: 567 888. Fax: 594 589
www.mohg.com
The Mandarin remains Macau's classiest hotel. Full five-star facilities and superb spa in garden setting. 435 rooms.
Pousada de São Tiago
Avda da Republica
Tel:378 111. Fax: 552 170
www.saotiago.com.mo
This piece of Macanese history includes part of a 17th-century Portuguese fortress built for its commanding views. Dark wood, marble, chandeliers and white linen add to the historic ambience. Good restaurants, an outdoor swimming pool and a delightful terrace. 22 rooms.
Westin Resort
1918 Estrada de Hac Sa, Coloane
Tel: 871 111. Fax: 871 122
www.westin-macau.com
Located on the quiet island of Coloane, the Westin is a luxury hotel overlooking the sea.

Guest rooms terrace down towards the beach and the extensive recreation facilities include an 18-hole golf course on the resort's roof, and a spa. 208 rooms.

Expensive

Lisboa
2–4 Avda de Lisboa
Tel: 377 666. Fax: 567 193
www.hotelisboa.com
This gaudy hotel is something of an icon of Macau, and famous for its casino. Rooms are grand and the decor highly ornate. The 18 restaurants and entertainment facilities are superb. 1,000 rooms.
Hyatt Regency
Estr. Almirante Marques Esparteiro, Taipa
Tel: 831 234. Fax: 830 195
www.macau.hyatt.com
Superb facilities, and well placed to explore the main parts of Macau and the islands. 326 rooms.

Moderate

Grand View Hotel
142 Estr Governador Albano de Oliveira, Taipa
Tel: 837 788. Fax: 837 777
www.grandview-hotel.com

De luxe hotel in the heart of Taipa Island. Great value, and fascinating views of Macau Jockey Club's race track. 407 rooms.
Hotel Royal
2–4 Estr da Vitoria
Tel: 552 222. Fax: 563 008
www.hotelroyal.com.mo
Convenient mid-range hotel at the foot of the Colina da Guia, in a quiet area close to central Macau. Spacious, comfortable rooms. Facilities include an indoor pool. 380 rooms.
Hotel Sintra
Avda D. Joao IV
Tel: 710 111. Fax: 510 527
www.hotelsintra.com
Sister hotel to the Lisboa, the Sintra is a pleasant, low-key three-star alternative. Rooms were renovated in 2004 and are large and comfortably furnished. A good location for central Macau. A shuttle runs to the Lisboa. 240 rooms.
Pousada de Coloane
Praia de Cheoc Van, Coloane
Tel: 882 144. Fax: 882 251
A long-time favourite with Hong Kong residents seeking a moderately priced hotel with character. The appeal

should be enhanced by the long-overdue renovations. 22 rooms.
Pousada de Mong Ha
Colina de Mong-Ha
Tel: 515 222. Fax: 556 925
www.ift.edu.mo/pousada/
Tucked away on a green hillside below 19th-century ruins, this romantic boutique hotel has beautifully decorated rooms with Portuguese and Oriental style. 20 rooms.
Ritz Hotel
Rua do Comendador, Kou Ho Neng
Tel: 339 955. Fax: 317 826
www.ritzhotel.com.mo
Small luxury hotel with five-star facilities located on Penha Hill. The bland exterior belies ornate, spacious interiors. Many rooms have views of Macau and the Portuguese consulate building. Facilities include mini-golf, squash and tennis. 163 rooms.

SHENZHEN

HOTELS

Luxury

Mission Hills Resort
1 Mission Hills Rd
Tel: 2801 0888. Fax: 2801 0713
www.missionhillsgroup.com

Just outside Shenzhen, China's No. 1 golf club boasts a record-breaking 10 championship courses. The Resort also features luxurious rooms and suites with balconies overlooking the greens. Non-golfers can enjoy the scenery,

tennis, pool, spa and the contrast to industrial southern China. 315 rooms.
Shangri-La Hotel Shenzhen
East Side Railway Station, Jianshe Rd
Tel: 8233 0888. Fax: 8233 9878
www.shangri-la.com/shenzhen

This leading five-star hotel is a handy recognisable landmark when emerging from the Lo Wu border crossing. High standards throughout hotel and spa. A popular meeting place for tourists and business travellers. 553 rooms.

Expensive

Hilton Panglin Hotel
2002 Jiabin Rd, Lo Wu
Tel: 2518 5888. Fax: 2518 5999
www.hilton.com
Opened in 2001, this giant hotel offers views of Shenzhen and Hong Kong from its 50th-floor revolving restaurant. 527 rooms.

Nan Hai Hotel
1 Gong Ye 1st Rd, Shekou Industrial Zone
Tel: 2669 2888. Fax: 2669 2440
www.nanhai-hotel.com
A low-rise resort hotel in Shekou, a town west of Shenzhen with efficient ferry connections to Macau and Hong Kong. 396 rooms.

Moderate

Four Points by Sheraton
5 Guihua Rd, Futian District
Tel: 8359 9999. Fax: 8359 2988
www.starwoodhotels.com/fourpoints
Brand-new Starwood hotel in the Futian Free Trade Zone. Five-star-quality facilities targeting the business traveller. 278 rooms.

Novotel Watergate Shenzhen
Water Building, 1019 Shennan Zhong Rd
Tel: 8213 7999. Fax: 8213 7311
www.accorhotels-asia.com/

This interestingly named business hotel is good value.Right in the main shopping district, rooms have computers and DVD players. 135 rooms.

Budget

Shenzhen Lido Hotel
45 Donmennan Road
Tel: (755)8225 9988. Fax: (755)8220 6963
www.szlido.com
Three-star hotel located in shopping area, a 10-minute walk from Lo Wu crossing. 265 rooms.

GUANGZHOU

HOTELS

Luxury

China Hotel by Marriott
Liu Hua Lu
Tel: 8666 6888. Fax: 8667 7288
www.marriott.com
This five-star hotel complex includes serviced apartments. Convenient location just across the street from the trade-fair grounds, which makes it a favourite with business people. 1,013 rooms.

Garden Hotel Guangzhou
368 Huanshi Dong Lu
Tel: 8333 8989. Fax: 8335 0467

www.thegardenhotel.com.cn
Spectacular hotel that claims to have the largest lobby in Asia. The 30-storey building is part of a stylish twin-tower complex that includes offices and apartments. 1,140 rooms.

White Swan Hotel
1 Shamian Nan Lu
Tel: 8188 6968. Fax: 8186 1188
www.whiteswanhotel.com
One of the finest hotels in China, the White Swan has a prime location on Shamian Island and incorporates top-class boutiques and restaurants as well as indoor tennis courts and two pools. 843 rooms.

Expensive

Dong Fang Hotel
120 Liu Hua Lu
Tel: 8666 9900. Fax: 8666 2775
www.dongfanghotel-gz.com
Large luxury hotel complex situated just opposite Liu Hua Park and the trade-fair headquarters. 900 rooms.

Gitic Riverside Hotel
298 Yan Jiang Lu
Tel: 8383 9888. Fax: 8381 4448
www.riverside-hotel.com.cn
Situated on the banks of the Pearl River, this four-star hotel offers spacious rooms, full facilities and good restaurants. 328 rooms.

Moderate

China Merchants Hotel
8–111 Liu Hua Lu
Tel: 3622 2988. Fax: 3622 2680
www.cmhotel.com.cn
Business hotel situated next to the trade-fair centre and close to Liu Hua Lake. 240 rooms.

Guangdong Hotel
309 Dongfeng Zhong Rd
Tel: 8333 9933. Fax: 8333 9723
www.guangdong-hotel.com
Convenient location, well equipped, comfortable and good value. 508 rooms.

Landmark Hotel Canton
8 Qiao Guang Lu, Haizhu Sq
Tel: 8335 5988. Fax: 8333 6197
www.hotel-landmark.com.cn
Located on the banks of the Pearl River, the 2004 face-lift has improved standards in decor and comfort. 672 rooms.

Budget

Guangdong Shamian Hotel
52 South Shamian St
Tel: 8121 8288. Fax: 8121 8628
www.gdshamianhotel.com
Small budget hotel on Shamian Island with comfortable rooms. 130 rooms.

Guangzhou Youth Hostel
No. 2, 4th St Shamian
Tel: 8121 8606. Fax: 8121 8298
Bargain accommodation on historic Shamian Island. Clean and comfortable.

Victory Hotel
53 North Shamian St
www.vhotel.com
Great-value three-star hotel with Old-World architecture, pleasant rooms and good facilities. 330 rooms.

TRANSPORT

ACCOMMODATION

ACTIVITIES

A – Z

LANGUAGE

ACTIVITIES

THE ARTS, NIGHTLIFE, SHOPPING AND SPECTATOR SPORTS

THE ARTS

Art Galleries and Exhibitions

The **Hong Kong Museum of Art** houses the territory's largest collection of traditional Chinese painting and calligraphy. A wider variety of work is displayed in the **Hong Kong Heritage Museum** in Sha Tin. As well as traditional Asian paintings and sculptures, the museum has held funky exhibitions on subjects as diverse as poster art and Tibetan treasures. Local artists and photographers have a space at the **Hong Kong Arts Centre** and the **Fringe Club** to showcase their work. There are also dozens of small commercial art galleries, mainly concentrated around Hollywood Road in Central. For what's showing, see the Art section of the free weekly *HK Magazine*.

Fringe Club
2 Lower Albert Road, Central
Tel: 2521 7251
www.hkfringe.com.hk
Open Mon–Sat noon–10pm.
Hong Kong Arts Centre
2 Harbour Road, Wan Chai
Tel: 2582 0200, www.hkac.org.hk
Temporary exhibitions only – mainly local artists. Open

10am–8pm during exhibitions.
Hong Kong Heritage Museum
www.heritagemuseum.gov.hk
1 Man Lam Road, Sha Tin
Tel: 2180 8188
Open Mon–Sat 10am–6pm, Sun 10am–7pm.
Hong Kong Museum of Art
10 Salisbury Road, Tsim Sha Tsui
Tel: 2721 0116
Open Fri–Wed 10am–6pm.
University Museum and Art Gallery
94 Bonham Road, Mid-Levels
Tel: 2241 5500
www.hku.hk/hkumag
Open Mon–Sat 9.30am–6pm, Sun 1.30–5.30pm.

Commercial galleries

Connoisseur Art Gallery
1 Hollywood Road, Central
Tel: 2868 5358
www.connoisseur-art.com
Open Mon–Sat 10.30am–7pm, Sun noon–6pm.
John Batten Gallery
64 Peel Street, Central
Tel: 2854 1018
www.johnbattengallery.com
Open Tues–Sat 1–7pm, Sun 2–5pm.
Schoeni Art Gallery
www.schoeni.com.hk/
21–31 Old Bailey Street, Central
Tel: 2869 8803
Open Mon–Sat 10.30am–6.30pm.
Good collection of contemporary Asian artists.

Wattis Fine Art
www.wattis.com.hk
20 Hollywood Road, Central
Tel: 2524 5302
Open Tues–Sat 10am–6pm, Sun 1pm–5pm.
Specialises in historical paintings, prints and maps.

Macau

The severe steely grey building of the Macau Museum of Art has five floors of exhibition space, mainly given over to traditional Chinese painting, calligraphy and ceramics, but there is also room for international visiting exhibi-

BUYING TICKETS

You can buy tickets for shows, concerts and some sporting events from any of the venues' box offices or Tom Lee music stores (noticeable by their bright yellow sign). If you have a credit card you can buy tickets over the phone via Urbtix (tel: 2111 5999) or HK Ticketing (tel: 3128 8288). Urbtix will also allow you to reserve tickets free of charge for three days (tel: 2734 9009 to book). You can also pay for tickets on the Internet at Cityline – www.cityline.com.hk or HK Ticketing – www.hkticketing.com. You are required to register (free) first.

TRANSPORT

tions. For an overview of Macau's art scene, there is a useful website at www.macauart.net

Macau Museum of Art
Av. Xian Xing Hai
Tel: 7919814
www.artmuseum.gov.mo
Open 10am–6.30pm.

Old Ladies' House Art Space
OX Warehouse (at the intersection of Av. Coronel Mesquita and Av. do Almirante Lacerda)
Tel: 530 026
http://www.olhartspace.org.mo
Open Wed–Mon noon–7pm.

WHAT'S ON LISTINGS

Listings and reviews are given in the freebies – *HK Magazine* and *BC Magazine* – available in bars and Western coffee shops, and also in the City pull-out section of the English daily *South China Morning Post*. The tourism websites, with a bit of navigation, will yield an event's calendar – try www.discoverhongkong.com and www.macautourism.gov.mo

Tap Seac Gallery
95 Av. Conselheiro Ferreira de Almeida
Tel: 335 141
Open Tues–Sun 10am–6pm.

Guangzhou

Gallery of Guangzhou Painting Academy
3 Zhongshan San Lu
Tel: 8384 3949
Open 10am–noon, 1–6pm.

Guangdong Museum of Art
www.gdmoa.org/english/
38 Yan Yu Lu, Ersha Island
Tel: 8735 1468

Concerts

Classical
The Hong Kong Philharmonic Orchestra, chief conductor Dutchman Edo de Waart, and the Hong Kong Chinese Orchestra, principal conductor Yan

Huichang, perform regularly when they are not on world tour. They, the Hong Kong Sinfonietta and visiting orchestras, both Western and Asian, hold concerts at the Hong Kong Cultural Centre and urban theatres. Recitals (sometimes free) are held at the Hong Kong Academy for Performing Arts.

Pop, Rock etc.
Despite the lack of a world-class concert venue, Hong Kong periodically attracts some big name acts from the world of pop, rock and jazz, as well as many fading stars including the hairy-chested Englebert Humperdinck. As a taster, Norah Jones, R.E.M. and Sting performed here in the first three months of 2005. Tickets are expensive, though – generally ranging between HK$500 and HK$900. You can also catch local Cantopop bands and Taiwanese pop stars – both are hugely popular. International acts tend to play at the Hong Kong Convention and Exhibition Centre, while Cantopop stars favour the Hong Kong Coliseum.

Hong Kong Convention and Exhibition Centre (HKCEC)
1 Expo Drive, Wan Chai
Tel: 2582 8888
www.hkcec.com.hk/

Hong Kong Cultural Centre
10 Salisbury Road, Tsim Sha Tsui
Tel: 2734 2009
www.lcsd.gov.hk/CE/CulturalService/HKCC

Hong Kong Coliseum
9 Cheong Wan Road, Hung Hom
Tel: 2335 7234
www.lcsd.gov.hk/CE/Entertainment/Stadia/HKC/

Hong Kong Academy for Performing Arts (HKAPA)
www.hkapa.edu/
1 Gloucester Road, Wan Chai
Tel: 2584 8500

Macau Cultural Centre
www.ccm.gov.mo/en/intro.htm
Av. Xian Xing Hai South
Tel: 700 699
Macau's main venue for performances, with a 1,000-seat auditorium.

MUSEUM PASS

A museum pass allows free access to six museums for a week – the Heritage Museum, Museum of Art, Science Museum, Space Museum, Museum of History and the Coastal Defence Museum. The HK$30 pass is available from these six museums or HKTB information centres.

Dance/Ballet

There is a vibrant dance scene in Hong Kong with performances by the home-grown Hong Kong Ballet, Hong Kong Dance Company and the offbeat City Contemporary Dance Company. Dance troupes from around the region, particularly from the mainland, can also be seen – perhaps the most spectacular are the Shaolin Monks who leap and tumble elaborate kung fu moves. Shows are usually held at the City Hall, urban theatres, or the Fringe Club *(see previous page)*.

City Hall
1 Edinburgh Place, Central
Tel: 2921 2840

Film

Hong Kong's movie-making studios churn out dozens of kung fu action films and soppy romantic comedies every year. While the quality doesn't always match the quantity, local cinema has risen in stature in recent years by its association with the Oscar-winning *Crouching Tiger, Hidden Dragon* (a joint production between Hong Kong, mainland China, Taiwan and the US), giving the world an appetite for leaping kung fu period dramas. Mainland director Zhang Yimou, already celebrated globally as an arthouse director for films such as *Raise the Red Lantern*, made *Hero* in the same mould. Look out for Hong Kong's very funny actor-director Stephen Chow

ACCOMMODATION

ACTIVITIES

A – Z

LANGUAGE

(*Shaolin Soccer*, *Kung Fu Hustle*), and the movies of critically acclaimed director Wong Kar-wai (*Chungking Express*, *Happy Together*, *In the Mood for Love* and *2046*). Hong Kong stars that have made it globally include Bruce Lee, Jackie Chan, Chow Yun-fat, Jet Li and Maggie Cheung. All-action Hollywood director John Woo (*Face/Off*) also hails from Hong Kong.

Cinemas

There are dozens of cinemas and multiplexes in Hong Kong that show a mixture of the latest Hollywood releases, local offerings and big-budget Japanese, South Korean and Thai movies. There are also several good arthouse theatres with European and Asian productions. Almost all non-English films will come with English subtitles, but beware of cartoons dubbed into Chinese. As evening shows tend to sell out quickly, it's best to buy in advance by a few hours. Tickets cost around HK$60–70, while discounts of around HK$20–30 are offered on tickets all day Tuesday and for morning and matinée shows.

Broadway Circuit
Tel: 2388 3188
You can book tickets for the following Broadway cinemas via www4.cinema.com.hk. The **ifc Palace**, IFC2, Central, is the city's most luxurious cinema with big comfy armchair seats, but tickets are standard price. It shows art-house movies as well as mainstream films, has a DVD store and café. **Cinematheque**, 3 Public Square St, Yau Ma Tei, near Temple Street market, shows art-house movies and has a small DVD shop and café. **Windsor**, Windsor House, Causeway Bay next to Victoria Park, shows mainstream films.

UA Cinemas
In Times Square, Causeway Bay; Pacific Place, Admiralty and Langham Place, Mongkok.
Tel: 2317 6666
Hollywood and local films.

Cine-Art House
Sun Hung Kai Centre, Wan Chai
Tel: 2827 4820
Shows art-house movies only.
Golden Gateway Multiplex
The Gateway, 25 Canton Rd, Tsim Sha Tsui
Tel: 2186 1313
In Macau, Hollywood movies are shown at the modern **Theatre**, Macau Tower, tel: 933 339.

Film Festivals

Every spring, Hong Kong holds its two-week **International Film Festival** (www.hkiff.org.hk). It's advisable to book ahead as tickets sell out fast. You can buy online on their website. The two-week **Lesbian and Gay Film Festival** (www.hklgff.com) is usually held around October to November. **Le French May** (www.french-may.com/), held in May, is a festival of French culture, and usually offers a run of French movies. Throughout the year various **mini-film festivals** are held. Check freebie magazines and the local press for details.

Museums

Hong Kong has some world-class museums. The Museum of History and the Heritage Museum offer great hands-on displays of life in the city in days gone by. The Space and Science Museums are fun places for children and often have superb visiting exhibitions. The Space Museum also has an Omnimax theatre. See the Places section of the book for full details.

Theatre

Most theatre productions are in Cantonese or Mandarin – although some of the larger theatres will put on English subtitles. The professional Hong Kong Repertory Theatre always provides subtitles to its shows. There are also local English-language drama troupes, but the quality is variable. Performances are usually held at the Fringe

Club, the Hong Kong Arts Centre or the Hong Kong Cultural Centre. Big-name musicals like *Mama Mia* and *Les Misérables* periodically make it to Hong Kong. The Hong Kong Arts Festival (www.hk.artsfestival.org/), which runs for about a month at the beginning of every year, features opera, concerts, musicals, ballet and drama by artists from all over the world.

Regular performances of **Cantonese opera**, shunned by the younger generation, but loved by the over-fifties, are held at the Sunbeam Theatre, 423 King's Road, North Point, tel: 2563 2959, and at other urban theatres. While the elaborate costumes, shocking make-up and slow-motion dance look and sound exotic, the strangled singing, atonal music and difficulty in following the story often make it impossible for foreigners to sit through an entire performance.

Macau

There is not much in the way of English-language drama in Macau. Your best bet is to visit during the one-month Macau Arts Festival held every year around March to April. Performances are held in the Macau Cultural Centre (see page 217).

NIGHTLIFE

Hong Kong has an extremely lively nightlife scene. There are plenty of Western-style bars and discos, some of which attract a mainly Western clientele, while others cater to a mix of locals and expats.

There are three districts in which most bars and clubs likely to appeal to visitors are located: Central, Wan Chai (including Causeway Bay) and Tsim Sha Tsui. Central is where most expats and trendy locals go after work, especially Lan Kwai Fong, SoHo and BoHo. All are packed with chic bars and restaurants. Wan Chai has a grungier drinking scene interspersed with girlie bars and tacky basement discos that keep going throughout the night. On Kowloon side, Tsim Sha Tsui's nightlife tends to be split between bars that are exclusively for locals and those aimed mainly at tourists.

Bars in Central and the swankier Causeway Bay and Tsim Sha Tsui joints are the most expensive, with non-happy-hour drinks costing HK$60 upwards. The grittier Wan Chai bars are the cheapest, with HK$40 beers as a rule.

For a list of bars and club nights check *HK Magazine* and *BC Magazine*. You can also try www.hkclubbing.com for party dates.

Central

Captain's Bar, Mandarin Oriental Hotel. Tel: 2522 0111. Where the captains of industry congregate after work.
Club 97, 9 Lan Kwai Fong. Tel: 2810 9333. One of the longest-running but still one of the hippest clubs in town. Friday night is gay night.
Club Feather Boa, 38 Staunton St. Tel: 2857 7156. Like a regency drawing room; amazing, eclectic and so SoHo.
Dragon-i, The Centrium, 60 Wyndham St. Tel: 3110 1222. Operates a guest-list-only entrance policy, but you may call in advance to request entry. One of the "to be seen" places for minor and would-be celebs.
Dublin Jack, 37–43 Cochrane St. Tel: 2543 0081. Rowdy Irish bar. Big screen sports and comedy tapes in the toilet. The first bar in Hong Kong to go completely smoke-free.
Fringe Club, 2 Lower Albert Rd. Tel: 2521 7485. Live bands downstairs, or a relaxing beer garden on the roof. Along with reasonable drinks prices, this place is a rare gem.
Hei Hei Club, 3/F On Hing Terrace, Wyndham St. Tel: 2899 2068. Two open-air balconies with comfy seating arranged

around jacuzzis and a pool plus a dance floor.
Le Jardin, 1/F, 10 Wing Wah Lane, Central. Tel: 2877 1100. The best outdoor bar in Central/Lan Kwai Fong. Laid-back atmosphere with a good mix of people.
Linq, G/F, 35 Pottinger St, Central. Tel: 2971 0680. Describes itself as a pre-club bar, but stays open until 2am on weekdays and later at weekends. Laid back and cool.
Nu, Winly Building, 1–5 Elgin St, SoHo. Tel: 2549 8386. Smooth lounge club, takes its music seriously. Occasionally hosts speed dating and tarot card parties.
Red Bar, Level 4, Podium, IFC2 Building, 8 Finance Rd. Tel: 8129 8882. Outdoor terrace with harbour views and resident DJs.
Staunton's, 10 Staunton St. Tel: 2973 6611. Long-running trendy bar next to the escalator.
Vodka Bar, 13 Old Bailey St. Tel: 2525 1513. Hip bar and gallery on the fringe of SoHo.
Yumla, Lower Basement, Harilela House, 79 Wyndham St. Tel: 2147 2382. Packed little dance club with great music (check www.yumla.com for DJ list).

Wan Chai and Causeway Bay

Beer Garden & Innside Out, 10 Hysan Ave, Causeway Bay. Tel: 2895 2900.
Unpretentious bar with outdoor seating, big-screen sports, peanuts on demand – shells must be thrown on the floor – big glasses of Hoegaarden and a wide range of other beers.
Carnegie's, 53–55 Lockhart Rd,

Wan Chai. Tel: 2866 6289. A rowdy, rocky two-tier bar that is packed and boisterous at weekends and fun most nights. Hosts live-music events.
Champagne Bar, Grand Hyatt, Wan Chai. Tel: 2588 1234. Intimate, opulent bar for expensive after-work entertaining.
Delaney's, One Capital Place, 18 Luard Road, Wan Chai. Tel: 2804 2880. Very popular Irish theme pub with good food.
Klong Bar and Grill, The Broadway, 54–62 Lockhart Rd, Wan Chai. Tel: 2217 8330. Named after Bangkok's network of tiny canals. There's optional pole dancing, zebra-patterned pool tables, and niches hiding faux opium dens.
Joe Banana's, 23 Luard Rd, Wan Chai. Tel: 2529 1811. This bar/club has been running for years, with a reputation as something of a meat market for expatriates. Smart-casual dress code.
Manhattan Club ING, Renaissance Harbour View Hotel, 1 Harbour Rd. Tel: 2836 3690. American-style club with R&B most nights, ladies' night on Thursday. A bit 'preppy' for some.
R66, Revolving Restaurant, 62/F Hopewell Centre, 183 Queen's Rd East, Wan Chai. Tel: 2862 6166. Skip the food and have a drink with great views of Hong Kong. There's just enough time to down a couple and do one complete circuit.
S, 8 Yiu Wa St, Causeway Bay. Tel: 2838 0044. A funky jet-black wine bar with chill-out music.
Strawberries, 48 Hennessy Rd, Wan Chai. Tel: 2866 1031. One of

several tacky Wan Chai disco bars that stay open until breakfast.
TOTT's Asian Grill and Bar, 281 Gloucester Rd, Causeway Bay. Tel: 2894 8888. This chic restaurant at the top of the Excelsior is a popular nightspot after dinner.
Viceroy, 2/F Sun Hung Kai Centre, 30 Harbour Rd, Wan Chai. Tel: 2827 7777. This Indian restaurant has a bar with seating on a terrace overlooking the harbour. Occasionally hosts clubbing nights with international guest DJs, and stand-up comedy nights.

Tsim Sha Tsui

Aqua Spirit, 1 Peking Rd. Tel: 3427 2288. Amazing views of the skyline in this trendy bar, but the price of the drinks will bring a tear to your eye.
Bahama Mama's, 4–5 Knutsford Terrace. Tel: 2368 2121. Caribbean-themed bar that spills out onto the street.
Balalaika, 2/F, 10 Knutsford Terrace. Tel: 2312 6222. Russian restaurant with vodka bar. Don fur hat and coat and down shooters in the walk-in fridge.
Chillax Bar & Club, G/F, The Pinnacle, 8 Minden Ave, Tsim Sha Tsui. Tel 2722 4338. One of the livelier of several bars and clubs

KARAOKE

Many bars and even restaurants have private rooms where groups get together to sing Chinese songs. There are TV screens showing music videos and the words to the song in Chinese. Words are highlighted when you are supposed to sing them. Some karaoke bars also employ "hostesses" to sing together with the customers, who are usually rowdy groups of Asian businessmen. A night out in one of these establishments will prove extremely expensive. Westerners unaccompanied by local Chinese will probably not be made very welcome.

sprouting up on Minden Avenue.
Felix, The Peninsula, Salisbury Rd, Tsim Sha Tsui. Tel: 2315 3188. Felix is a tower-of-power destination, a sublime Philippe Starck-designed bar perched on top of the legendary Peninsula Hotel since opening in 1994. Check out the celebrated urinals.
Rick's Café, 53–59 Kimberley Rd. Tel: 2311 2255. Loud basement bar/club, usually packed.
Someplace Else, Sheraton Hotel and Towers, Tsim Sha Tsui. Tel: 2721 6151. Popular, comfortable rendezvous point with live music late at night.

Macau

Apart from hotel and restaurant bars and, of course, the casinos, Macau's nightlife is centred along Avenida Dr Sun Yat-sen – a strip of bars along the waterfront near the Cultural Centre.
Café Madeira, Macau Tower. Tel: 963 399. Long wine-and-port list, great place for a drink with sea views. Closes at midnight.
Embassy Bay, Mandarin Oriental. Tel: 793 3831. Typical hotel bar, with live cover band, dance floor, big-screen sports and cigar lounge.
Oparium, 1399 Vista Magnifica Court, Avda. Dr Sun Yat-sen. Good range of beers, outdoor seating, and live cover band. Typical of many bars in this strip.

Shenzhen

3D Bar (Beerworld), Bar Street, Citic Plaza, Shen Nan Central Rd. Tel: 2598 6011. Part of a chain of prefab bars in a shopping plaza. Amazing variety of bottled beers, popular with expats.
Class Club, 5/F Century Plaza Hotel, 1 Chun Feng Road, Luo Hu. Tel: 8236 3999. Shenzhen's "in" spot, with two dance floors, international DJs, and a very pretentious crowd.
True Color, 4/F Dongmen Friendship City, Jie Fang Rd, Louhu. Tel: 8230 1833. Cool bar with floor-to-ceiling windows, stage for live music, occasional international DJs and a restaurant with live jazz.

Guangzhou

Guangzhou also has a buzzing nightlife scene, with a range of clubs and other late night options as well as more standard bars. For some incisive reviews, try www.guangzhouhotel.com/bardisco.htm

Gay/Lesbian Nightlife

Hong Kong has a small but thriving gay scene, though lesbians are stuck with a few local-style karaoke bars in Causeway Bay office blocks. The bars and clubs that are most welcoming to foreigners are located in Central. On the Internet, www.fridae.com is a Singapore-based gay and lesbian resource with nightlife listings for Hong Kong.
OA2, 42 Yiu Wa St, Causeway Bay. Tel: 2838 5809. A cramped karaoke lesbian bar, with seating at the back. Attracts a mainly younger crowd of girls.
Propaganda, 1 Hollywood Rd, Central. Tel: 2868 1316. Long-running gay club, packed at weekends with great music.
Rice Bar, 33 Jervois St, Sheung Wan. Tel: 2851 4800. Refined lounge bar mainly for gay men. Recently turned non-smoking.
Works, 30–32 Wyndham St, Central. Tel: 2868 6102. Hot and sweaty club decked out in black – a serious cruising joint for men.

Live Music Venues

Most hotel bars will have either a resident Filipino band to warble out some golden oldies, or a jazz band. Many bars also have cover bands that play dance and pop. See live music listings in HK Magazine to find out who's playing.
48th Street Chicago Blues Bar, 2A Hart Ave, Tsim Sha Tsui. Tel: 2723 7633. Small, friendly bar with nightly jazz and blues.
Bohemian Lounge, 3–5 Old Bailey St, Central. Tel: 2526 6099. Opulent bar in rich red and purple with live jazz or latin dance performers Thursday–Saturday.
Dusk Till Dawn, 76 Jaffe Rd, Wan Chai. Tel: 2528 4689.

MACAU'S CASINOS

After tycoon Stanley Ho's monopoly was lifted at the end of 2001, two Las Vegas-backed companies have opened casinos in Macau and since licensees can also sub-let, the industry is now wide open – and booming as never before.

Traditionally Macau's dens of vice were a world apart from Las Vegas – inside it was serious business, few smiles, austere croupiers and scruffy carpets pocked with cigarette burns. Macau's newest casinos have tried to capture some of the glamour of the American gambling houses, to mixed results. In the Sands Macao, for example, instead of buxom waitresses serving alcohol, men dressed in traditional peasant garb with tea in urns on their back refill your plastic cup. Ho's newest venture – the Greek Mythology Casino in the New Century Hotel – was described by one punter as 'unbelievably tacky', with faux-marble pillars, a plastic statue of Zeus and lino-covered floors.

Casa Real Casino, Casa Real Hotel, Avda do Dr Rodrigo Rodrigues. Tel: 726 288.
Casino Kingway, Hotel Kingsway, Rua Luis Gonzaga Gomes. Tel: 702 398.
Diamond Casino, Holiday Inn, Rua de Pequim. Tel: 783 333.
Fortuna Casino, Hotel Fortuna, Rua de Cantao. Tel: 786 333.
Galaxy Casino, Waldo Hotel, Avda de Amizade. Tel: 886 620.
Golden Dragon Casino, Hotel Golden Dragon, Rua de Malaca. Tel: 727 979.
Greek Mythology Casino, Hotel New Century, Avda Padre Tomas Pereira, Taipa. Tel: 835 223.

Jai Alai Casino, Estr da Pelota Basca. Tel: 726 086.
Kam Pek Casino, Centro Comercial, Rua de Foshan. Tel: 780 168.
Lisboa Casino, Hotel Lisboa, Avda de Lisboa. Tel: 377 666.
Macau Jockey Club Casino, Grandview Hotel, Estr Governador Albano de Oliveira, Taipa. Tel: 837 788.
Macau Palace Casino Avda de Amizade. Tel: 727 218.
Mandarin Oriental Casino, Mandarin Oriental, Avda de Amizade. Tel: 567 888.
Marina Casino, Pousada Marina Infante, Taipa–Coloane Causeway. Tel: 838 333.
Pharoah's Palace Casino, The Landmark, Avda de Amizade. Tel: 788 111.
Sands Macao, Avda de Amizade. Tel: 883 388.
Taipa Casino, Hyatt Regency, Taipa. Tel: 831 234.
All casinos are open 24 hours.

Rowdy bar with cover band playing rock, indie and pop tracks. **Gecko**, 15–19 Hollywood Rd, Ezra's Lane (alley next to the escalator), Central. Tel: 2537 4680. Funky lounge and wine bar with live jazz during the week.

SHOPPING

Shopper's Paradise

Hong Kong has frequently been called a shopper's paradise, and it is certainly true that most Hong Kong citizens are insatiable shoppers. Shopping places range from colourful night markets and glitzy shopping malls, to multi-storey department stores and bustling narrow streets full of antiques and bric-a-brac. These days, Hong Kong may not be the bargain basement it once was, but shopping may nonetheless prove one of the most compelling activities of any trip to the territory for many visitors. There is certainly no shortage of supply.

Shopping Advice

The Hong Kong Tourism Board offers two golden rules for shoppers:
● Shop around and compare prices before you make any decision to buy, particularly for an expensive purchase.
● Always deal with reputable establishments, such as members of the Hong Kong Tourism Board's Quality Tourism Services Scheme (identifiable by the logo of a red junk set next to a big golden Q with the Chinese character for quality written in black inside). The sign should be displayed prominently on the premises).

Make sure when buying electrical goods that you get an international guarantee and not just a local Hong Kong guarantee.

Sometimes goods that seem suspiciously cheap may not have this guarantee. It is rare for local retailers to accept responsibility for faulty goods. Instead, you will have to return them to the manufacturer for repair.

The problem of retailers cheating tourists was rife a few years ago, but has been brought much more under control. However, if you do have a problem you should contact the HKTB or the **Consumer Council** (Tel: 2929 2222). Both organisations are keen to protect Hong Kong's shopping reputation and will offer whatever assistance they can. Calling in a police officer in a case of very obvious cheating can also be helpful, as shopkeepers do not wish to waste their time getting into disputes and do not like to have their reputation publicly damaged by the appearance of the police.

Shopkeepers may often appear to be rather rude and

...ND ELECTRICALS

...d electrical wares
...d buys in Hong
Kong.....ay particular attention in camera shops that you are not being conned. Most camera and electronics stores are in Causeway Bay, Tsim Sha Tsui and Mong Kok. They seldom have price tags on the items, so bargain, compare prices and beware. Most resident expatriates prefer the camera stores in Stanley Street, Central. There is not such an extensive range there, but the shopkeepers are friendly, the goods are reasonably priced and there are few reports of cheating. With electronic goods, remember to check for correct voltage, adaptors, etc.

impatient – although the situation has improved in recent years. Foreigners can sometimes assume rudeness just because of the way that Hong Kong English sounds. There is a fine line between rude and unhelpful shopkeepers, and those who just practise the normal Hong Kong behaviour of trying to do things quickly.

Where to Shop

The prime shopping malls are Central, Admiralty and Causeway Bay on Hong Kong Island, and Tsim Sha Tsui and Mong Kok in Kowloon. Shopping hours vary, but the good news is that shopping basically goes on until late seven days a week. Even during public holidays, most shops are open, except during Chinese New Year. As a guide, shops in Central close around 7pm, but the other main areas tend to stay open till 10pm, sometimes even later.

Shopping Malls

The best-known shopping malls on Hong Kong Island are Landmark in Central, Pacific Place in Admiralty, Times Square in Causeway Bay

and City Plaza in Taikoo Shing. In Kowloon, the linked Ocean Terminal and Harbour Centre complexes plus Festival Walk in Kowloon Tong can keep you busy. The newest addition to Hong Kong's trademark shopping malls is the IFC Mall in Central – a vast selection of swanky shops and snack bars wrapped in a cocoon of shiny steel and glass just above the Hong Kong Airport Express station.

Markets

Hong Kong has a number of lively and interesting shopping markets. **Cat Street**, off Hollywood Road in Central, is a flea market offering inexpensive trinkets and bric-a-brac. The surrounding area is famous for fine arts and antiques.
Stanley Market, on the south side of the island, is famous for sports and casualwear, linen, tableware, silk and leather garments. Open 10am–7pm daily.
Temple Street, Hong Kong's most popular night market, runs from Jordan to Yau Ma Tei in Kowloon. Cheap clothing, watches, pens, sunglasses, CDs, electronic gadgets and luggage abound in its colourfully lit stalls. There are also Chinese fortunetellers and Chinese opera singers practising. Open 6pm to midnight.

Tung Choi Street is a busy street market in Mong Kok and is less tourist-oriented than Temple Street. Specialities include local women's fashions, jewellery and accessories. Open 3–10pm.

Jewellery fans may like to check out the **Jade Market**, located under the flyover near Kansau Street in Yau Ma Tei. Open daily 10am–6pm.

What to Buy

Antiques & works of art

The network of antique shops located around Hollywood Road and Cat Street offers an extraordinary range of Asian antiquities and artworks at a very wide

range of prices. The Chinese department stores scattered around Hong Kong also offer many inexpensive antiques and handicrafts from mainland China.

Ivory

For many years, Hong Kong was the international centre of carved ivory. However, the ban imposed by the Convention on International Trade in Endangered Species (CITES) means that you now have to obtain an import licence from your country of residence in order to take any ivory out of Hong Kong.

Bookshops

Bookazine, Shop 309–313 Prince's Building, 10 Chater Rd, Central.
Commercial Press, 3/F Star House, 3 Salisbury Road, Tsim Sha Tsui.
Dymocks, level 2, IFC Mall, Central; 1/F Prince's Building, 10 Chater Rd, Central; Star Ferry Concourse, Central.
Page One, 2/F Century Square, 1–13 D'Aguilar St, Central; Shop 3202, Zone A, Harbour City, Canton Rd, Tsim Sha Tsui; 9/F Times Square, 1 Matheson St, Causeway Bay.
Red & Book, 2/F Arts Centre, Wan Chai has a good selection of art books.
Swindon, 13–15 Lock Rd, Tsim Sha Tsui; 310 Ocean Centre, Harbour City, Tsim Sha Tsui.

Computers

Hong Kong is a major exporter of computers, components and accessories, and you will find the most up-to-date models at great prices. There are a number of arcades devoted solely to selling computers and accessories. If you are buying a computer, make sure that the keyboard is in English and not English with Cantonese symbols. Ask to see it before you buy. The best retailers are found in Star House in Tsim Sha Tsui near the Star Ferry, Windsor House in Causeway Bay, and Whampoa Gardens in Hung Hom, Kowloon.

Clothing

Hong Kong has a superb range of clothing to suit all ages, tastes and budgets. Although many visitors from South-East Asia flock to Hong Kong for the latest names in international fashion, most Western visitors will find they get much better buys on the big names at home. The factory outlets in Wan Chai, Tsim Sha Tsui and Mong Kok, however, are extremely popular with tourists. These are essentially seconds and over-runs from Hong Kong's export industry, and are available at a fraction of the selling price overseas. The Chinese products emporia such as the CRC department stores have great bargains on Chinese-made silks.

Custom Tailors

Having your own suit made to measure is still a popular luxury for visitors to Hong Kong. The territory has some of the legendary tailors of old Shanghai, who have passed on their skills to the next generation. The speed and quality of craftsmanship and the range of fabrics here are all excellent. Such personal tailoring is no longer a massive bargain, but still worthwhile. A few places can produce your suit within 24 hours, but you won't usually see the best-quality results. Expect your tailor to take about a week if you want a high-quality garment. There are a lot of tailors in Tsim Sha Tsui and a few in Wan Chai and Causeway Bay. The Shanghai Tang store in Central also offers a Shanghainese tailoring service for either Western- or Mandarin-style suits.

Jewellery

Hong Kong is the world's fourth largest exporter of jewellery, and there is a wide range of designs available in retail outlets throughout the territory. Because Hong Kong is a free port and there is no tax on the import or export of precious metals, prices are good. Particularly popular jewellery includes jade items (though you should avoid buying expensive pieces without expert advice) and bright-yellow 24-carat gold, called *chuk kam* in Cantonese. Jewellery stores specialising in *chuk kam* are usually very crowded,

and the atmosphere is more akin to that of a betting shop than an exclusive store. These items are sold by the weight of the gold only, so you pay no premium for the design. There are many fine jewellery stores selling a vast range of gem-set designs – here, you pay for the craftsmanship as well as the materials. Another good buy in Hong Kong are pearls, which come in all shapes, sizes and colours. The practice of bargaining is much less common in jewellery stores now, but you can certainly try your luck by asking for a discount.

Leather goods

Many shops stock a wide range of leather shoes, bags, wallets and luggage. There are top-quality, brand-name goods, as well as very inexpensive wallets and bags from discount stores in the main shopping areas of Tsim Sha Tsui and Causeway Bay.

Sportswear

Hong Kong has many chain stores selling inexpensive sportswear and sports shoes (try Marathon Sports or Royal Sporting House). In Mong Kok, the streets east of Tung Choi street market are devoted to sports stores.

Macau

Macau is a good place to buy Chinese antiques and artefacts, and an excellent place to buy well-crafted Asian furniture in wood or wicker. Many Hong Kong expats buy their furniture here and have it delivered to Hong Kong, often free of charge. Shipping prices may be lower than expected.

BARGAINING

Contrary to popular belief, the practice of bargaining for goods in Hong Kong is a dying art. Price differences are usually so marginal that it is hardly worthwhile trying to bargain. Shopkeepers who are not used to bargaining will probably react rather impatiently to your efforts. If you settle by cash you may get a slightly better deal than if you use a credit card – in many cases, shops will add an extra few percent to the price if you pay by credit card.

Don't waste time trying to bargain in department stores or modern shops. They frequently offer marked discounts to induce sales but are not amenable to any bargaining. Small family-run stores may do so, and in markets you should certainly attempt to use your bargaining skills. Remember, though, that if you buy from a market there are no guarantees and there's no possibility of exchanging goods. Even in street markets, it is highly unlikely that you'll be able to reduce the asking price by much more than about 10 to 20 percent.

Many antique stores are clustered in Rua de São Paula, the busy lane which leads up to the facade of São Paulo. You are free to bargain hard here. Otherwise, Macau is rarely thought of as a shopping mart, except for its magnificently priced wines, brandies and ports, which are restricted upon return to Hong Kong. Though it is a duty-free port like Hong Kong, the array of goods available is not nearly as extensive. Some items, such as cameras or stereo systems, are more costly in Macau because of the smaller number sold.

Shenzhen

Shenzhen is now a major shopping destination for Hong Kongers. There is a wide variety of merchandise at prices much lower than you will ever find in Hong Kong. Designer clothing and accessories can be bought for less than a fifth of the price in Europe or North America.

Lo Wu Commercial City, immediately on the right as you emerge from customs, is the place everyone heads to, a vast shopping mall packed with electronics, clothes and all kinds of chinoiserie. Shops are generally open 7 days a week from about 10am until 8 or 9pm. Most people venture no further, but there are also some great bargains to be had in the main shopping area

of Dongmen in the centre of Shenzhen (take the new subway, or find a taxi).

Whatever you are buying, remember to bargain hard!

Clothing & textiles

The best tailors in Shenzhen cluster together in **Bu Cheng** – Fabric City – in the Dongmen district. Customers are welcome to choose their fabrics in one shop and then get them made up by the tailor of their choice. A pair of trousers, for example, can be made in a week and should cost less than RMB80. The Dongmen Fabric Market on Hu Bei Lu is also worth visiting.

Lo Wu Commercial City also has plenty to offer for those looking for a tailor-made suit or other custom-made clothing. Most tailors' shops are around the fabric market on the fifth floor. There are literally hundreds of clothing, footwear and accessories shops spread throughout the complex.

Jewellery

Lo Wu Commercial City is also well endowed with jewellery shops, and there can be amazing bargains. The main focus is on pearls (mostly of the freshwater variety), but jade and various precious and semi-precious stones are easy to find, too.

Electronics

Shenzhen's main electronic-goods stores are gathered around a single block on Huaqiang Lu, with names like Electronic City and Aihua Computer City – take a taxi or bus 101 from Lo Wu. The first floor of Lo Wu Commercial City also has plenty of electronics shops. The major bargains are in domestically manufactured items.

Guangzhou

Don't expect the glitz and variety of goods available in Hong Kong to be on offer here, although Guangzhou does still have interesting shopping and good

bargains. The main shopping areas are Zhongshan Wulu, Beijing Lu, Renmin Nanlu, Zhongshan Silu and Xiajiu Lu-Shangjiu Lu. The main open-air market is at Qingping Lu, near Shamian Island.

There are several large department stores worth a visit for their wide array of foreign merchandise, at prices lower than in Hong Kong. Nanfang Dasha (49 Yanjiang Xilu) offers a good choice of local products. Xihu Lu Baihuo Dasha, on Xihu Lu, has a huge choice, especially foreign goods, at amazing prices. Xin Da Xin, at the corner of Beijing Lu and Zhongshan Wulu, offers a good range of Chinese goods, including silk.

Antiques

The largest private market for antiques is the Daihe Lu Market, which sprawls over several lanes.

Antiques that date from before 1795 may not be legally exported. Any antique over a century old must carry a small red wax seal or have one affixed by the Cultural Relics Bureau before it can be taken out of China.

Beware of fakes, as the production of new "antiques" complete with "official" seal is a thriving industry in China. Despite

JADE

Jade holds a greater fascination for the Chinese than any other stone. Traditionally, it is worn for good luck, as a protection against sickness and as an amulet for travellers. There are several types: nephrite, jadeite and a local variety, *nanyu* jade. Do not buy from open-air private markets, as there are plenty of imitations in the market. In Guangzhou, buy from established shops such as the Jade Shop (12–14 Zhongshan Wulu), Baoli Yuqi Hang (220 Zhongshan Silu), Guangzhou Antique Shop (696 Wende Lu), and the jewellery shops of the China, Garden and White Swan hotels.

PEARLS

For centuries, pearls have been the indispensable ornament of the nobility, especially emperors. Most of the pearls on sale in Guangzhou are saltwater southern pearls called *hepu*, cultured in silver-lipped oysters. The largest of these lustrous pearls can have a diameter of 12–16 mm (0.47–0.63 in). Recommended shops include the following: Guangzhou Gold and Silver Jewellery Centre (109 Dade Lu) and Sun Moon Hall (Equatorial Hotel, Renmin Beilu).

the pitfalls, there is still much to buy: *kam muk* (gilded sculptured wood panels), vintage watches, tiny embroidered shoes for Chinese women with bound feet and beautiful Shiwan porcelain.

Popular buys are calligraphy works, jewellery boxes, paintings, porcelain and silver jewellery.

Clothing & textiles

Guangdong province is a major production centre for ready-to-wear clothes and shoes. Look for down jackets (typically costing only one-fifth the price you would pay elsewhere) and cashmere sweaters and scarves. The Bingfen Fashion Market on Haizhu Square, Gong Lu Fashion Market on Zhongshan Erlu in Dongshan District, the night market under the Quzhuang Overbridge and the Xihu Lu night market are also good hunting grounds for apparel.

SPORT

Facilities

Top **hotels** in Hong Kong generally have **swimming pools**, **gyms** and **tennis courts** available free to their guests. A few allow non-guests to use their facilities for a

fee – for example the Marriott Hotel in Admiralty charges HK$285 on weekdays and HK$340 on weekends for an all-day pass. There are also scores of gyms, including international chains like Fitness First and California. However, if you're not a member, daily rates, which range from HK$150 upwards, are quite expensive.

A health craze has sparked the opening of several trendy **yoga and pilates clubs**, mostly concentrated in Central. *HK Magazine* is packed with their ads. By posing as a resident, you can usually pick up a free introductory class, but be prepared for a hard sell afterwards.

The government-run Leisure and Cultural Services Department (LCSD) have **sports centres**, with tennis, badminton and squash courts and swimming pools, all over the city. Visitors to Hong Kong can use their sports facilities, but you must go in person to the centre to book a court. You should be able to walk in and find an available court during the daytime on weekdays, but evening and weekend slots are usually booked days in advance. For a list of centres see www.lcsd.gov.hk/leisurelink/en/ls_booking_1.php.

The **Hong Kong Squash Centre** is at 23 Cotton Tree Drive, Admiralty, tel: 2521 5072. For **tennis** try King's Park Tennis Court, Jordan, tel: 2385 8985, Victoria Park Tennis Court, Causeway Bay, tel: 2570 6186 and Causeway Bay Sports Ground, tel: 2890 5127. Hourly rates are around HK$50.

There are good LCSD **swimming pools** in Victoria Park, Causeway Bay (tel: 2570 4682), and Kowloon Park, Tsim Sha Tsui (tel: 2724 3577). Entry fee is HK$19 per person. Most pools – which are unheated – are closed between November and March.

There are **ice-skating rinks** at City Plaza shopping mall in Tai Koo Shing, and Festival Walk shopping mall in Kowloon Tong. Price, including skate hire, is between HK$45 and HK$60.

Bowling is not ver the few alleys that do scattered in remote s malls in the New Territ..... The most convenient for tourists are the Olympian Super Fun Bowl, in Olympian City shopping mall, tel: 2273 4772 (Olympic MTR station on the Tung Chung line), and the South China Athletic Association Bowling Centre, 88 Caroline Hill Rd, Causeway Bay, tel: 2890 8528.

The only public **golf course** in Hong Kong is the Jockey Club Kau Sai Chau course on an island off Sai Kung in the southeastern New Territories (www.kscgolf.com/eng/course.html, tel: 2791 3388). There are also a handful of private members' clubs which are open to visitors only on weekdays. Try Hong Kong Golf Club, which has three 18-hole courses in Fanling in the northern New Territories (www.hkgolfclub.org/golf/index.jsp, tel: 2670 1211) and three nine-hole courses at Deep Water Bay at 19 Island Rd (tel: 2812 7070), on the south side of Hong Kong Island.

There are **bicycle trails** around Tai Mei Tuk reservoir in the New Territories, from Sha Tin to Tai Po market, around Shek O village and on Cheung Chau island. Bikes can be hired for around HK$40 per day at all these places. You will have to leave your passport as deposit.

Spectator Sports

During the **horse-racing** season (September to June), locals swarm to the city's two big racing stadia in Happy Valley on Wednesday nights, and Sha Tin on weekends. You can make your own way to the track and join the punters in the stands, or take the HKTB's Come Horse-Racing Tour which includes transfer, entry to the visitors' box, buffet meal and drinks. Come in March for the Hong Kong Derby, April for the Queen Elizabeth II Cup and December for the Hong Kong International Races.

TRANS

ACCOMMODATION

ACTIVITIES

A – Z

LANGUAGE

The city's single biggest sporting event is arguably the **Hong Kong Rugby Sevens** – three days of heavy drinking, silly hats and manic singing in the stands while teams from all over the world fight it out on the pitch. The tournament is held at the Hong Kong Stadium in Causeway Bay (www.hksevens.com.hk). You can buy tickets online or from the Rugby Football Union shop at Room 2001, Sports House, 1 Stadium Path, Causeway Bay (tel: 2504 8311). Tickets sell out quickly. More demure is the **Hong Kong Cricket Sixes** held in November at the Kowloon Cricket Club.

The **Macau Grand Prix** (http://gp.macau.grandprix.gov.mo) is held every November; hotels get booked out so plan ahead. Races – car, motorbike and formula cars – are exhilarating since they take place along a 6.2-kilometre (3¾-mile) street circuit, so for one weekend normality is suspended, with tens of thousands of racing fans crowding into this tiny enclave. To buy tickets, contact the Macau Grand Prix committee on tel: 7962242 or buy online at www.macauticket.com

Hiking & Rock Climbing

An oft-quoted "little-known fact" is that around three-quarters of Hong Kong is actually countryside, and if you have the time there are plenty of great hikes on well-marked trails, including circling or descending The Peak, mountain climbs on Lantau Island and spectacular coastal walks in the wilds of Sai Kung. The Country and Marine Parks Authority list walks on their website (http://parks.afcd.gov.hk/newparks/eng/hiking/index.htm), otherwise there's a good paperback – *Hong Kong Pathfinder* by Martin Williams – that picks out some good hikes. For your own safety bring maps, water and a mobile phone. A company called Walk Hong Kong organises hiking tours all over Hong Kong, see www.walkhongkong.com

Every November, teams race to complete the 100-kilometre (62-mile) **Maclehose Trail** which runs east–west across the New Territories in the Hong Kong Trailwalker charity event. The record to date is held by a Gurkha team in 2004 – they finished in 11 hours 57 minutes.

If you are into rock climbing there are at least 19 sites dotted around country parks, from headland crags at Shek O to Lion Rock in Kowloon. See www.hongkong-climbing.com for a good overview as well as a list of indoor climbing walls. The most convenient climbing wall for tourists is at the YMCA in Tsim Sha Tsui, which has two U-shaped walls.

Diving & Watersports

While certainly no match for what's on offer in nearby Thailand and the Philippines, Hong Kong does have a fair few diving schools which brave the territory's murky water. Pollution and over-fishing have taken their toll, but octopus and barracuda are sometimes spotted, and there are several wreck and reef dives. There is even a small amount of coral in Mirs Bay in the northeastern New Territories. Email the Hong Kong Underwater Club at sec@hkuc.org.hk to book a dive. They go out every fortnight. A day's diving with all equipment hire costs around HK$550.

Windsurfing is popular. You can hire boards at Cheung Chau's Kwun Yam Wan Beach. Windsurfing and wakeboarding are also available at beaches at Stanley and Sai Kung, amongst others.

OTHER ACTIVITIES

Cultural Tours

The HKTB runs free "meet the people" tours, which provide more than the usual shopping-and-skyscrapers look at the city.

You can join an early-morning tai chi (shadow boxing) class at 8am at the Avenue of Stars in Tsim Sha Tsui on Monday, Wednesday, Thursday and Friday. Other "classes" include an architecture tour, how to shop for pearls and jade, how to taste Chinese tea, how to listen to Cantonese opera, an antiques lesson and a class in kung fu. All classes are free. See the HKTB for times and booking.

Junk trip

The distinctive diamond-shaped junk with bright red sails, emblematic of Hong Kong, was replaced long ago by giant container ships and sleek turbojets. The last remaining authentic junk, the Duk Ling, is owned by the HKTB and, as a visitor you can book a free one-hour cruise on the boat. There are several departures every Thursday afternoon leaving from Tsim Sha Tsui and Central. You must register first with the HKTB office in person.

Children's Activities

There is a great deal on offer for children in Hong Kong. Travelling on its public transport is adventure enough for some, with its trains, trams, taxis, minibuses, double-decker buses, ferries and junks.

Hong Kong now has two large theme parks. The new kid on the block is **Disneyland** (Lantau, tel: 1 830 830; www.hongkongdisney-land.com), which opened in 2005 and is at or near the top of most children's must-see list. Just 30 minutes by MTR from Central, the 126-hectare (310-acre) site includes four themed areas – Main Street USA, Fantasyland, Adventureland and Tomorrowland. Entrance fees are HK$295 for adults (HK$350 at peak times), HK$210 (HK$250) for children aged 3–11, and HK$170 (HK$200) for under-65s.

Ocean Park (Aberdeen, tel: 2552 0291) is a home-grown theme park located on the south side of Hong Kong Island. Its animal collections include giant pan-

das, sea lions, birds, butterflies and dolphins. The coral-reef-themed aquarium includes a dramatic shark tunnel. There are also various stomach-churning rides. Admission charges are: adults, HK$185, children (3–11) HK$95.

A must-see for most visitors, including kids, is the view from **The Peak**. The Peak Tower is undergoing a face-lift in late 2005 and will be closed until March 2006, when it will reveal various new attractions. **Madame Tussaud's** is also reopening in 2006 after renovation.

Some Hong Kong museums are particularly child-friendly. In Kowloon, visit the highly interactive **Science Museum** (2 Science Museum Road, Tsim Sha Tsui East; tel: 2732 3232; closed Thursday). On the ground floor, the Children's Zone under-fives make giant bubbles and experiment. Among the 17 other galleries, older children are drawn to the transport simulators and the computer lab.

The **Museum of History** (100 Chatham Road, Tsim Sha Tsui; tel: 2724 9042; closed Tuesday) is a modern museum that recreates the "Hong Kong Story". Younger children love the volcano simulation and life-size examples of the mammals that once roamed Kowloon. The walk-through Hong Kong street scenes are excellent.

The **Space Museum** (10 Salisbury Road, Tsim Sha Tsui; tel: 2721 0226, closed Tuesday) has exhibitions, but best of all is its dome-shaped cinema screen, which shows Omnimax films and the Sky Show (Adults HK$32, Children HK$16).

Perhaps an unlikely hit with children, the Hong Kong Jockey Club's **Racing Museum** (2/F Happy Valley Stand, Happy Valley Racecourse; tel: 2966 8065; closed Monday) focuses on horses rather than gambling – dress up as a jockey, and try out the horse simulators.

Adventurous types love clambering around the battlements and tunnels at the extremely well-designed **Museum of Coastal Defence** (175 Tung Hei Road, Shau Kei Wan; tel: 2569 1500; closed Thursday). Explore 600 years of coastal history and walk around the hillside at this historic fort that once protected the eastern approach to the harbour.

If it's raining or very hot, you will need a few indoor activities on your itinerary. **Ice skating** is a cool option. Kids can skate in decent-sized rinks in a shopping mall while you shop. City Plaza (Tai Koo Shing; tel: 2844 8633) and Festival Walk (Kowloon Tong; tel: 2844 2223).

For space in the city, head to the free public parks and play-grounds. In Causeway Bay there's **Victoria Park** (tel: 2570 6186), with mini-playgrounds, boat pond, small roller-skating rink, and outdoor swimming pool. Cross the road bridge to the **Central Library** (66 Causeway Road, Causeway Bay; tel: 3150 1234; closed Wednesday morning) for air-conditioning, children's books, a playroom, readings and information about what's on for children.

Connecting Admiralty to Central, **Hong Kong Park** (tel: 2521 5041) is good for a few hours of fun. Enjoy its 250-square-metre (300-sq. yd) children's playground, water features, huge aviary and a reasonable open-air restaurant.

Kowloon Park (tel: 2724 3344) is a green haven in the heart of Tsim Sha Tsui. Its playground, maze and sculpture park are useful diversions. A selection of swimming pools offers more excitement than the average hotel swimming pool.

For a unique Hong Kong experience, take to the water to see the rare **pink dolphins** that live in the Pearl River Delta. Hong Kong Dolphinwatch Ltd (Tel: 2984 1414, www.hkdolphinwatch.com) runs tours every Wednesday, Friday and Sunday morning. A coach collects visitors from Central and Tsim Sha Tsui for a 2 to 3 hour junk trip. Adults HK$320, Children (3 to 11 years) HK$160.

The **outlying islands** are an easy day out with children. Take a ferry to Cheung Chau or Lamma Island and set your own pace. The tanks of live fish and seafood outside the islands' renowned restaurants will fascinate, plus the seafood restaurants are relaxed and family-friendly. Enjoy a stroll to the beach, hike over the hills or hire bikes and explore the traffic-free islands.

For a day on the **beach** on Hong Kong Island visit Deep Water Bay, Repulse Bay and Chung Hom Kok (near Stanley). The beaches are kept clean and are patrolled by lifeguards.

All sights are detailed in full in the Places section of the book.

DIRECTORY

A dmission Charges

Government-owned museum and gallery admissions are good value in Hong Kong. Average charges are around HK$10 for adults and HK$5 for seniors and students. Children under three are free, and many museums are free to all on Wednesdays. To make your money go further, the HK$30 Museum Pass gives one week's unlimited access to six of the city's most popular museums.

Privately owned venues are more expensive. Adults pay HK$95 at Madame Tussaud's, while children aged 3 to 11 years cost HK$55. A day of fun at Ocean Park is HK$93 for children and HK$185 for adults. At cinemas, tickets average HK$60 for adults with a small reduction for

children. Admission to all parks and beaches is free.

B udgeting for Your Trip

Hong Kong has yet fully to recover from the economic crisis of 1998. As a result, lower rents and less confidence in the economy has tended to lower prices in the past few years. An additional factor is that the Hong Kong dollar is pegged to the US dollar, so how far your money goes in Hong Kong and China will always be relative to the strength and weakness of the greenback.

Hotel prices can vary throughout the year. The busiest times at Hong Kong hotels are during the main public holidays, and major trade fairs. Outside these times prices can drop considerably.

Researching your options will pay off, as many hotels have regular promotions on their websites, and travel agents and online hotel-booking sites negotiate special rates *(see hotels, page 209)*.

Once in Hong Kong, transportation is a bargain. For HK$15 (US$2) you can travel up to 10 stops on the MTR or cross Hong Kong Island by public bus. It costs HK$2 to ride the length of the island by tram and on Hong Kong's other iconic transportation, the Star Ferry, you will spend HK$2.20 to cross the harbour.

Discovering the range of food in Hong Kong is part of the experience, and prices can vary dramatically. You can expect to pay US$10–$15 or less per person at a very reasonable Chinese restaurant. A meal for two in a

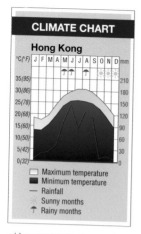

CLIMATE CHART

Hong Kong

- ☐ Maximum temperature
- ■ Minimum temperature
- — Rainfall
- ☼ Sunny months
- ☂ Rainy months

mid-range restaurant can cost upwards of US$100 with wine. At the best restaurants diners expect to pay US$250 plus for two.

To stretch the budget further, look out for special menus and budget set menus at cafés and restaurants. "Business lunch" set menus are great value.

There are bargains to be had at the best hotels. The hotel buffet is an institution and a great way to sample a huge variety of cuisine, or satisfy different tastes within a group for a reasonable price. It's an event in itself and a treat for gastronomes.

Standard drinks in Hong Kong cost around US$5 and can be double in luxury hotel bars and the trendiest venues. Look out for Happy Hours.

Business Hours

Office hours in Hong Kong are 9am to 5.30pm or 6pm. Small shops, grocers and markets are open before 8am, but major stores and shopping centres generally open around 10am. Banks open between 8.30am and 4.30pm, but times may vary between branches and banks.

While shops in Central close by 7 or 8pm, elsewhere it's late-night shopping every night. In particular, many shops in Cause-

way Bay, Tsim Sha Tsui and Mong Kok stay open until 10 or 11pm. Hong Kong is anticipating the opening of the first 24-hour shopping centre in 2006, but for now the usual opening times for shopping centres is 10am until 10pm, 7 days a week, including public holidays.

Bars and restaurants are free to choose their own opening times. Things start to quieten down in the main entertainment districts after 1am. If you want to drink and party all night you will find venues.

In Macau, restaurants and bars are open late, but after midnight most of the action is centred around the 24-hour casinos. In Shenzhen and Guangzhou shops and shopping centres are open in the evening and although locals like to dine early, there are many places to eat and drink late at night.

C limate

Hong Kong has a humid subtropical climate. There are, however, four distinct seasons. The ideal time for travelling to Hong Kong is from the end of September to early December, when the weather is warm, the air is relatively dry and it seldom rains. The average daytime temperature is around 24°C (75°F), with humidity around 70 percent.

Despite the latitude, winter (late December to early March) temperatures can be slightly chilly, especially in the rural areas, so it is advisable to bring light woollens and sometimes a coat. The average daytime temperature is 17°C (63°F), with humidity around 75 percent.

Temperatures and humidity rise abruptly in spring, when daytime temperatures shoot up from 20°C (68°F) in March to 28°C (82°F) in May. In summer, which lasts until early September, temperatures hover around 30°C (86°F) and humidity is consistently above 70 percent. Even at night it is rare for the temperature to dip below 26°C (79°F), and even when it doesn't rain you will quickly be dripping with sweat. Wear light clothes, but bring something with long sleeves for the summer – because many

TYPHOONS

From June to early September, it is not uncommon for Hong Kong to experience tropical storms or typhoons (the name derives from *dai fung* – big wind). If you are in Hong Kong when a typhoon hits, you will find that virtually everything comes to a complete standstill.

The Hong Kong Observatory has standard typhoon warnings that vary according to how close a typhoon is to Hong Kong. Usually, this begins with a typhoon number one signal, which may shortly escalate to a number three. When the number eight signal is raised, it means Hong Kong may suffer a direct hit. Schools, offices and shops close immediately and everyone goes home. A rare typhoon number ten is almost certain to

mean serious damage, as the storm sweeps through the territory causing floods and sometimes deaths. Watching typhoon news bulletins can be dramatic and exciting, but when everything closes you will be stuck for anything to do. Hotels, however, do continue to operate. In fact, locals often go to hotel restaurants as they are the only places likely to be open during a typhoon. Stay inside during a typhoon, as fatalities have been known to occur in both urban and rural areas, mainly due to objects and structures that fall in the strong winds.

The frequency of direct hits is erratic: of the thirteen since 1946, only one (typhoon York in 1999) has occurred in the past twenty years.

ELECTRICITY

The voltage in Hong Kong is 200/220 volts, 50 cycles. For a place of such international standing, it is surprising that Hong Kong still does not seem to have standardised plug fittings. However, hotels will certainly have adaptors to make any appliance work.

restaurants and shops have very effective air-conditioning.

Macau's climate is the same as Hong Kong's. Temperatures in Guangzhou are slightly higher in summer, slightly lower in winter, and there is rather more rain through the year.

Crime & Safety

One of the great joys of Hong Kong is the low level of crime and the resultant freedom from fear of crime. In the main commercial and entertainment areas you are safe to walk alone any hour of the day, and most of the night. Tourists are more obvious targets for pickpockets in busy areas, but normal precautions should suffice.

Both Guangzhou and Macau are considered safe destinations for tourists. Avoid touts and do not be tempted to pursue goods and services offered to you on the street.

More caution is required in Shenzhen. Hong Kong residents have reported muggings and a few have reported being held against their will. Dress down for a visit to Shenzhen and leave your jewellery behind. Stick to busy public areas. When shopping, do not let the lure of a bargain make you forget your common sense.

Customs Regulations

Hong Kong is a free port, so you can bring as many gifts as you like in and out of the territory.

Cars can also be brought in for personal use without payment of duty. Firearms must be declared and handed into custody until departure. Duty-free allowances for visitors are 200 cigarettes and 50 cigars or 250g tobacco and 1 litre of wine or spirits.

Departure tax

Hong Kong imposes a HK$120 Air Passenger Departure Tax on all passengers aged 12 years and above departing Hong Kong International Airport. This is normally included in the price of the airline ticket.

D isabled Travellers

The Hong Kong Council of Social Services has compiled a useful accessibility guide for buildings and tourist attractions, www.hkcss. org.hk/rh/accessguide/ default.htm

Taxis are often the best way to get about in Hong Kong, and reasonably priced. The train networks have a very inconsistent level of access. Station announcements are in Cantonese, Mandarin (Putonghua) and English.

Easy-Access Travel, is a subsidiary of the Hong Kong Society for Rehabilitation, has a fleet of specially adapted buses so it can cater for visitors with limited mobility. Day trips, full itineraries and advice are available. Email: enquiry@easyaccesstravelhk.com, tel: 2772 7301, www.easyaccesstravelhk.com

E mbassies & Consulates

Australia, Harbour Centre, 21–4/F, 25 Harbour Rd, Wan Chai. Tel: 2827 8881.
Canada, One Exchange Square, 11/F, 8 Connaught Place, Central. Tel: 2810 4321.
France, Admiralty Centre, Tower II, 26/F, 18 Harcourt Rd, Admiralty. Tel: 3196 6100.
Germany, 21/F United Centre, 95 Queensway, Admiralty. Tel: 2105 8712.
Japan, 46/F One Exchange Square, 8 Connaught Place, Central. Tel: 2522 1184.
New Zealand, Rm 6505, Central Plaza, 18 Harbour Rd, Wan Chai. Tel: 2877 4488.

EMERGENCY NUMBERS

For police, fire and ambulance services in Hong Kong and China, dial 999. In Macau call 999 for emergencies, or 919 for police.

Singapore, Unit 901, 9/F Tower 1, Admiralty Centre, 18 Harcourt Rd, Admiralty. Tel: 2527 2212.
South Africa, 27/F Great Eagle Centre, 23 Harbour Rd, Wan Chai. Tel: 2577 3279.
United Kingdom, 1 Supreme Court Rd, Admiralty. Tel: 2901 3000.
United States, 26 Garden Rd, Central. Tel: 2523 9011.

Entry Requirements

Visas & passports

Nationals of most developed countries do not require a visa for entry to Hong Kong or Macau, but you will need one if you plan to visit mainland China. *See panel.*

For those taking up employment in Hong Kong, it is necessary to obtain a work permit from the Immigration Department, usually in advance of entering the territory. Your company should be able to assist with the necessary paperwork. Hong Kong residents should carry a Hong Kong identity card, which is issued by the Immigration Department.

All other visitors are supposed to carry photographic identity such as a passport with them, but it is unlikely that you will be stopped by police officers and asked to produce identification.

G ay & Lesbian Travellers

Hong Kong's gay scene may not yet have come of age but it had its long-overdue coming-out party with its first Pink Parade in October 2004, and the city's Gay and Lesbian film festival has become part of the alternative arts calendar. For information on events and happenings, look for HK Magazine and its sister publication G Magazine.

To sample the local scene, visit Hong Kong's self-proclaimed "first Internet gay bar". New Wally Matt Lounge, G/F Humphrey's Avenue, Tsim Sha Tsui is open from 5pm to 4am daily, and is a friendly pub with free computers. On Hong Kong side, try Rice Bar, 33 Jervois Street, Central, open 7pm until late, for an evening drink in a sophisticated and welcoming venue (see page 220).

H ealth & Medical Care

No vaccinations are required for Hong Kong, but it is advisable to consider inoculations against Hepatitis A. Tap water is safe in Hong Kong but you may find bottled water more palatable. The most important thing is to keep well hydrated in the heat and humidity. Eat in licensed cafés and restaurants and avoid eating food from street stalls.

Medical services

Hong Kong
Adventist Hospital, 40 Stubbs Rd, Happy Valley. Tel: 2574 6211.
Central Medical Practice, 1501 Prince's Bldg, Central. Tel: 2521 2567.
Hong Kong Central Hospital, 1B Lower Albert Rd, Central. Tel: 2522 3141.
Prince of Wales Hospital, 30–32 Ngan Shing St, Sha Tin, New Territories. Tel: 2632 2211.
Queen Elizabeth Hospital, 30 Gascoigne Rd, Kowloon. Tel: 2958 8888.
Queen Mary Hospital, Pokfulam Rd, Hong Kong. Tel: 2816 6366.

Macau
S. Januário Hospital, Estrada do Visconde de S. Januário. Tel: 313 731.
Kiang Wu Hospital, Estrada Coelho do Amaral. Tel: 371 333.

Shenzhen
Shenzhen People's Hospital, Dongmen Road North. Tel: 2553 3018.

CHINESE VISAS

All visitors to China require a visa. These can be obtained from your nearest China embassy before you travel. When in Hong Kong you can contact a travel agent or go direct to the Ministry of Foreign Affairs, 7/F Lower Block, China Resources Building, 26 Harbour Road, Wan Chai, or to the China Travel Service, CTS House, 78–83 Connaught Road, Central. Tel: 2853 3533. In Kowloon, CTS is at 1/F Alpha House, 27 Nathan Road, Tsim Sha Tsui. Tel: 2315 7106; 24-hour hotline, tel: 3413 2300.

If you plan on visiting Hong Kong as a side trip from the mainland, make sure that you have a double- or multiple-entry China visa.

Guangzhou
Guangzhou Can Am International Medical Centre, 5/F Garden Hotel, 368 Huanshi Dong Lu. Tel: 8386 6988.
Guangzhou No. 1 People's Hospital, 602 Renmin Road North. Tel: 8108 2090.

I nternet

Internet access is available in all hotel business centres. More and more hotels offer broadband connections in their rooms for guests with laptops. Internet cafés are not common in Hong Kong, but free Internet access is available at many coffee shops around the SAR. Branches of chains Pacific Coffee, Starbucks and Mix offer two or three computers for free use by their customers – although you may have to wait at busy times.

L eft Luggage

Facilities are available at Hong Kong Airport, and in Kowloon, at Hung Hom Station and the Hong Kong China City Building.

FACT FILE

Area: The Hong Kong Special Administrative Region covers a total area of 1,103 square kilometres (426 sq. miles), comprising Hong Kong Island, the Kowloon peninsula, the New Territories and 262 outlying islands.
Geography: Hong Kong lies on a latitude of 22° 15 North and longitude of 114° 10 East.
Population: Hong Kong's population is approaching 7 million, and population density is 6,300 people per square kilometre (2,400 per sq. mile).

Of the half a million or so non-Chinese living in Hong Kong, the three biggest groups are the approximately 133,000 people from the Philippines, 96,000 Indonesians and 32,000 US passport holders.
Weights and Measures: Imperial, metric and traditional Chinese measures are all legally accepted weights and measures in Hong Kong. Distance is most often measured in kilometres. Clothes and shoes also mix Asian, European, British and American sizings.

Lost Property

To report lost or stolen property, contact the Hong Kong Police. Call 2860 2000 to find out the location of the nearest police station. If you are think you left your property in a taxi it may be worth contacting the taxi lost property line which will inform all taxi drivers. Tel: 1872 920.

To report a lost credit card, call American Express on 2811 6122, MasterCard on 2511 6387 and Visa on 2810 8033.

Maps

Maps with place names in both English and Chinese are useful. If you can point at a place name written in Chinese characters with a friendly smile, many a misunderstanding can be avoided.

The laminated Insight Fleximap Hong Kong is durable, detailed and easy to use, with a full street index. The Hong Kong Tourist Board provides welcome packs which include maps and airport, seaport and border crossings from mainland China. Maps of Macau can be picked up free of charge on arrival in Macau at the ferry terminal. Bookshops throughout the SAR stock maps of Guangzhou and Shenzhen.

Media

Newspapers & magazines

Hong Kong has a large number of newspapers and magazines, most of which are published in Chinese. Hong Kong continues to enjoy a free press despite being part of China, and the territory is noted as a media centre for the region.

The most influential newspaper in Hong Kong is the daily English-language *South China Morning Post*. A second English daily is the *Hongkong Standard*. Two of the most popular Chinese-language dailies are the rather sensationalist *Oriental Daily*

News and the *Apple Daily News*.

One magazine worth looking out for is the weekly English-language *HK Magazine*, which is published every Friday and distributed free at most popular bars, restaurants and bookshops in the territory. It is aimed at residents, but tourists who want an opinionated insider's view will find its restaurant and entertainment reviews worth a read.

Radio & television

Over a dozen radio stations are broadcast in Hong Kong, though there is now only one dedicated English-language channel: RTHK. Some other stations offer an element of programming in English. The BBC World Service is available free 24 hours a day.

For local news, Hong Kong's two TV stations, TVB and ATV, each broadcast one English-language channel and one Chinese-language channel. If you are staying in a hotel you should have access to a good selection of regional and international broadcasters in English via cable and satellite.

Money Matters

The Hong Kong dollar is the standard unit of currency and comes in denominations of HK$1,000, $500, $100, $50, $20 and $10 notes plus HK$10, $5, $2 and $1 coins. The dollar is divided into 100 cents, and there are coins of 50¢, 20¢ and 10¢ denominations. The dollar rate fluctuates against most major international currencies but it is pegged to the US dollar at approximately 7.8 Hong Kong dollars to the US dollar.

There are three note-issuing banks in Hong Kong: Hongkong and Shanghai Bank, Standard Chartered Bank and the Bank of China. Most high street banks will exchange foreign currency and generally display exchange rates on digital boards. They usually offer better rates than the money-changers in the major tourist areas, although there's usually a $50 charge for a single transaction. Cash machines are plentiful in the urban areas, and allow the withdrawal of local currency with most major credit cards.

Macau's official currency, the

PUBLIC HOLIDAYS

The fact that many Hong Kong residents work a five-and-a-half-day week and have short periods of annual leave is compensated by a relatively large number of public holidays every year – 17 in total. These are as follows:

- **1 January:** New Year's Day
- **January/February:** Lunar New Year (three-day holiday)
- **March/April:** Good Friday and Easter Monday; Ching Ming Festival (5 April)
- **May/June:** Dragon Boat Festival; Buddha's Birthday (11 May); Labour Day (1 May)
- **1 July:** SAR Establishment Day
- **September/October:** The day following Mid-Autumn Festival
- **1 October:** National Day

(2 days)
- **October:** Chung Yeung Festival
- **25 December:** Christmas (2 days)

Macau

As for Hong Kong, but with Macau Special Administrative Region Establishment Day (**20 Dec**) instead of the 1 July holiday.

China

Official state holidays are:
- **1 January:** New Year's Day
- **1 May:** Labour Day
- **1 October:** National Day
Most shops and offices close down for a week or so at Chinese New Year, and for a few days around Labour Day and National Day.

pataca (MOP$), is divided into 100 avos. There are banknotes in denominations of 1,000, 500, 100, 50, 20 and 10 patacas and 10, 5, 2, and 1 pataca coins. The pataca is linked to the Hong Kong dollar, which is accepted as currency in Macau.

Hong Kong dollars are also widely accepted in Guangzhou and Shenzhen, but if you are staying more than a day in mainland China it is worth changing your money to Chinese currency, renminbi (RMB). The basic unit is the yuan, often called kuai. One yuan is worth ten jiao. Banknotes come in 100, 50, 10, 5 and 1 yuan denominations: plus 5, 2 and 1 jiao.

Tipping

Tipping is customary in Hong Kong in bars, restaurants and hotels. A 10-percent service charge is added to the bill in many restaurants, but it is still customary to add a further 5 percent to go direct to the staff. Taxi drivers do not expect to be tipped, but rounding up the fare to the nearest dollar or two is appreciated.

In places frequented by tourists in Macau, Shenzhen and Guangzhou tipping is increasingly common practice; follow the same guidelines as Hong Kong.

Postal Services

Airmail stamps are available from convenience stores and vending machines outside post offices. The General Post Office in Central, located close to the Star Ferry pier, also sells a selection of cards and gifts.

Most post offices are open 9.30am to 5pm Monday to Friday and 9.30am to 1pm on Saturday. On Kowloon side, the main post office is located at 10 Middle Road, Tsim Sha Tsui, and is also open on Sundays, 9am to 2pm.

If you choose to mail presents and purchases rather than carry them home, Hong Kong Post is cheap, efficient and can also courier documents and parcels.

In Hong Kong, Macau, Shenzhen and Guangzhou hotels will assist guests with posting mail and packages.

In Macau, the main post office is located in picturesque Senado Square. If you are tempted by antique and reproduction furniture, shops can assist in arranging shipping. Shenzhen shoppers rely on the post office on the ground floor at the Lo Wu shopping centre to ease their burden after bargain-hunting. In China it is probably much simpler to use the postal services at business and tourist hotels.

Public Toilets

Toilet facilities at tourist attractions in Hong Kong are generally clean, well maintained and always free of charge. Public toilets in other locations are of a variable standard, and soap and paper may be absent. Shopping centres and restaurants usually have clean facilities. To be on the safe side, always carry a small pack of tissues.

There are few public toilets to be found in Macau, and clean public toilets are a rarity in Shenzhen. However, in recent years Guangzhou has opened some acceptable new public toilets, complete with star rating. Patrons must pay a small fee of one or two yuan at these new

Student Travellers

Students over the age of 11 years do not benefit from many travel discounts in Hong Kong, Macau and the mainland. Some cultural events offer slightly reduced ticket prices for students with identification.

Telecommunications

Hong Kong is well known for having one of the most advanced telecommunications systems in the world. Virtually the entire network consists of fibre-optic cabling with digital switching, which means a whole host of advanced telecommunications services are available to local users. Phones can be used on the MTR subway system. Hong Kong has one of the highest rates of mobile phone penetration – at 117 percent there are more phone subscribers than residents.

Mobile phones can be rented at Hong Kong International Airport. To avoid roaming changes, you can buy pre-paid SIM cards with a Hong Kong number and fixed number of minutes from convenience stores or the telephone companies' shops. These cards are compatible with tri-band and dual-band phones.

Local telephone calls are free of charge, so it is acceptable to

TRANSPORT

ACCOMMODATION

ACTIVITIES

A – Z

LANGUAGE

use telephones in shops, bars and restaurants. Using a public telephone booth usually costs HK$1 for five minutes and calls can be paid by phone card or coins. Stored-value phone cards are available from retail stores of telephone companies and convenience stores. All hotels offer international direct-dial services at an inflated price and charge for local calls from guest rooms.

International dialling codes:
• Hong Kong: **852**
• Macau: **853**
• Shenzhen: **86-755**
• Guangzhou: **86-20**

In Hong Kong:
• Directory Assistance: 1081 (in English)
• Collect Calls: 10010
• Overseas IDD: 10013

International access codes:
AT&T: 800 96 1111
MCI: 800 96 1121
Sprint: 800 96 1877

Time Zone

Hong Kong, Macau, Shenzhen and Guangzhou all operate on the same time zone (Beijing time). This is GMT +8 hours (EST +13 hours). There is no daylight savings time, so from early April to late October, when Europe and America put their clocks forward by 1 hour, Hong Kong is 7 hours ahead of London and 12 hours ahead of New York.

Tourist Information

The Hong Kong Tourism Board (HKTB) is the official government-sponsored body representing the tourism industry of Hong Kong, and offers many useful services and helpful publications. HKTB also provides information packs for tourists arriving at the airport and the land crossing at Lo Wu. Out-of-hours computer terminals provide 24-hour access to the www.DiscoverHongKong.com website.

At the HKTB's Visitor Information and Services Centres you can pick up useful publications including the weekly Hong Kong Diary and the monthly Official Hong Kong Map. *A Guide to Quality Shops and Restaurants* is a handy but dense book that lists all establishments that have been accredited by the by the HKTB, and includes special offers and vouchers that are exclusive to visitors. The centres also provide a tour-reservation service for selected tours, and stock an interesting selection of souvenirs.

HKTB visitor centres

• **International Airport**: (only accessible to arriving visitors), 7am–11pm daily
• **Lo Wu Terminal Building**: Arrival Hall, 2/F, 8am–6pm daily
• **Hong Kong Island**: Causeway Bay MTR station (Near Exit F), 8am–8pm daily
• **Kowloon**: Star Ferry pier, Tsim Sha Tsui, 8am–8pm daily
Visitor Hotline (multilingual)

2508 1234 8am–6pm daily
Tourist information is available at www.DiscoverHongKong.com

CTS offices

China Travel Service (CTS) is China's state travel agency and can arrange tours, tickets and visas for travel to the mainland, although CTS offices do not provide a tourist information service.
Hong Kong: G/F CTS House, 78–83 Connaught Road, Central. Tel: 2853 3533.
Kowloon: 1/F Alpha House, 27 Nathan Road, Tsim Sha Tsui. Tel: 2315 7106.

Macau

The Macau Government Tourist Office runs offices at the Macau ferry terminal in Hong Kong and upon arrival in Macau. There is also a useful **tourist information centre** on the Largo do Senado square, open 9am–6pm daily. Visitors can contact the tourist hotline (853) 333 000 or view the website www.macautourism.gov.mo

Tourist offices overseas

Australia
Level 4, Hong Kong House, 80 Druitt Street, Sydney, NSW 2000
Tel: 61 2 9283 3083
Fax: 61 2 9283 3383
Canada
Ground Floor, 9 Temperance Street, Toronto, Ontario M5H 1Y6
Tel: 1 416 366 2389
Fax: 1 416 366 1098
United Kingdom
6 Grafton Street, London W1S 4EQ
Tel: 44 20 7533 7100
Fax: 44 20 7533 7111
USA
115 East 54th Street, Second Floor, New York, NY 10022-4512
Tel: 1 212 421 3382
Fax: 1 212 421 8428
Singapore
9 Temasek Boulevard, #34–03 Suntec Tower Two, Singapore 038989
Tel: 65 6336 5800
Fax: 65 6336 5811

A BRIEF INTRODUCTION TO CANTONESE

Hong Kong's official languages are Chinese and English. The main Chinese dialect is Cantonese, spoken by more than 90 percent of the population and an inseparable part of the sound and rhythm of the city. Mandarin Chinese *(Putonghua)*, the official language of the People's Republic of China, is gaining in popularity. This reflects the importance of doing business with the mainland and inbound tourism rather than government directives.

There are eight dialects or varieties of Chinese that share some similarities and a writing form, but they are not mutually intelligible. The written form of Chinese was originally derived from pictures or symbols that represented objects or concepts, so there is no correlation between the apperance of Chinese characters and the sound that they represent.

Cantonese is spoken in Hong Kong, Macau and the southern provinces of Guangdong and Guangxi. Outside China, Cantonese is the most widely spoken form of Chinese due to the history of worldwide migration from Hong Kong and its neighbouring provinces.

Hong Kong people use a standard form of Cantonese when they write, or in a business situation, but speak colloquial Cantonese in everyday conversation. Colloquial Chinese is rich in slang, and some spoken words do not have characters.

To confuse the Chinese learner further, Hong Kong (like Taiwan) uses a slightly different style of characters to the rest of China. During reforms initiated by Mao in the fifties to increase literacy, the PRC simplified its characters. Hence the characters used on the mainland are referred to as Simplified Chinese while Hong Kong's more complex characters are called Traditional Chinese.

Tones

If all this was not enough to master, many an enthusiastic linguist has been defeated by Cantonese tones. Tone is not used within a sentence to indicate stress as in many European languages; instead, each word has a distinct pitch that goes higher, lower or stays flat within each word. Among the Cantonese there is no real agreement as to how many tones there are – some say as many as nine – but most people use six in daily life (which makes Putonghua's four tones seem more accessible).

The Jyutping transliteration system devised by the Linguistic Society of Hong Kong classifies the six main tones as: 1, high falling/high flat; 2, high rising; 3, middle; 4, low falling; 5, low rising; 6, low. For the new learner, just hitting three tones to boost their intelligibility is a triumph.

Each word has one syllable, and is represented by one distinct character. A word is made up of three sound elements. An initial e.g., "f ", plus a final sound e.g. "an", plus a tone.

Tone is an essential part of each word. A few rare words just have a final sound and a tone, e.g. "m" in "m goi" (thank you).

Therefore, when combined with a tone, "fan" has seven distinct and contradictory meanings: to divide (high rising 1); flour (high falling 2); to teach (middle flat 3); fragrant (high flat 1); a grave (low falling 4); energetic (low rising 5); and a share (low flat 5).

The wealth of sound-alike words (homonyms) that can be easily mispronounced play a part in many Cantonese traditions and the development of slang. However, for the visitor or new learner tones that utter bafflement is a common reaction to your attempt simply to say the name of the road you wish to visit. Persevere and attempt to mimic the way a Cantonese speaker says each part of the phrase.

Pronunciation

j as in the "y" of **y**ap
z is similar to the the sound in
bei**ge** or **j**ar or the zh in Guang**zh**ou
c as in **ch**ip
au as in h**ow**
ai as in b**uy**
ou as in n**o**
i as in h**e**

Numbers

one	jat
two	ji
three	saam
four	sei
five	ng
six	luk
seven	cat
eight	baat
nine	gau
ten	sap
eleven	sap jat
twelve	sap ji
twenty	ji sap
twenty-one	ji sap jat
one hundred	baak
zero	ling
140	jat sei ling
235	ji saam ng

Common words and phrases

Good morning	zou san (joe san)
Good afternoon	ng on
Good night	zou tau
Goodbye	bai bai
Hello (on phone)	wai!
Thank you (service)	m goi
Thank you (gift)	do ze
You're welcome	M sai m goi
No problem	mou man tai
How are you?	Nei hou maa? (neigh ho marr)
Fine, thank you	gay ho, yau sum
Have you eaten?	sik zou faan mei a?
yes	hai
no	m hai
OK	hou aa
so-so	ma ma
My name is…	ngor geeu
yesterday	kum yut
today	gum yut
tomorrow	ting yut

Nouns

hotel	zau dim
key	so si
manager	ging lei
room	haak fong
telephone	din wa
toilet	ci so
bank	ngan hong
post office	yau jing guk
passport	wu ziu
restaurant	zaan teng
bar	zau ba
bus	ba si
taxi	dik si
train	fo ze

Questions

Questions are often followed by "a"

Who?	bin go a?
Where?	bin do a?
When?	gei si a?
Why?	dim gaai a?
How many?	gei do a?
How much does that cost?	gei dor chin a?
Do you have…?	yau mo … a?
What time is the train to Guangzhou…?	Guangzhou ge for che, gay dim hoy a?

People

mother	maa maa
father	baa baa
son	zai
daughter	neoi
baby	be be
friend	pang jau
boyfriend	naam pang jau
girlfriend	neoi pang jau
husband	lou gung
wife	lou po

Adjectives

small	sui
big	dai
good	ho
bad	mm ho
expensive	gwai
cheap	peng
thin	sau
fat	fei
slow	maan
fast	faai
pretty/beautiful	leng
hot	jit

cold	dung
very…	hou …
very cold	hou dung
delicious	ho sick

Taxis

taxi	dik si
Please take me to	m goy chey ngor hur-ee .
straight on	jick hur-ee
left	hai jor bin
right	hai yau bin

Health and Emergencies

I have (a) …	ngo…
headache	tau tung
stomach ache	tou tung
toothache	nga tung
cough	kau sau
fever	faat sui
flu	gam mou
I have a headache	ngo tau tung
I am sick	ngo jau beng
doctor	ji sang
nurse	wu si
ambulance	gau surng che
police	ging chaat

Food and drink

breakfast	zou caan
lunch	ng caan
dinner	maan caan
eat	sik faan
rice	faan
boiled rice	baak faan
fried rice	cau faan
noodles	min
vegetables	coi
meat	juk
beef	ngau juk
pork	zyut juk
lamb	joeng juk
chicken	gai
prawn	ha
fish	jyu
tea	ca
coffee	gaa fei
water	sur-ee
beer	be zau
white/red wine	baak/hung zau
I am a vegetarian	ngo sik zaai
My bill, please!	maai daan, m goi!
a little	seeu seeu
enough	gau la

FURTHER READING

Fiction

Clavell, James. *Taipan*. Antheneum & Dell, 1966. The rise of an influential 19th-century British merchant family in Hong Kong.

Elegant, Robert. *Dynasty*. William Collins & Sons, 1977. Written by a foreign correspondent based in Hong Kong, this is the tale of a powerful Eurasian family in the colony from 1900 to 1970.

Mason, Richard. *The World of Suzie Wong*. 1957, Pegasus Books, 1994. An English artist falls in love with a local lass in this, the book that made Wan Chai famous.

Mo, Timothy. *The Monkey King*. Paddleless Press, 2000. A brilliant account of a dysfunctional family living in colonial Hong Kong.

Morris, Jan. *Hong Kong*. Vintage, 1997. Wonderfully insightful text from the doyenne of modern travel writers.

Row, Jess. *The Train to Lo Wu*. Dial Press, 2005. Highly acclaimed philosophical short stories about Hong Kong, this book is unusual and thought-provoking.

Theroux, Paul. *Kowloon Tong*. Penguin, 1998. Witty and amusing tale reminiscent of Graham Greene, with characters familiar to anyone who has spent time in Hong Kong.

Xi Xi. *Marvels of a Floating City*. Renditions Paperbacks, 1997. *A Girl Like Me and Other Stories*. Renditions Paperbacks, enlarged edition, 1996. Short stories from Hong Kong's most prominent female fiction writer, Zhang Yan, aka Xi Xi.

History and Current Affairs

Booth, Martin. *Gweilo: Memories of a Hong Kong Childhood*. Bantam, 2005. A thoroughly enjoyable memoir, amusing and affectionate.

Coates, Austin. *Myself a Mandarin*. OUP China, 1988. Evocative memoirs of 1950s Hong Kong.

Endacott, G.B. *A History of Hong Kong*. OUP Hong Kong, 1958 and 1973. The established "Bible" of Hong Kong history, this is an extensive study of the former British colony, from ancient to modern times.

Hong Kong Government. *Hong Kong 2005*. A detailed review of contemporary Hong Kong. *Updated annually*.

Keay, John. *The End of Empire in the Far East*. John Murray, 1997, 2005. Explores the legacy of the British Empire in Asia with some fascinating detail, and a new afterword on the remarkable development of the Chinese economy.

Vines, Stephen. *Hong Kong: China's New Colony*. Texere Publishing, 2000. A thorough overview of the economy, media and political set-up of modern Hong Kong.

Welsh, Frank. *A History of Hong Kong*. HarperCollins, 1997. A social, economic and political history of the territory.

Wordie, Jason. *Streets*. (Hong Kong University Press, 2002). A fascinating guide to the history of individual streets on Hong Kong Island.

Nature / Walking Guides

Stokes, Edward. *Exploring Hong Kong's Countryside: A Visitor's Companion*. HKTB, 1999, 2001,

2002; *The Wilson Trail: Hiking Across Hong Kong*. HKCP Foundation, 2003; *Hong Kong's Wild Places: An Environmental Exploration*. OUP, 1995. These books explore the scenic beauty of the Hong Kong countryside.

Williams, Martin. *Hong Kong Pathfinder*. Asia, 2000, 2004. 23 walks in rural Hong Kong.

Macau

Doling, Annabel. *Macau on a Plate*. Hong Kong University Press, 1996. The best book on Macau's unique cuisine.

Porter, Jonathan. *Macau : The Imaginary City : Culture and Society, 1577 to Present*. Westview Press, 2000. Recommended to anyone who is interested in learning more about Macau.

China

Becker, Jasper. *The Chinese*. OUP, 2002. Fine analysis of contemporary China and what makes the country tick, from the former *South China Morning Post* correspondent.

Chang, Gordon. *The Coming Collapse of China*. Random House, 2001. Strong on polemic, Chang's book may seem overly subjective, but is backed up by solid research and ultimately convinces.

Studwell, Joe. *The China Dream: The Elusive Quest for the Greatest Untapped Market on Earth*. Grove Press, 2003. Salutary observations and cautionary tales for those contemplating doing business in China.

TRANSPORT

ACCOMMODATION

ACTIVITIES

A – Z

LANGUAGE

HONG KONG ATLAS

The key map shows the area of Hong Kong covered by the
atlas section. An index of street names and places of interest
shown on the maps can be found on the following pages.
For each entry there is a page number and grid reference

Map Legend

▭▭	Motorway with Junction
▭ ▭ ▭	Motorway (under construction)
▭▭▭	Dual Carriageway
▬▬	Main Road
▬▬	Secondary Road
▬▬	Minor road
▬ ▪ ▪	International Boundary
▬ ▬ ▬	Province Boundary
▬▪▬	National Park/Reserve
▬ ▬ ▬	Ferry Route
✈✈	Airport
✝✝	Church (ruins)
✝	Monastery
▉▟	Castle (ruins)
∩	Cave
★	Place of Interest
※	Viewpoint
⌐	Beach
▭▭	Motorway
▭▭	Dual Carriageway
▭▭	Main Roads
▭▭	Minor Roads
▭▭	Footpath
▬▪▬	Railway
▭	Pedestrian Area
▭	Important Building
▭	Park
🚇Ⓜ	Metro
🚌	Bus Station
❶	Tourist Information
✉	Post Office
✝	Cathedral/Church
✡	Synagogue
🛇	Statue/Monument

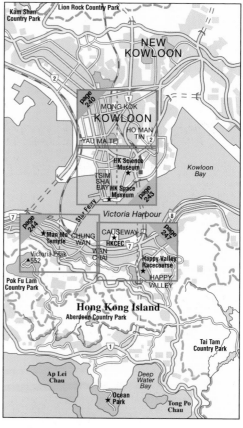

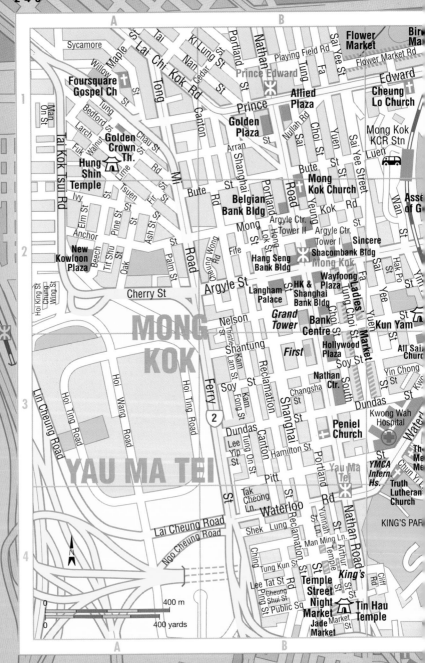

Sycamore

Foursquare
Gospel Ch

Tai Lai Chi Kok Rd
Maple St
Willow St
Ki Lung St
Nan St
Cedar St
Portland St
Nathan
Playing Field Rd
Sai Yee St
Fa St
Tung St

Flower
Market

Bir
Ma

Prince Edward

Edward

Cheung
Lo Church

Allied
Plaza

Prince

Man On St
Tung St
Bedford St
Larch St
Chau St
Fuk Wa St
Walnut St
Lime St

Golden
Crown
Th.

Hung
Shin
Temple

Golden
Plaza

Nullah Rd
Choi St

Canton Rd
Arran St

Yuen St
Sai Yee Street
Luen Wan

Mong Kok
KCR Stn

Tai Kok Tsui Rd
Ivy St
Elm St
Tit Shu St
Anchor St
Beech St
Pine St
Ash St
Fir St
Tsuen St
Mi St

Shanghai St
Bute St

Bute

Portland St
Yeung

Mong
Kok Church

Asse
of G

Belgian
Bank Bldg

Kok Rd

Mong
Lok St
Hong Lok St

Argyle Ctr.
Tower II

Argyle Ctr.
Tower I

Sincere

Shacombank Bldg

New
Kowloon
Plaza

Oak St
Palm St

Fife St

Hang Seng
Bank Bldg

Mong Kok

Fa Yuen St

Hak Po St

Yim

Cherry St

Argyle St

Cheung Wong Rd
Road

Langham
Palace

HK &
Shanghai
Bank Bldg

Wayfoong
Plaza

Sai Yee St

Kun Yam

MONG

KOK

Hoi Ting Road
Hoi Wang Road

Nelson St

Thistle St
Kam St
Lam St

Shantung St

Grand
Tower

First

Bank
Centre

Hollywood
Plaza

Soy St

Ladies' Market
Tung Choi St

All Sai
Chur

Lin Cheung Road

Ferry St
2

Soy St

Fong St

Changsha St

Shanghai St
Canton Rd
Reclamation St

Nathan
Ctr.

Nathan Road

South St

Dundas

Yin Chong
St

St Kwe

Dundas St
Lee Yip St
Tung On St
Hamilton St

Peniel
Church

Kwong Wah
Hospital

Water

Th
Me
Me

Chun Y.L.

YAU MA TEI

Pitt

Portland St

Yau Ma
Tei

YMCA
Intern.
Hs.

Truth
Lutheran
Church

Waterloo

Reclamation St

Nathan Road

KING'S PAR

Lai Cheung Road

Shek Lung St

Man Ming Ln.
Temple St
Arthur St

King's
Rd

Cliff Rd

Ngo Cheung Road

Ching St

Tung Kun St

Lee Tat St
Cheung
Ping St

Temple
Street
Night
Market

King's
St

Tin Hau
Temple

Jade
Market

Shui St
Public Sq

Market St

0   400 m

0   400 yards

West

① Kowloon Hospital ✚

Kowloon Rehab. Ctr. ✚

Argyle St

✝ Fuk Cheung St

Baptist Church

MA TAU WAI

1

Lomond Rd

St John's Ln.

Kadoorie Ave

Braga Circuit

Tin St

Kwong

Kadoorie Ave St

Guliane Tweed Rd

Dunbar Rd St

Perth Shek

Hop Yat Church

St Mark's Church ✝

King Tak

Ku St

Mormon Church

Farm Rd

Sheung Hong

Sheung Wo St

Sheung Shing St

Rd

2

Kau Pui Lung Rd

Argyle

Metropole YWCA

Man Fuk Rd

Man Wan Rd

Princess

Shing St

Sheung Shing St

Foo St

Sheung Lok St

Chinese Church of Christ

Julia Ave

Soares Ave

Emma Ave

Pentecostal Tabernacle

Kowloon Central Library

oon Chamber ommerce

Pui Ching Rd

Sheung Hin St

Fat

Sheung

Kwong

✝

Tin Hill Rd

Rd

Ho Man Tin St

Tin Hill

Chung

Good

Hau

Shepherd St

St

HO

MAN

St

KO SHAN ROAD PARK

3

Ko Shan Rd

Margaret

Chung Man St

Carmel Village St

Hau

Man

Sheung Lok St

Ko Shan Theatre

Road

Ho Man

🚌 Oi Man Shopping Centre

St

TIN

Fat Kwong St

Shun Yung St

Ko Shan Rd

Chatham Rd North

Wo Chung St

4

King's Park Rise

Chi Man St

① Road

Wylie Rd

Road

Chung

Hau St

Fung St

Yau Valley Rd

ARK ✚

D

E

A
B

1

Yan Cheung Road

Chinese
Meth. Ch

So
Kow
Magis

Eaton

Kansu St

Pak Hoi St

Cheong
St

Man
Man Sing St Wai St
Man Yuen St
Man Ying St
Man Wui
St

Saigon
St

Ferry
St

Wai Ching St

Canton

Ning

Battery

Nanking St

Reclamation St

Shanghai
St

Po
St

Temple St

Woosung
St

Parkes St

Nathan

Chi Wo St

**Kowloo
Union**

Jordan
Rd

Jordan

Jordan

Union
Square

Lin Cheung Road

**City Golf
Club**

Min St

Bowring
St

Kwun
Chung St

Shanghai
St

Temple
St

Woosung St

Parkes St

St

Pilkem St

Austin
Rd

**Prudential
Centre**

Tak Shing S

Kowloon
Station

**The
Waterfront**

Wui Cheung Road

2

Austin Road West

Canton
Rd

Austin

Austin

Hillwoo

HI
Obser

**BP International
House**

**St Andrew's
Church**

Observato

KOWLOON Piazza

TSIM

SHA

TSUI

**China
HK City**

*Royal
Pacific*

**China
Ferry
Terminal**

*Marco
Polo
Prince*

*Marco Polo
Gateway*

Harbour

City

CHINESE
GARDEN

Bird Lake

PARK

Kimbe

Miramar

Granville

Cameron L

Can

Kowloon Park

Canton
Rd

ORNAMENTAL
GARDEN

Silver-
cord

Haiphong Rd

**Kowloon
Mosque**

Humph
Ave

Carnar

Hankow

Ashley

Lock Rd

Tsim
Tsui

3

Victoria

Harbour

**Ocean
Centre**

Peking

Rd

China
Travel Service

Middle

Rd

Rd

2

3

5

6

7

4

8

P

Ocean Terminal

**Marco
Polo HK**

Star House

Salisbu

**HK Space
Museum**

Dr.

4

HK Tourist Board

**Star
Ferry
Pier**

i

**HK Cultural
Centre**

**Clock
Tower**

★

**HK Museum
of Art**

0   400 m

0   400 yards

A
B

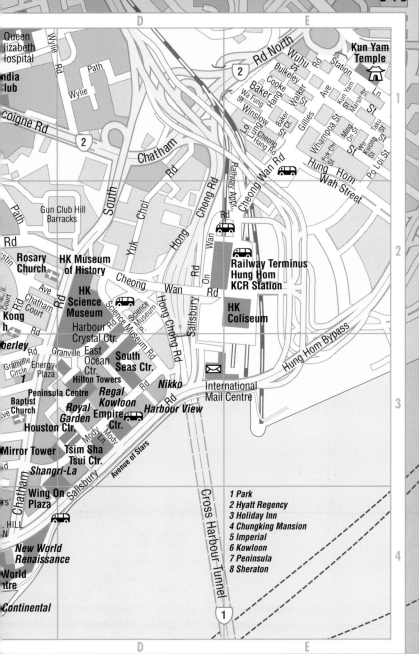

Queen
lizabeth
lospital

ndia
lub

coigne Rd

Rosary
Church

HK Museum
of History

Gun Club Hill
Barracks

HK
Science
Museum

Harbour
Crystal Ctr.

East
Ocean
Ctr.

South
Seas Ctr.

Hilton Towers

Peninsula Centre

Baptist
Church

Royal
Garden

Regal
Kowloon

Empire
Ctr.

Houston Ctr.

Mirror Tower

Tsim Sha
Tsui Ctr.

Shangri-La

Wing On
Plaza

New World
Renaissance

World
ntre

Continental

Rosary
Rd

Chatham
Court

Kong
h

berley

Granville
Circle

Energy
Plaza

Granville

Nikko

Harbour View

Avenue of Stars

Salisbury

Rd North
Wuhu

Bulkeley

Cooke

Baker

Winslow

Walker

Gillies

Wa Fung
St

Cheong
Hang Rd

Whampoa St

Kun Yam
Temple

Kun yam

Ave

Station

Marsh St

Taku
St

Po Loi St

Hung Hom
Wah Street

Chatham

South

Yuk
Choi

Hong

Chong

Rd

Railway App.

Cheong Wan Rd

Cheong

Wan

Rd

Railway Terminus
Hung Hom
KCR Station

HK
Coliseum

Hung Hom Bypass

Science
Museum
Rd

Hong Chong Rd

Salisbury

International
Mail Centre

Cross Harbour Tunnel

1 Park
2 Hyatt Regency
3 Holiday Inn
4 Chungking Mansion
5 Imperial
6 Kowloon
7 Peninsula
8 Sheraton

SHEUNG WAN

Night Market

Chung Kong Rd

Connaught Rd West

7

Des Voeux Rd

Queen St

Ko Shing St

Wo Fung St

West St

Wing Lok St West

New Market St

Bonham Strand W

Western Market

Shun Tak Centre

Wing On Ctr.

Victoria

Ha

Vicwood Plz.

Sincere

Queen's Rd

Hollywood Rd

New St

Po Yan St

Tai Ping Shan St

Possession St

Lok Ku Rd

West

Bonham Strand

Morrison

Jer-vois St

Burd St

Cleverly St

Kwai Wa Ln

Hillier St

Des Voeux Rd C.

Man Wa Ln

Wing Wo St

Man Mo Temple

Lam Kuo St East

Wan Lok St

Sheung Wan

Strand

Martin St

Bonham Rd

Park

Rd

Hospital Rd

Tung Wah Hospital

Sui Tsing Paak Temple

Cat Street Galleries

Ladder St

Gough St

Ki Ling Lane

Wellington St

Peel St

Gage St

Graham St

Gutzlaff St

Cochrane

Ce

Lyttelton Rd

Robinson Rd

Breezy P.

Nethersole Hospital

Caine Ln.

Kui Ln Fong

Museum of Medical Sciences

Shin Wong Rd

Bridges St

Caine Rd

Aber-deen St

Staunton St

Elgin St

Lyndhurst Te

Hollywood Rd

Robinson Rd

Conduit Rd

Castle Rd

Seymour Rd

Ohel Leah Synagogue

Pentecostal Tabernacle

Mid-Levels Escalator

Shelley St

Old Bailey St

Chancery Ln.

Arbuthnot Rd

St

1 Wing Lung Bank Building
2 International Building
3 Wang Kee Building
4 Hang Seng Bank Building
5 Hang Seng Bank Building
6 Wing Hang Bank Building
7 Korea Centre
8 Guangdong Building
9 Queen's Theatre
10 King's Theatre
11 Shell House
12 Central Building
13 Gloucester Tower
14 Landmark
15 St George's Building
16 Prince's Building
17 Legislative Council Building
18 New World Tower
19 HK Diamond Exchange Building
20 Bank of East Asia Building
21 Bank of Canton Building
22 Standard Chartered Bank Building
23 Bank of China
24 Bank of America Tower
25 Peregrine Tower
26 Lippo Tower

BUN SAN KUI (Mid-Levels)

Peel St

Mosque St

Mosque Junction Rd

Jamia Mosque

Roman Cath. Cathedral

Conduit Rd

Lugard Rd

Glenealy

Hornsey Rd

Canossa Hosp.

Robi

Old Peak Rd

May Rd

SHAN TENG (The Peak)

Austin Rd

Lugard Rd

Mount

Old Peak Rd

Trequnter

Brewin

0   400 m

0   400 yards

A   B

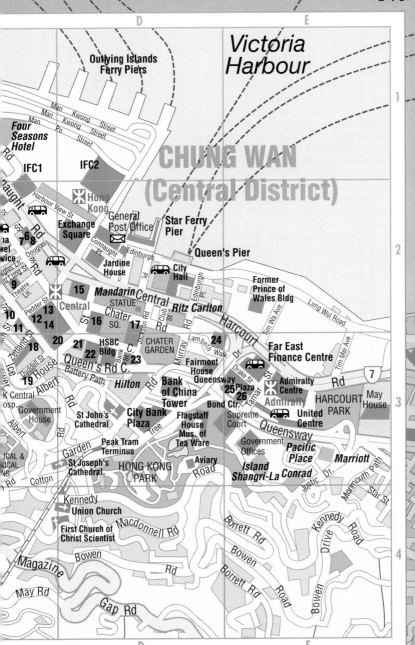

Victoria Harbour

Outlying Islands
Ferry Piers

Man Kwong Street
Man Kwong Street
Man Po Street

Four
Seasons
Hotel

IFC1   IFC2

CHUNG WAN
(Central District)

Harbour View St

Hong
Kong

Exchange
Square

General
Post Office

Star Ferry
Pier

Connaught Pl

Edinburgh

Queen's Pier

Jardine
House

City
Hall

Former
Prince of
Wales Bldg

Lung Wui Road

15 Mandarin Central

Central

STATUE
SQ.

Chater

Ritz Carlton

Harcourt

16   17

20   21   24

HSBC
Bldg

CHATER
GARDEN

Fairmont
House
Queensway

Far East
Finance Centre

22   23

Queen's Rd C.

Battery Path

Hilton

Bank
of China
Tower

25 Plaza
26

Admiralty
Centre

Admiralty

HARCOURT
PARK

May
House

St John's
Cathedral

City Bank
Plaza

Flagstaff
House
Mus. of
Tea Ware

Bond Ctr.

Supreme
Court

United
Centre

Queensway

Government
House

Peak Tram
Terminus

Aviary

Government
Offices

Pacific
Place

Marriott

St Joseph's
Cathedral

HONG KONG
PARK

Island
Shangri-La

Conrad

Kennedy
Union Church

First Church of
Christ Scientist

Macdonnell Rd

Borrett Rd

Kennedy

Road

Magazine

Bowen

Rd

Bowen

May Rd

Gap Rd

Borrett Rd

Road

Bowen

Star St

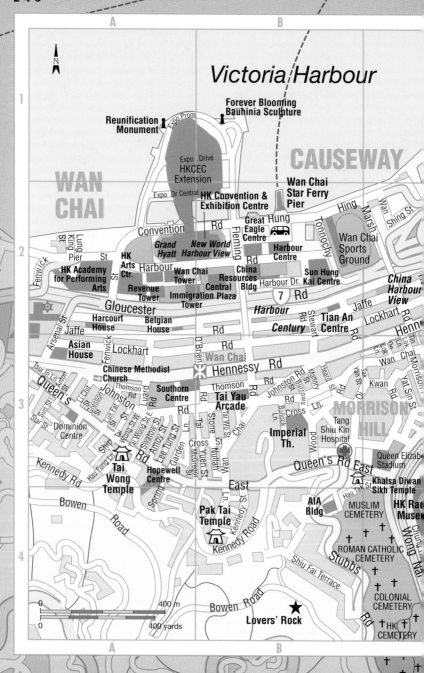

N

Victoria Harbour

Forever Blooming Bauhinia Sculpture

Reunification Monument

Expo Prom

CAUSEWAY

WAN CHAI

Expo Drive
HKCEC Extension

Expo Dr Central

HK Convention & Exhibition Centre

Convention Rd

Wan Chai Star Ferry Pier

Hing

Wan Shing St

Great Eagle Centre

Hung
Fleming

Tonnochy

Marsh

Wan Chai Sports Ground

Grand Hyatt

New World Harbour View

Harbour Centre

HK Arts Ctr.

Harbour

Wan Chai Tower

China Resources Bldg

Sun Hung Kai Centre

China Harbour View

HK Academy for Performing Arts

Pier St
Lung King St
Fenwick

Revenue Tower

Central

Harbour Dr.

7 Rd

Jaffe

Lockhart Rd

Immigration Tower

Harbour

Stewart Rd

Tian An Centre

Henn

Gloucester

Harcourt House

Belgian House

Rd

Century

Jaffe

Asian House

Lockhart

Rd

Wan Chai

Hennessy Rd

Johnston Rd

Wan Chai Rd

Lok

Yat Sin St

Morrison St

Chinese Methodist Church

Thomson Rd

Southorn Centre

Thomson Rd

Tai Yau Arcade

Mallory

Burrows St

Heard St

Cross Rd

MORRISON HILL

Queen's

Dominion Centre

Johnston

Luard Rd

Tai Wo St E.

Lee Tung St

Amoy St

Stone Nuttah St

Tai Wo St

Cross St

Bullock Ln.

Tang Shiu Kin Hospital

Yan St

Kwan

Kennedy Rd

Ship St

Hau Fung Ln

Swatow St

Garden

Yuen St

McGregor

Imperial Th.

Wood Rd

Queen Elizabeth Stadium

Tai Wong Temple

Hopewell Centre

Spring

Cross St

East

Queen's Rd East

Hau Tak St

Khalsa Diwan Sikh Temple

HK Rac Muse

Bowen

Kennedy St

Kennedy Road

Pak Tai Temple

East

AIA Bldg

MUSLIM CEMETERY

HK RA

CEMETERY

ROMAN CATHOLIC CEMETERY

Chung Wong Nai

Stubbs

Shiu Fai Terrace

COLONIAL CEMETERY

Bowen Road

★ **Lovers' Rock**

HK CEMETERY

0 — 400 m
0 — 400 yards

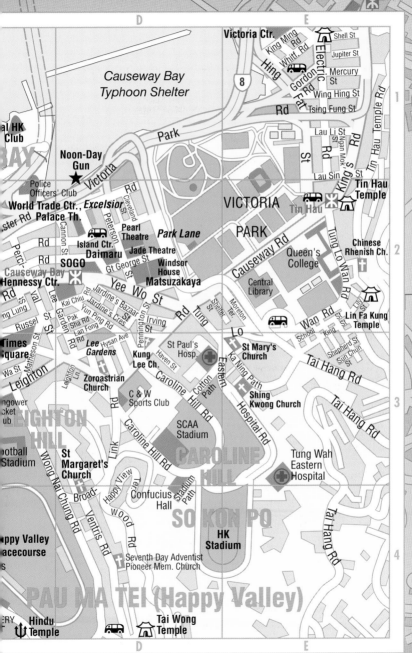

D

E

Victoria Ctr.

Shell St

King Ming Rd

Whitf. Rd

Jupiter St

Hing

Gordon Rd

Electric

Mercury St

Fat

Wing Hing St

8

Rd

Tsing Fung St

Causeway Bay
Typhoon Shelter

Tin Hau Temple Rd

Lau Li St

Nyan Mok St

King's Rd

1

Park

St

Lau Sin St

al HK
Club

Noon-Day
Gun

★

Victoria

Rd

VICTORIA

Tin Hau
Temple

Police
Officers' Club

Tin Hau

Chinese
Rhenish Ch.

World Trade Ctr., Excelsior

ster Rd Palace Th.

Cleveland Rd

PARK

Tung Lo Wan Rd

Perciv

Cannon St

Peterson

Pearl
Theatre

Park Lane

Causeway Rd

Queen's
College

2

Rd

Island Ctr.

Rd

SOGO

Daimaru

Jade Theatre

Windsor
House

Central
Library

Causeway Bay

Hennessy Ctr.

Yee Wo St

Matsuzakaya

Lin Fa Kung
Temple

ng Lung

Kai Chiu

Jardine's Bazaar

Jardine's Cres.

Irving St

Tung

Moreton Ter.

Shelter St

Wan

Rd

King

Russel

St

St

Pak Sha Rd

Yun Ping Rd

Lan Fong Rd

Pennington St

Lo

School

Shepherd St

Sun Chun St

Wa St

Matheson St

Lee
Garden

Hysan Ave

St Paul's
Hosp.

St Mary's
Church

Tai Hang Rd

Times
Square

Leighton

Lee
Gardens

Kung
Lee Ch.

Haven St

Caroline

Ka Ning Path

Tai Hang Rd

3

ngower

cket

ub

Leighton Ln

Zoroastrian
Church

C & W
Sports Club

Hill Rd

Cotton Path

Eastern

Shing
Kwong Church

EIGHTON

HILL

Link

Rd

SCAA
Stadium

Hospital Rd

Tung Wah
Eastern
Hospital

ootball
Stadium

Wong Nai Chung Rd

St
Margaret's
Church

Caroline Hill Rd

CAROLINE

HILL

Tai Hang Rd

Broad-

Happy View Ter.

Confucius
Hall

Stadium Path

SO KON PO

ppy Valley

acecourse

s

wood Rd

Ventris Rd

HK
Stadium

4

Seventh Day Adventist
Pioneer Mem. Church

PAU MA TEI (Happy Valley)

ERY

F

Hindu
Temple

Tai Wong
Temple

D

E

STREET INDEX

ART & PHOTO CREDITS

GENERAL INDEX

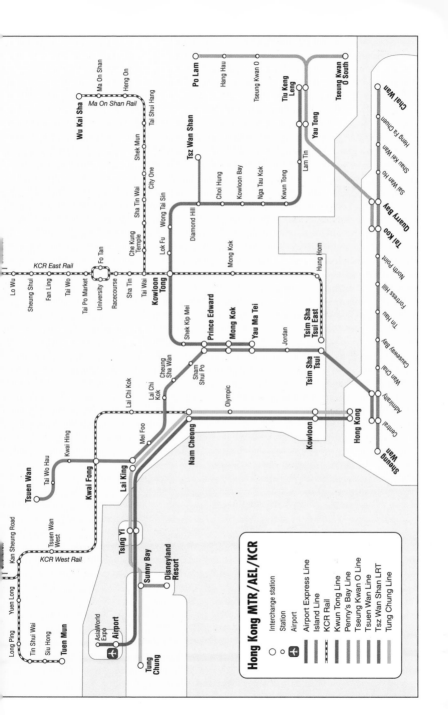

Hong Kong MTR/AEL/KCR

○ Interchange station
• Station
✈ Airport

━━━ Airport Express Line
━━━ Island Line
┅┅┅ KCR Rail
━━━ Kwun Tong Line
━━━ Penny's Bay Line
━━━ Tseung Kwan O Line
━━━ Tsuen Wan Line
━━━ Tsz Wan Shan LRT
━━━ Tung Chung Line